INSIGHT GUIDES

NEW YORK CITY

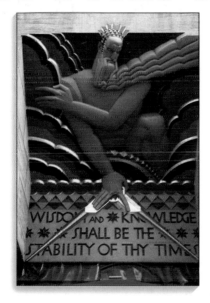

WISDOM AND KNOWLEDGE SHALL BE THE STABILITY OF THY TIMES

Discovery CHANNEL

APA PUBLICATIONS

Part of the Langenscheidt Publishing Group

INSIGHT GUIDE
NEW YORK CITY

Editorial
Project Editor
Martha Ellen Zenfell
Editorial Director
Brian Bell

Distribution

UK & Ireland
GeoCenter International Ltd
The Viables Centre, Harrow Way
Basingstoke, Hants RG22 4BJ
Fax: (44) 1256 817988

United States
Langenscheidt Publishers, Inc.
46–35 54th Road, Maspeth, NY 11378
Fax: 1 (718) 784 0640

Canada
Thomas Allen & Son Ltd
390 Steelcase Road East
Markham, Ontario L3R 1G2
Fax: (1) 905 475 6747

Australia
Universal Press
1 Waterloo Road
Macquarie Park, NSW 2113
Fax: (61) 2 9888 9074

New Zealand
Hema Maps New Zealand Ltd (HNZ)
Unit D, 24 Ra ORA Drive
East Tamaki, Auckland
Fax: (64) 9 273 6479

Worldwide
**Apa Publications GmbH & Co.
Verlag KG (Singapore branch)**
38 Joo Koon Road, Singapore 628990
Tel: (65) 6865 1600. Fax: (65) 6861 6438

Printing

Insight Print Services (Pte) Ltd
38 Joo Koon Road, Singapore 628990
Tel: (65) 6865 1600. Fax: (65) 6861 6438

©2003 Apa Publications GmbH & Co.
Verlag KG (Singapore branch)
All Rights Reserved
First Edition 1991
Fourth Edition 1999
Updated 2003

CONTACTING THE EDITORS
We would appreciate it if readers
would alert us to errors or out-
dated information by writing to:
**Insight Guides, P.O. Box 7910,
London SE1 1WE, England.
Fax: (44) 20 7403 0290.
insight@apaguide.co.uk**

ABOUT THIS BOOK

This guidebook combines the interests and enthusiasms of two of the world's best-known information providers: Insight Guides, whose titles have set the standard for visual travel guides since 1970, and Discovery Channel, the world's premier source of nonfiction television programming.

Insight Guides' editors provide both practical advice and gen-eral understanding about a destination's history, culture, institutions and people. Discovery Channel and its website, www.discovery.com, help millions of viewers explore their world from the comfort of their home and also encourage them to explore it firsthand.

How to use this book

The book is carefully structured to convey an understanding of New York City and its culture and to guide readers through its many sights and attractions:

◆ The first section, with a yellow color bar, covers the city's fascinating **History** and **Culture** in lively authoritative chapters written by specialists.

◆ The **Places** section, with a blue bar,

EXPLORE YOUR WORLD
DISCOVERY CHANNEL

provides full details of all the sights and areas worth seeing. The chief places of interest are coordinated by number with specially drawn maps.

◆ The **Travel Tips** listings section, with an orange bar, at the back of the book, offers a convenient point of reference for information on travel, accommodation, restaurants, shopping, culture, nightlife and other practical aspects of the city. Information in this section may be located quickly using the index printed on the back cover flap, which also serves as a handy bookmark.

The contributors

This new edition builds on another, earlier edition that was edited by **Martha Ellen Zenfell**, and rated by *New York* magazine as one of the best contemporary guidebooks to New York City. Zenfell collaborated then – as now – with New York update editor **Divya Symmers**, who wrote the original Downtown chapters as well as this edition's essay on Green Spaces.

The History chapters were written by Insight Guides stalwart **John Gattuso**, now editor-in-chief of Discovery Travel Adventures. Other writers include **A. Peter Bailey**, who drew on his life in Harlem to pen that piece for us; **Michele Abruzzi**, **John Wilcock** and **John Strausbaugh**. The articles called "Metropolis of the Mind" and "Aiming for the Top" were written by **Samuel G. Freedman** and **Daniel Goleman** respectively, both *New York Times* veterans, and are reprinted here with permission.

The pictures in any Insight Guide are always very important; in this case, Zenfell looked through thousands of slides to make the final selection published here, aided by photographers **Catherine Karnow**, **Tony Perrottet**, **Douglas Corrance** and **Bill Wassman**, among others.

Thanks for encouragement, information and on-site help to **Clay** and **Rona Edmunds**, **Brook Hersey**, **David Whelan** and **Stacy Cochran**. This edition was comprehensively updated by writer, broadcaster and TV producer **Kathy Novak**, who also wrote the "Media in Manhattan" chapter.

Map Legend

—— ——	State Boundary
— — —	County Boundary
—•—•—	National Park/Reserve
— — — —	Ferry Route
Ⓜ	Subway
✈ ✈	Airport: International/Regional
🚌	Bus Station
Ⓟ	Parking
❶	Tourist Information
✉	Post Office
✝ † ⳩	Church/Ruins
†	Monastery
☾	Mosque
✡	Synagogue
⌂ ⌂	Castle/Ruins
∴	Archeological Site
∩	Cave
⚑	Statue/Monument
★	Place of Interest

The main places of interest in the Places section are coordinated by number with a full-color map (e.g. ❶), and a symbol at the top of every right-hand page tells you where to find the map.

INSIGHT GUIDE
NEW YORK CITY

Maps

CONTENTS

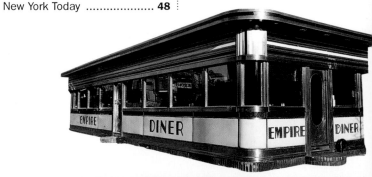

Christmas
cheer in
Rockefeller
Center

METROPOLIS OF THE MIND

New York could easily have become the ultimate urban nightmare. But the creative energy of its polyglot population turned it into a city of dreams

A beggar staggers up the aisle of a Broadway local subway and into the next car. In his wake sits a woman reading *One Hundred Years of Solitude* by Gabriel García Márquez, the Colombian Nobel laureate. On a sidewalk not far from Times Square, near a souvlaki stand and a pornographic bookstore, 10 men bend over five chessboards. A window is thrown open and the sound of an English horn wafts in. It is impossible to know its source – lights burn in dozens of nearby apartments. And in a sense, that sound has no single origin; it is born out of New York itself.

Snapshots of a city

These are scenes – snapshots, if you will – of the intellectual life of a city, New York City. This life of the mind is not a graft on the metropolitan body; it is something organically, naturally, often anonymously part of the constitution of New York. It is the contrast, or perhaps the coexistence, between life ascendant and life descendant: chess next to pornography, a book and a beggar. It is that English horn music, moving on the air like a transparent streamer, as much a part of the sophisticated urban atmosphere as oxygen.

Certainly, there is a public face to intellectual accomplishment in this city. The intellectual life here has its rituals, like museum openings, and its own venues. There are professional philosophers and critics who by their presence give definition to the proper noun New York Intellectual. But those people, places and events represent only the surface stratum of something deeper.

Intellectual life in New York is not a cerebral speakeasy where a panel slides open in a door and you whisper "Kierkegaard sent me." Rather, it is a range of mental endeavor –

Sinology and sculpture, poetry and particle physics – and it is a rich and polyglot marketplace of lectures, galleries, museums, plays, concerts, libraries, films and, of course, dinner parties. It is the casual way great minds have always moved through the landscape: Thomas Wolfe stalking the streets of Brooklyn, Sonny

Rollins practicing his saxophone on the Williamsburg Bridge. It is a painter named Mizue Sawano who used to go to the Brooklyn Botanic Garden once a week to sit with her easel beside the Lily Pools. The lily pads there reminded her of Monet's lily pads, she said, and they inspired her own art.

All this amounts to a kind of aura. Stephen Tim, a director of scientific affairs at the Brooklyn Botanic Garden, found an analogy in his studies. "The process is osmosis," he explained. "You absorb the intellectual life, the culture. Without even consciously learning from it, you are stimulated by it. It is almost a passive thing that happens. You cannot stop it."

PRECEDING PAGES: Outer Boroughs outlook and the Verrazano Narrows bridge; Zabar's is a deli with a difference; Central Park transportation; Ms Liberty of Times Square.
LEFT AND RIGHT: Manhattan taste and style.

Culture and intellect

Culture and intellect not only transform the individual, they give identity to the mass, to the city as a whole. In his book *The Art of the City: Views and Versions of New York*, Peter Conrad writes, "Every city requires its own myth to justify its presumption of centrality," and he then goes on to cite artistic annotators of New York, from the songwriter George M. Cohan to the painter Saul Steinberg, whose famous cover for *The New Yorker* suggests an earth largely occupied by Manhattan.

Alexander Alland, Jr, former chairman of the anthropology department at Columbia

University, puts the myth into words: "The intellectual life is why I am a New Yorker. It's why I stay here. I spend my summers in Europe, and when they ask me if I'm an American, I say, 'No, I'm a New Yorker.' I don't know about everyone else, but for me that's a positive statement."

New York began its rise to intellectual primacy in the 1850s. It is easy now to forget that throughout the colonial era and the early 19th century New York was at best the third city of the nation, behind Boston and Philadelphia. What shifted the gravity was the migration of the publishing industry to New York from Boston. Initially, the publishers were simply

seeking more customers – New York had the largest population – but their relocation set off a chain reaction that altered the city. With publishing houses came writers and editors and illustrators.

Meanwhile, the city had begun to change in other ways. At the top of the New York economic scale, the captains of commerce and industry began to endow museums and to support individual artists; at the bottom, each wave of immigrants enriched and diversified the intellectual community. City College, established in 1849, acted as the great pedagogue for those without wealth and later came to be known as "the poor man's Harvard."

As more creative people lived in New York, even more were drawn to it. Scale is the key word: the number of college graduates living in New York City today collectively would constitute a very large city.

With size comes sustenance for all sorts of specialized intellectual communities. Greenwich Village became an urban version of the artists' colony, a home to creators of all stripes, the neighborhood that gave Eugene O'Neill a stage in the 1920s (at the Provincetown Playhouse) and Bob Dylan a bandstand in the 1960s (at Folk City). Miles uptown, Harlem has been home to a black intelligentsia that has included the writers Langston Hughes, James Weldon Johnson, James Baldwin and Ralph Ellison, the political theorist W.E.B. Du Bois and the photographer James Van Der Zee, whose record of his era appeared decades later in the striking album *Harlem on My Mind.*

The notion of pop culture versus high culture is rendered almost meaningless, because the esoteric can enjoy a mass audience: such demanding playwrights and composers as Tom Stoppard and Stephen Sondheim can have hits on Broadway, while a gospel-music version of *Oedipus at Colonus* – could anything seem more unlikely? – can be a sell-out at the Brooklyn Academy of Music.

Intellectual life also interacts with political life. From A. Okey Hall, the hack figurehead for Boss Tweed, to Edward I. Koch, New York's mayors have often doubled as authors. Former governor Mario Cuomo, a native of Queens, is a published author who spices his speeches with knowing references to Thomas More and Teilhard de Chardin. Before the senator Daniel Patrick Moynihan became a politician, he was a respected and provocative academic. A debate on an issue now decades old – whether or not Julius and Ethel Rosenberg were Soviet spies – has been known to fill the Town Hall and argued with ferocity.

Like politics, religion in New York is a matter not only of passion or rote, but also of intellectual rigor. There are almost a dozen Roman Catholic colleges in the city; there is an Islamic Seminary on Queens Boulevard. And in the *shulbels* – the houses of study – of Crown Heights and Flatbush and the Upper West Side, Hasidim gather to carry on theological debates that are centuries old. The

lished here. Most of the leading critics of theater, film, art, dance and music make their pronouncements from Manhattan.

Artists

From the time Walt Whitman published *Leaves of Grass* in 1855, artists have been bards of New York. Whitman is the common ancestor in an artistic family that includes novelist Theodore Dreiser and photographer Alfred Stieglitz, painter Ben Shahn and poet Delmore Schwartz, composer Duke Ellington and film maker Woody Allen, Diane Arbus, photographer of the bizarre, and Martin Scorsese, direc-

Society of Ethical Culture and Fieldston, its affiliated school in Riverdale, similarly provide education, advocacy and a sense of community for nonbelievers.

The intellectual force of New York sends ripples far beyond the city. The principal network news in the United States originates not from the nation's capital but from New York. Two major news magazines, *Time* and *Newsweek*, and two national newspapers, *The New York Times* and *The Wall Street Journal*, are pub-

---

LEFT: traditional wedding at St Patrick's Cathedral.
ABOVE: life's riches: if you can make it here, you can make it anywhere.

tor of *Mean Streets*, *Taxi Driver*, and *New York, New York*. These artists have drawn on New York for subject matter, and their work, in turn, has informed the world's impression of the city.

But the point here is not name-dropping. Without any of those figures, important as they are, intellectual life in New York would proceed with just as much vigor. It is, remember, largely a private and a personal affair. Manifested in individual taste and style, at its heart it has little to do with celebrity or vogue.

The intellectual sweep of New York allows almost unparalleled opportunities for eclecticism, for search and discovery. Literary agent Flora Roberts, for instance, who can count among her clients Stephen Sondheim and Maya Angelou, has work that situates her at high levels of the literary and theatrical worlds. "For me there are two great thrills," she says. "One is going to Carnegie Hall to hear Marilyn Horne doing Rossini. The other is looking at a Goya. I grew up in New York, and I remember when I first heard Laurence Olivier scream in *Oedipus*. I think of the audience at *Death of a Salesman* leaping up out of their seats to try to keep Lee J. Cobb from killing himself. In New York, there's this marriage of feeling."

One public hub of intellectual activity is a great bookstore, and in New York the Strand is

Strand's owner recalls eavesdropping on an argument about whether Douglas R. Hofstadter's *Gödel, Escher, Bach* or Martin Heidegger's *Being and Time* was more difficult to read. His employees, typically writers or musicians, have included poet Tom Weatherly (Americana aisle) and poet/rock singer Patti Smith (typist). "I always consider that after graduating from Columbia," says Craig Anderson of the rare-book department, "the Strand is where I really got my education."

Nancy Graves pursued her education at Vassar and Yale and her studies in painting in Paris and Florence. For all that, her move to

arguably the best. Occupying a former clothing store at Broadway and East 12th Street in Manhattan, the Strand carries some two million volumes of such vast variety that on a single table the tomes range from *The Sonata Since Beethoven* to *Civil Aircraft of the World*. Over the years, the Strand has counted among its regular customers writers Anaïs Nin and Saul Bellow, Senator Mark Hatfield, David Hockney, the painter, and the late William J. Casey, director of the CIA.

Zero Mostel, the comedian, once extemporized in the rare-book department on the relative artistic merits of the Mexican painters Diego Rivera and David Siqueiros. The

New York was to affect her art profoundly. "I couldn't sleep for my first two weeks here," she recalls. "I remember the energy and the hostility. The chaos. I enjoy it. The anonymity, even. You may have a career and be somewhat visible in your field and yet have the sense of a private life."

Certainly few of the vendors in the flower district along the Avenue of the Americas recognize Ms Graves, when she comes to buy dried vegetables, as an artist with several

ABOVE: The late English eccentric Quentin Crisp was a longtime resident of the Big Apple.
RIGHT: New York taxi driver.

national exhibitions to her credit. Nor do the shopkeepers in Chinatown, her source for lotus roots and fans, or the cashiers at Balducci's, where she gets brussel sprouts. These are not the makings of dinner or some sort of talisman; they are among the organic bits of New York that Miss Graves uses in the direct casting for her sculptures.

She has also drawn on the industrial resources of the city – the foundry that casts her work – and on its academic sector. When she made a film about the moon as a personal art project, she studied the fossil collections at the American Museum of Natural History. And,

again, there are the circles: Miss Graves numbers many dancers among her friends and, as well as many other activities, has served on the board of the Mabou Mines theater troupe. "The fact of being in New York allows people to contact you," she says. "It's not just artists reaching out, but others reaching in."

In fact, artists tend to define the resurgent neighborhoods of the city. When Ms Graves first moved to Soho years ago, "it was hard to get cabs to go there." When that neighborhood became so expensive, artists advanced on a different set of frontiers. They moved to the area variously referred to as Alphabetland, Alpha-

FAMOUS NEW YORKERS

Here's a sample of some of the people who were born or spent most of their lives in the New York City area:

Lauren Bacall	actress	Vince Lombardi	football star
Pat Benatar	singer	Walter Matthau	actor
Mel Brooks	film director	Joseph Papp	theater impresario
Cab Calloway	orchestra leader	Buddy Rich	jazz drummer
Al Capone	gangster	Richard Rogers	Broadway composer
Mary Cleave	NASA astronaut	Franklin D. Roosevelt	American president
Lou Gehrig	baseball hero	Theodore Roosevelt	American president
Rita Hayworth	actress	Jerry Travers	golf star
Michael Jordan	basketball star	Mike Tyson	boxer
Larry King	TV personality	Cornelius Vanderbilt	transportation magnate
		Mae West	actress
		Malcolm X	black activist

betville or Alphabet City (Avenues A, B, C, and so forth on the Lower East Side of Manhattan), across the Hudson to Hoboken and Jersey City, across the East River to Greenpoint and Williamsburg, and to a part of Brooklyn they simply call DUMBO, for Down Under Manhattan Bridge Overpass. Trendy stores, bars and restaurants followed, rents soared, and artists are constantly on the lookout for other territories to colonize.

Ethnic mix

If artists define much of the New York landscape, geographically and intellectually, then the Southeast Asians of Elmhurst and with Iranians like Bahman Maghsoudlou.

Until he went into self-exile from the theocracy of the Ayatollah Ruhollah Khomeini, Mr Maghsoudlou was a leading film scholar in Iran. His own estimate is that 90 percent of Iran's artists fled the nation in the years after the Iranian revolution. His words are a reminder of what America and New York still mean. "It is a country of dreams, a city of dreams, to everybody all over the world," Mr Maghsoudlou says. "Whatever happens anywhere in the world – if it is violent revolution, if it is radical change, if it is disaster – people of those coun-

so, emphatically, do immigrants and refugees. The German influx of 1848, the Irish flight from famine, migrations of Jews, Italians, Greeks, Chinese, Koreans and Vietnamese – all have brought knowledge and culture from abroad to New York, making an American city cosmopolitan. In 1933, the New School for Social Research acknowledged that rich resource by founding the University in Exile (now the Graduate Faculty of Political and Social Science) as a graduate school to be staffed by European scholars who escaped the Nazi regime. The international dynamic continues today, with the Soviet Jews of Brighton Beach, with the West Indians of Jamaica, with

tries rush to America. In our own countries, we cannot paint, write, put on a play. Here you have freedom of expression. You can lecture. You can say what you want."

Predictably, life for Iranians has not been entirely easy here. Mr Maghsoudlou did fairly well for himself, operating a film-distribution company, studying at Columbia, writing a book on Iranian cinema. However, he also knows a film director who is driving a cab and other intellectuals who are working as doormen.

The same process occurred, too, with the Polish intellectuals who clustered in New York after martial law was declared back in their homeland. Janusz Glowacki is a journalist, novelist, and playwright whose Kafkaesque tragic comedy *Cinders* was mounted by the New York Shakespeare Festival. Like Mr Maghsoudlou, Mr Glowacki grappled with the mix of freedom and foreignness. No longer was he writing with the fear of censorship; but, on the other hand, New York's world of agents and grant applications was a strange one. Crime, particularly a murder in his apartment building, was shocking, but Mr Glowacki survived, helped along by his circle of expatriate Polish writers and professors.

That Broadway local subway, the one with the beggar and the woman reading *One*

knowingly of the writings of C.S. Lewis and G.K. Chesterton, he was, in his parish, surrounded by "sin". He gazed out of his window to see cocaine being sold in the alley below; if some New Yorkers can pooh-pooh such commerce, it deeply disturbs Father Rutler. New York, he says, puts a tangible face on the theological idea of Satan.

Meditation

But, as much as Janusz Glowacki or Nancy Graves, Father Rutler finds intellectual stimulation in the city, finds his circles; in the Roman Catholic theological body Opus Dei or in

Hundred Years of Solitude, ran to South Ferry in Lower Manhattan. Not far from there, wedged in amid the towers of Wall Street, sits Our Lady of Victory Church, where Father George Rutler has been a priest. He remembers his time there vividly. Although he ministered to the people of the financial district, he himself rejected the consumer society they served.

He is someone who might have good reasons to abhor New York. A man of faith and ideas, who reads Greek and Hebrew, who speaks French, Italian and Latin, who talks

LEFT AND ABOVE: The great melting pot: two of the many faces of New York City.

conversation with a fellow Dartmouth graduate who stops in occasionally to discuss St Augustine – in French. There are times, in the evenings and on weekends when much of the city is deserted, when Father Rutler takes his daily hour of meditation in the form of a solitary run around the empty streets of his parish. And in the silence, paradoxically, New York becomes a stimulating and catalytic place. "When you see all the misery of this city," Father Rutler says, "it makes the grandeur of it stand out in greater relief. When you see the skyline of New York at night, it's the closest we've invented to the medieval depictions of the heavenly Jerusalem." ❑

Mare glaciale.

AM

IRCVL9 ARCTIC9

Caput de bona ventura

zipagri ni sula

OCEANVS OCCIDENTALIS

EQVINOC

Terra incognita

Canus chuis

monte fregol

Alleg

rio decrusid

270 260 250 280 290 300 310 320 330 340 350 360

90

vnus gd9 cotinet miliar. 6.

Decisive Dates

1000–1500 Algonquin tribes hunt for animals on the island later known as Manhattan.

1524 Italian explorer Giovanni da Verrazano, under the patronage of Francis I of France, sights the territory but doesn't land.

1609 Englishman Henry Hudson weighs anchor on the island, then sails the *Half Moon* up the river that now bears his name.

1624 The Dutch West India Company establishes a trading post on the southern tip of the island at the current site of Battery Park.

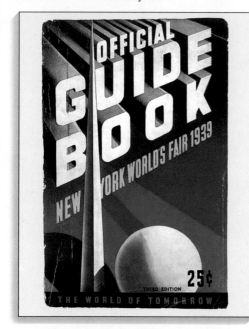

1626 The provincial director general of the New Amsterdam settlement, Peter Minuit, purchases Manhattan from the local Indians for 60 guilders' worth of trinkets – the equivalent of $24.

1630s Dutch farmers settle land in what is now Brooklyn and the Bronx.

1643 Conflict with local Algonquin tribes leaves about 80 Indians dead at the Panovia Massacre.

1647 Peter Stuyvesant becomes director general and soon suppresses political opposition.

1653 Stuyvesant builds a fence along Wall Street to protect New Amsterdam from British incursion.

1664 In the first year of the sea war between England and Holland, Stuyvesant is forced to surrender the town to the British without a fight. New Amsterdam is renamed New York, after King Charles II's brother, James, Duke of York.

1673 The Dutch recapture New York and rename it New Orange, again without fighting.

1674 New York is returned to the British as a result of the Anglo/Dutch Treaty of Westminster.

1690 With a population of 3,900, New York is now the third-largest town in North America.

1735 Newspaper publisher Peter Zenger is tried for slandering the British crown. He is acquitted, establishing the precedent for press freedom.

1765 In accordance with the Stamp Act, unfair taxes are levied aginst the colonists.

1770 A series of skirmishes between the Sons of Liberty and British soldiers culminate in the Battle of Golden Hill.

1776 The Revolutionary War begins and the colonies declare their independence from Great Britain. George Washington, in command of the colonial troops, loses the Battle of Long Island. British troops occupy New York until 1783.

1789 New York becomes capital of the newly-founded United States of America, but only retains this status briefly.

1789 George Washington is inaugurated at the site of the Federal Hall, Wall Street.

1790 A first official census reveals that New York now has a population of 33,000.

1792 An open-air money market is founded beneath a buttonwood tree on Wall Street.

1807 Robert Fulton, sailing along the Hudson River, establishes the first successful steamboat company.

1811 An important decision is made affecting the city's future appearance: all streets are to be laid out in the form of a grid.

1820 An official Stock Exchange replaces the outdoor money market on Wall Street.

1825 The economic importance of New York increases sharply as a result of the construction of the Erie Canal, connecting the Hudson River with the Great Lakes.

1830 Irish and German immigrants begin arriving in great numbers. The city's population soon tops 200,000.

1835 Manhattan between South Broad and Wall Street is ravaged by the "Great Fire".

1857 William Marcy "Boss" Tweed, elected to the County Board of Supervisors, launches a career of notorious corruption.

1858 Calvert Vaux and Frederick Law Olmsted submit plans for the city's Central Park.

1860 New York becomes the largest city in the US.

Brooklyn's population increased 10 times in the previous 30 years.

1861 The Civil War begins.

1863 The Draft Riots rage in the city for three days. Around 1,500 people are killed.

1870s William Marcy "Boss" Tweed is arrested; he later dies in jail.

1877 The Museum of Natural History opens.

1880 Metropolitan Museum of Art opens.

1883 Brooklyn Bridge officially opens. First performance is held at the Metropolitan Opera.

1886 Unveiling of the Statue of Liberty, a gift from France, on Liberty Island.

1892 Ellis Island in New York Harbor becomes the point of entry for immigrants to the US.

1898 New York's five boroughs are united under one municipal government.

1902 The Flatiron Building is completed.

1904 A subway system is established.

1911 The Triangle Fire alerts the public to the appalling living conditions of immigrants.

1913 Construction of the world's tallest skyscraper, the Woolworth Buildings, begins. It is superseded in 1930 by the Chrysler Building.

1929 Wall Street crashes, and with it comes the start of the Great Depression.

1931 The Empire State Building opens.

1933 Fiorello LaGuardia is elected mayor and uses federal money to fight the devastating effects of the Depression.

1939 Ten years after its foundation by Abby Aldrich Rockefeller, the Museum of Modern Art moves into its new home on 53rd Street.

1941 United States enters World War II.

1946 The United Nations begins meeting in New York. The permanent buildings on East 42nd–48th streets are completed six years later.

1959 The Guggenheim Museum opens its doors for the first time. Work begins on Lincoln Center.

1965 A 16-hour-long power cut paralyzes the city.

1970 Economic decline sets in as firms start leaving the city in ever-increasing numbers. This decline continues until around 1976.

1973 World Trade Center opens.

1975 As the city's chronic financial situation reaches its peak, impending bankruptcy is avoided only via a bridging loan from the federal government.

PRECEDING PAGES: detail from map, *circa* 1500.
LEFT: the World's Fair comes to Queens, 1939.
RIGHT: Mayor Giuliani's successful "get tough on crime" campaign in the 1990s offended many liberals and was the object of protests.

1977 A second power cut occurs, this time 27 hours long. Much looting and vandalism.

1982 The IBM Building opens, followed by the AT&T Building in 1983.

1983 Trump Tower is completed on Fifth Avenue.

1986 Battery Park City opens.

1987 "Black Monday" on Wall Street. Shares suffer a sudden 30 percent drop in value.

1990 David Dinkins becomes the city's first African-American mayor.

1993 A bomb explodes below the World Trade Center. Many are injured.

1993 Former prosecutor Rudolph Giuliani beats David Dinkins to become mayor of New York.

1997 Giuliani is re-elected mayor. His "get tough on crime" campaign is highly effective, with double-digit figure declines in crime transforming the Big Apple into one of the safer large cities in the US.

1998 The city celebrates the Centennial of Greater New York, marking the amalgamation of the five boroughs in 1898.

2000 Former first lady Hillary Rodham Clinton is elected as New York's junior senator.

2001 On September 11, terrorists highjack two passenger planes and crash them into the World Trade Center. Nearly 3,000 people are killed. Michael Bloomberg is elected mayor.

2003 Mayor Bloomberg's law to ban smoking in bars, clubs and restaurants is implemented. ❏

BEGINNINGS

From a tranquil hunting ground, New York grew to become a prosperous

trading post and, briefly, the nation's capital

Anthropologists say that people use mythology to imagine their own beginnings. It seems fitting, then, that according to local myth New York City began not with a divine urge to create but with a real-estate deal – and a swindle at that. In 1626, a Dutch official by the name of Peter Minuit bought Manhattan Island from the Indians for a box of trinkets worth 60 guilders, or about $24. Today in downtown Manhattan, $24 buys less than one square inch of office space.

The Algonquin

The Indians Minuit did business with were of Algonquin stock, a family of loosely associated tribes ranging along the northeast coast. They led fairly settled lives, moving seasonally within tribal territory and making their livelihoods from hunting, fishing and planting.

Despite occasional skirmishes, their relations with Europeans in the first years of contact were cordial, if not exactly friendly. But when the Dutch set up house for good in Manhattan, the peace deteriorated. Theft, murder and squabbles over land rapidly escalated into a cycle of revenge that kept both Indians and colonists in a constant state of fear. At its worst, in 1643, a detachment of Dutch soldiers fell on two Indian camps, savagely murdering about 120 men, women and children, and then, two years later, massacred 1,000 more in villages north of Manhattan.

In 1655 the Indians launched the so-called Peach War to avenge the murder of an Indian woman caught stealing from an orchard. Two thousand warriors terrorized the town for three days, killing 100 colonists, setting fire to houses and slaughtering cattle. In the end, however, the Algonquin were overwhelmed. Outnumbered by the well-armed Dutch, under constant threat of attack from the neighboring Iroquois, and rid-

LEFT: statue in St Patrick's Cathedral of Elizabeth Bayley, educator and devout New Yorker.
RIGHT: Peter Stuyvesant governed "New Amsterdam" from 1647 to 1664.

dled with European diseases, the tribes were muscled out of their own territory. It was perhaps inevitable that the Indians would be pushed off their land from the first moment that Europeans set eyes on it. In 1524 Giovanni da Verrazano sailed into the Lower Bay and remarked on its "commodiousness and beauty" which he

believed was "not without some properties of value." Verrazano took glowing descriptions back to his patrons in France, but no one in Europe paid much attention to the new land until 1609, when Henry Hudson sailed into New York Harbor flying a Dutch flag.

English by birth, Hudson was hired by a Dutch trading company to discover the elusive Northwest Passage to India. Although he didn't have much luck finding the legendary shortcut, he did stumble into the Upper Bay and agreed with Verrazano that "this was a very good land to fall with and a pleasant land to see." After tangling with a group of Indians, he pointed his ship, the *Half Moon*, up the river that would later bear his name, and sailed to the site of Albany before realizing he wasn't headed for the Pacific Ocean. The voyage wasn't a total loss, though. Along the way, he discovered a woodland that was brimming with commercial possiblities. He was especially interested in the pelts worn by local Indians. Fur meant big money in a cold country like the Netherlands, so he sent samples back to his trading company, explaining there was plenty more where they came from.

Hudson's employers were not impressed. But

WHAT'S IN A NAME?

The name Manhattan comes from the Native American word for island, which is *menatay*.

loons on tiny Nut Island (Governor's Island) just off the tip of Manhattan. Within a few months, late arrivals crowded the camp, and the group decided to move to Manhattan. They planted their new settlement at the southern end of the island, naming it New Amsterdam.

One of the first men to be appointed by the company to govern the small village was Peter Minuit, who arrived in 1626 and immediately made his fateful deal with the Indians at the site of Bowling Green, plunking down a chest of beads, knives and hatchets in

when word of his discovery leaked out, independent merchants sailed for the New World determined to bring back a fortune in pelts. One corporation in particular – the Dutch West India Company – pulled ahead of its competitors, and in 1621 acquired exclusive trading rights to New Netherland, a territory stretching from Cape May (New Jersey) into New England.

Trading posts

To seal its claim, the company built trading posts along the coast and rivers, and sent a boat load of French-speaking Protestants known as Walloons to occupy them. In the summer of 1623, Dutch ships dropped off about 50 Wal-

exchange for the entire island. Unfamiliar with the European notion of private property, the Indians probably didn't understand what they were giving away. On the other hand, it's been argued that Minuit didn't understand the division of tribal territory and may have paid off a group of sachems that had no claim to Manhattan in the first place.

Life in tiny New Amsterdam was tumultuous, to say the least. There were Indian raids to worry about, and rumors concerning the English, who made no secret about their imperialist ambitions in the New World. Drinking seems to have been a favorite pastime among the lustier sorts, with boozy knife-fights finishing a close second. The town itself was little more than a cluster of wood houses and mud streets huddled around a rude fortification. In its first few years, the Walloons and Dutch were joined by a motley collection of convicts, slaves, religious zealots and profiteers who had nowhere else to go, as well as an occasional group of Indians wandering in to trade. In all, the people of New Amsterdam represented four continents, at least eight nationalities, and spoke as many as 15 languages. It was an explosive mix, made all the more volatile by the short-sightedness of Dutch leadership.

In 1647 the company decided to put New

Stuyvesant made few friends in New Amsterdam, but he got things done. During his 17-year rule, he established the town's first hospital, prison, school and post office. In order to keep both the English and Indians at arm's length, he built a wood barricade from river to river at the present site of Wall Street (hence the name). He was so successful at attracting settlers that New Amsterdam doubled in population to about 1,500 people.

New York, New York

But Stuyvesant's success provided no defense against intervention. Wedged into the North

Amsterdam back on the straight and narrow, and they knew just the man to do it. Peter Stuyvesant was a hard-bitten soldier who had formerly served as the governor of Curaçao, where he lost his right leg in a tussle with the Portuguese. Upon arriving in New Amsterdam, "Peg Leg" Pete made no bones about his intention to rule with an iron hand. He quickly cracked down on the smuggling and tax evasion, and made much use of the whip and branding iron on the town's rowdier citizens.

LEFT: a fanciful view of a meeting between Native Americans and European colonists.
ABOVE: lower Manhattan in the 1730s.

American coast with the English on either side, it was only a matter of time before the Dutch got squeezed out. In 1664, King Charles II dispatched Colonel Richard Nicholls to New Amsterdam with four warships and instructions to seize the town. Stuyvesant was ready to start a war, but the townspeople refused to fight. They were hopelessly outnumbered by Nicholls' men, and glad for the opportunity to get out from under Stuyvesant's rule. Without firing a single shot, the English raised the Union Jack over Fort Amsterdam and renamed the town New York in honor of the King's brother. The Dutch recaptured the town about 10 years later during the Second Anglo-Dutch War, but a quick deal at the negotiating table put it back in British hands, again without shedding a single drop of blood.

The British didn't fare much better than the Dutch at keeping a lid on their new possession. In 1712, a group of slaves set fire to a house and killed nine whites who rushed to put it out. Six of the would-be revolutionaries committed suicide rather than face the cruel colonial court. Others were banished, burned alive or tortured to death. Apprehension over the

FREEDOM OF THE PRESS

John Peter Zenger, publisher of the *New-York Weekly Journal*, was thrown into jail for slander in 1734. After a long trial, Zenger was acquitted, establishing the principle of press freedom.

the real test of New York's independence came in 1765 with passage of the Stamp Act. After a 100-year struggle for supremacy in North America, the English decided it was time to show the colonies who was boss. King George III launched a battery of legislation designed to assert his authority over colonial affairs and fill the royal coffers. The new laws prohibited colonial currency, curtailed trade, and, in accordance with the Stamp Act, levied a tax on everything from tobacco to playing cards.

incident lingered until 1741, when a series of mysterious fires touched off a shameful anti-slave hysteria. Fearing what they thought was a bizarre black-Catholic conspiracy, white New Yorkers executed more than 30 slaves.

Pirates and smugglers

The British were also having a difficult time keeping a handle on their increasingly independent subjects. Despite efforts to control trade between the mother country and the colonies, pirates and smugglers – including the infamous Captain Kidd – swarmed to New York in order to fence their ill-gotten merchandise and avoid paying hefty customs taxes. But

To the feisty colonials, these restrictions were worse than the old Navigation Acts and smacked of the same arbitrary use of power. The rallying cry went out, "No taxation without representation" – and New Yorkers hit the streets with a vengeance.

Spurred on by a group of agitators known as the Sons of Liberty, angry mobs stormed Fort James and terrorized all the government officials. By the time the stamps actually arrived in New York, there wasn't a bureaucrat in town who was brave enough to distribute them. Heavily pressured by a colonial boycott, the British finally relented, and the volatile Stamp Act was repealed.

The Redcoats are coming

King George wasn't a man who took defeat lightly. In 1767 his new prime minister, Charles Townshend, lashed out with a new tax on imported items like paper, lead and tea. This time the King sent along an extra contingent of redcoats. The Sons of Liberty despised the soldiers and took every opportunity to make their lives miserable. They erected a symbolic Liberty Pole and taunted soldiers. The year long battle of nerves finally exploded in January 1770, when rebels and redcoats faced off at the Battle of Golden Hill.

Following the example of their Boston

According to legend, the statue was melted down into musket balls and fired at British troops.

After General George Washington chased the British out of Boston, he came down to New York for a rematch against General Howe, but this time he lost his shirt. British troops beat back Washington's fledgling army from Brooklyn, through Manhattan, to a resounding defeat at White Plains. The battle at Fort Washington was especially tragic. While Washington led his men across the Hudson River, a single regiment defended them from Washington Heights. But, rather than follow the rest of the army, the commanding officer decided to dig

cousins, New Yorkers protested against the hated Tea Tax by staging their own "Tea Party." On April 22, 1774, a mob of angry citizens boarded an English cargo ship and dumped the tea into the harbor. One year later, the "shot heard 'round the world" was fired at Lexington, Massachusetts, and the American Revolution was off and running. When the Declaration of Independence was read to crowds in New York, a mob raced down Broadway to topple the statue of King George III in Bowling Green.

in at Fort Washington and face the British head-on. It was a fatal error of judgment. Watching from New Jersey, General Washington wept as more than 5,000 men were slaughtered by the superior British force. They settled in for a brutal seven-year occupation.

When Washington eventually returned to New York in 1785 it was to celebrate America's victory and to bid farewell to his officers. If the General had had his way he would have retired to Virginia, never to serve again. But four years later he was back in New York, his hand on a Bible, taking the oath of office at Federal Hall. For a single year, New York was the nation's capital. ❏

LEFT: the Battle of Saratoga against the Redcoats.
ABOVE: detail from painting of George Washington en route to New York to fight the British.

Tms florishing city bicame, on the 25 december 1855, a prey to the flames. The fire broke out at nine in the evening, in
high north-east wind; together with the intensity of the cold, having paralysed the effect of the pumps, nothing could stop
miles distance (9 or 15 leagues). It is impossible to describe the awful horrible sight and desolation which the return of
piers amounting to above 3000 men. Seventeen clusters of the most vast and rich buildings were devoured; from 1000 to
impossible to estimate the immense losses occasioned by this unfortunate event, which are valued to above 260 millions o
dreadful fire plunged many families in misery. Fortunately the harbour was preserved; they have only to deplore the loss
fire was consumed in an instant. The president of the bank, though ill, came from Philadephia to New-York, and upor
they may cover a part of the reimbursements to the insured victims.

METZ, (Mozel) : printed and published by DÉMBOUR, E

nd richest part of the town. Ever since the great fire in Moscow, there has been no example of such disastrous an event. A
violence of the fire. It was a dreadful despairing night for this unfortunate city; the flames were perceived at 50 or 40
ore sensible. The courage and endeavours of man proved fruitless, and likewise the labours of the beautiful corps pum-
nt; storehouses in wgich were heaed quantities of goods, and other valuable objects were equally lost. It would be
my people perished in the flames, and that part of the town, so handsome and élégant, is but a heap of ruins. This
ship, the PARIS, arrived since two days from China, with a cargo valued to 200,000 dollars, which having caught
y of the burnt city, he ordered six millions of dollars to be advanced by the bank, to the directors of assurances, that

grapher, the successor of LACOUR and Cᵉ, of NANCY.

BRAVE NEW WORLD

New York's glittering prosperity was scarred by riots and the Civil War, forcing
Tiffany's to turn out military regalia and Brooks Brothers to sell uniforms

At the turn of the 19th century, New York was still a small town. The population stood at about 35,000 people and, although an outbreak of yellow fever scared some residents to the open spaces of Greenwich Village, most stayed where they were, huddled in the crooked lanes south of Canal Street.

Since the Revolution, there had been plenty to keep New Yorkers busy. A public debate raged over the new Constitution; a group of brokers hammered out the New York Stock Exchange in the shade of a buttonwood tree on Wall Street; five people were killed during a riot against Columbia University doctors who were robbing graves to supply their anatomy labs; and an occasional buffalo hunt was held, animals shipped in from the western territories.

Politically, the town was split between Democrats and Federalists, represented by the city's two most prominent lawyers: Aaron Burr, who would serve as Vice-president under Thomas Jefferson, and Alexander Hamilton, the nation's first Secretary of Treasury. After years of feuding, the two schemers finally had it out on the field of honor. In 1804, Aaron Burr shot and killed his rival in a duel at Weehawken, New Jersey.

But it wasn't until the opening of the Erie Canal in 1825 that the sparks really started to fly. The Erie Canal took 12 years to build, stretched over 350 miles (565 km) from Buffalo to Lake Erie, and provided a vital link between New York and the ripe markets of the midwest. Almost overnight, New York was transformed into a maritime giant as ships from all over the world jammed into the East River Harbor (now South Street Seaport) carrying goods destined for the heartland. Fueled by cheap immigrant labor, the city became an industrial dynamo too. Business boomed, the population soared to 312,000 (1840), and real estate prices went

through the roof. Wheeler-dealers like John Jacob Astor and Cornelius Vanderbilt made a killing in real estate and shipping, and the banking industry rose to national prominence. In 1835 the city celebrated its new affluence by hosting the World's Fair at the magnificent, although short-lived, Crystal Palace.

Immigrant labor

But while wealthy businessmen were "lapping up the cream of commerce," the people who actually did the work – most of them poor immigrants from Germany and Ireland – were struggling to keep their heads above water. Although a trickle of Irish immigrants had arrived in time to work on the Erie Canal, the floodgates didn't really open until the 1840s, when the Potato Blight in Ireland and the failed revolution in Germany sent thousands to the New World.

The immigrants piled into overcrowded tenements owned by slumlords like John Jacob Astor who grew fat (literally in Astor's case)

PRECEDING PAGES: in 1835, the Wall Street area was ravaged by a huge fire, damaging public buildings.
LEFT: Jewish refugees arrive in New York Harbor.
RIGHT: a fashionable gentleman in 1818.

on exorbitant rents. The dilapidated Five Points district – the largest Irish community outside Ireland – was particularly rancid, with frequent outbreaks of cholera and yellow fever, and gangs like the Bowery Boys and Plug Uglies marauding the streets.

So-called native Americans organized against foreigners, declaring that "Americans will never consent to allow the government established by our Revolutionary forefathers to pass into the hands of foreigners." The highly secretive nativists – whom newspaper editor Horace Greely called

TAMMANY HALL

If an Irish lad got himself arrested, a Tammany lawyer bailed him out – as long as he voted Democratic.

Slavery

By the 1850s, however, it seemed less likely that the country would be overrun by foreigners than split apart by domestic conflicts. Thanks largely to a highly vocal Bostonian named William Lloyd Garrison, slavery was fast becoming the issue of the day. Disparaged as fanatics and demagogues, New York abolitionists tried to bring their message to the people only to find themselves facing angry bankers and businessmen who were heavily invested in Southern crops.

"know-nothings" because they responded to every question that was asked them with the stock answer, "I know nothing" – focused their bigotry on the Irish, who they linked with a trumped-up "Catholic conspiracy" against god-fearing Yankees.

The Irish weren't scorned by all New Yorkers, however. The Democratic politicos at Tammany Hall saw the Irish as a keg of electoral power just waiting to be tapped: if an immigrant needed naturalization papers, a Tammany man was there to pull the right strings; if someone got it trouble, it could be sorted out. A simple enough deal, tit-for-tat. And all the Irish had to do was cast Democratic votes.

"The city of New York belongs almost as much to the South as to the North," the *Evening Post* reported. Even Mayor Fernando Wood supported the "continuance of slave labor and the prosperity of the slave master." When civil war seemed inevitable, he proposed that New York City declare itself independent in order to protect its business with the South.

In February 1860, a dark-horse candidate by the name of Abraham Lincoln spoke at Cooper Union, a free college established a year earlier by philanthropist Peter Cooper. Despite an ill-fitting suit, painfully tight shoes and an initial touch of stage fright, Lincoln's reasoned words and powerful delivery riveted the audience.

Copies of the Cooper Union address were distributed throughout the country, and Lincoln himself recognized that it was a critical turning point in his bid for the US presidency.

In November, Abraham Lincoln was elected without a single Southern electoral vote, and five months later Fort Sumter was bombarded by Confederate artillery. At the Plymouth Church of Brooklyn, abolitionist minister Henry Ward Beecher shrieked for "war redder than blood and fiercer than fire." And that's exactly what he got.

> ### THE DRAFT RIOTS
> The Draft Riots of 1862 left 1,000 people killed, 8,000 wounded and around 300 buildings damaged.

Among the war-weary lower classes, defeatism turned to rage when Lincoln pushed for a conscription law in 1862. Bad enough that Lincoln had dragged them into a war. But a draft? That was outrageous. When it was learned that wealthy young men could buy their way out of the army for $300, the poverty-stricken masses were unable to contain themselves.

On a steamy July morning a mob of several thousand stormed the Third Avenue draft office, routed police, and set fire to the entire block. Their appetite for carnage whetted, the mob

The Civil War

In April 1861, Lincoln called for volunteers to put down the rebellious Southerners and New York responded dutifully, producing 8,000 soldiers, including Irish and German regiments. Patriotism was suddenly in vogue. Even local businesses got in on the act. Tiffany's started crafting military regalia, and Brooks Brothers churned out uniforms. As the war dragged on and hope of a speedy victory faded, however, New York's fighting spirit started to sag.

LEFT: the wealthy residents of 1850s New York drove fashionable carriages through Central Park.
ABOVE: New York sent 8,000 troops to the Civil War.

rampaged for three more days while what little was left of the civil guard tried to cope. Apparently unsatisfied with beating policemen to death, the mob turned its attention to the few blacks who were unable to escape. An orphanage for black children was burned on Fifth Avenue, and 18 black men were lynched, their mutilated bodies left hanging from lampposts. The Draft Riots were the most barbaric display of violence New York had ever seen, and in the end, armed regiments were recalled from the Union Army to deal with them.

The Civil War ended two years later. Within months, Abraham Lincoln's body lay in state at New York's City Hall. ❑

DAWN OF THE MODERN AGE

Despite corruption and mass exploitation, the city went from

strength to strength – until the bottom fell out of the Stock Market

Historians put the founding of New York at 1625, when the Dutch first settled on lower Manhattan. But the New York most people envision – the financial giant bristling with skyscrapers, the dream-city of immigrants – that New York didn't really start until after the Civil War. The late 19th century was Manhattan's Big Bang, a time of explosive growth and wondrous achievements. The American Museum of Natural History was established in 1877, and the Metropolitan Museum of Art in 1880. The Metropolitan Opera opened in 1883, the same year as the Brooklyn Bridge opened (a few days after which a dozen people were trampled to death when someone got it in his head that the span of the bridge was about to collapse). Three years later, the Statue of Liberty was dedicated in New York Harbor.

Tenement city

Mass immigration continued after the Civil War, although most of the new arrivals were now coming from southern and eastern Europe as well as China. Italians – most from the southern provinces – crammed into the dilapidated tenements around Mulberry Street or in Greenwich Village. Jews forced out of Russia by anti-semitic pogroms flooded into the Lower East Side. And Chinese immigrants settled around Mott Street. In 1898, the unification of the five boroughs under a single city government brought New York's population to 3.4 million people – half foreign-born, and two-thirds living in tenements.

As far as politics was concerned, the city was run by Tammany Hall, and Tammany Hall was run by William Marcy Tweed. A 300-pounder of voracious appetites, "Boss" Tweed started out as a chairmaker, worked his way up the ranks of the Democratic machine, and then landed a position on the County Board of Supervisors. Within a few years, he was the

PRECEDING PAGES: Riverside Drive, 1896.
LEFT: the Brooklyn Bridge opened in 1883.
RIGHT: detail from the movie poster of *Metropolis*.

most powerful politician in New York City, if not the entire state.

Tweed established his influence the old-fashioned way – patronage, graft and kickbacks. The foundation of Tammany power was the loyalty of the lower classes, who saw Tweed as a sort of Robin Hood figure, stealing from the

rich and cutting the poor in for a slice of the pie, however small. As one observer put it, "The government of the rich by the manipulation of the vote of the poor is a new phenomenon in the world."

Although Tweed did his share of do-gooding for the poor, most of his energy was spent lining his own pocket. City contracts, for example, were commissioned on a simple percentage basis. Jobs were padded with extra funds, and a percentage of the total – sometimes the overwhelming percentage – wound up fattening Tweed's wallet. In one spectacular morning, Tweed and his cronies raked in a cool $5.5 million. Ironically, the contract in question was for the New York City Courthouse (a.k.a. the "Tweed Courthouse") immediately behind City Hall. As far as opposition went, Tweed simply bought off anyone who stood in his way. He kept the police department in his back pocket and had a number of judges on the payroll. And if money wasn't enough to cool the fires of reform, a visit from the police, health inspector or local Plug Uglies did the trick. But after 17 years as New York's unofficial monarch, Tweed's reign came to an end.

After litigation lasting three years, he was locked away in the Ludlow Street Prison – which, as luck would have it, he had been

the century, J. P. Morgan was well on the way to creating the first American company to hit the billion dollar mark (US Steel); John D. Rockefeller struck pay dirt with Standard Oil, and Andrew Carnegie plunked down a tidy $2 million for a brand-new concert hall. He named it after himself, of course, and even managed to get Tchaikovsky to conduct at the opening gala.

March of the upper crust

Pushed out of their downtown haunts by immigrants, the upper crust began a 50-year march up fashionable Fifth Avenue, leaving a trail of extravagant mansions as they moved farther

responsible for building. Tweed hardly led the life of a typical jailbird, though. During one of his frequent visits to his Madison Avenue brownstone, Tweed ducked out the back door and was spirited away to Spain. He was recaptured, thrown back into jail, and died of pneumonia less than two years later.

Tweed's corrupt empire had little if any effect on the new breed of "social Darwinists" who seemed to be pulling in money hand over fist. Cornelius Vanderbilt consolidated his vast railroad empire; the Astor family continued to collect rents from hundreds of tenements, and financier Jay Gould cornered the gold market, precipitating the Panic of 1869. By the end of

BUILT TO LAST	
The city has scores of places or organizations that date from the 19th century. Here's 10 of them:	
1857	Haughwout Building, Soho
1873	Central Park
1880	White Horse Tavern, Greenwich Village
1883	Brooklyn Bridge
1886	Puck Building, Soho
1889	Claremont Riding Academy, Upper West Side
1891	Carnegie Hall
1894	Veniero's pastry shop, 11th Street
1894	Bowery Savings Bank, East Village
1899	Brooklyn Children's Museum

and farther uptown. It was at this time that the elite came to be known as the Four Hundred because of Mrs Astor's habit of inviting 400 guests to her annual ball. "There are only about four hundred people in fashionable New York society," an insider explained. "If you go outside the number, you strike people who are either not at ease in a ballroom or else make other people not at ease. See the point?"

While the Four Hundred gorged themselves on lavish parties, the downtown scene was as wretched as ever. Two thousand immigrants poured into the new Ellis Island Immigration Station every day, cramming tenements and

women. With stairways locked or obstructed by flames and only a few slow elevators to take workers down, many were trapped inside. Spectators wept out loud as girls jumped from the eighth and ninth floors and thudded against the pavement. In all, the blaze only lasted about 10 minutes, but over 140 workers were killed, most of them women no more than 20 years old. Although the two men who owned the company were acquitted, the tragedy stimulated sweeping labor reforms.

World War I came and went with minimal impact on New York City. Doughboys, as the US infantrymen became known, returned home

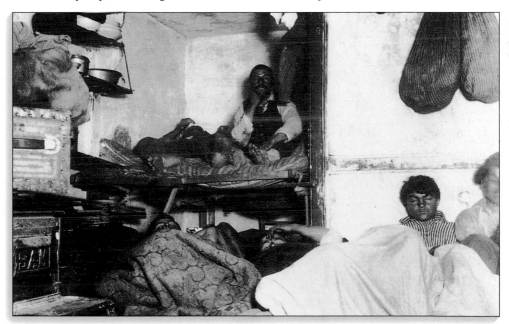

sweat shops with more people than they could possibly handle. Despite the work of reformers like photo-journalist Jacob Riis, it wasn't until tragedy struck that people took notice of the horrid conditions.

On March 25, 1911, just as the five o'clock bell sounded, a fire broke out on the top floors of the Triangle Shirtwaist Company, a garment industry sweatshop near Washington Square Park. There were about 600 workers crowded inside, most of them young Jewish and Italian

LEFT: the streets of New York, *circa* 1900.
ABOVE: photograph by Jacob Riis of the desperate tenement life endured by immigrants to the city.

to find business still booming, the population still growing, and an era of good feelings taking hold of the city. Prohibition kicked off the "Roaring Twenties" on a somewhat dreary note, but somehow the good times seemed better and the parties wilder now that drinking was taboo.

Prohibition backfired

In fact, Prohibition backfired in New York even more than in other cities. The liquor trade turned into a gold mine for organized crime, especially the mafiosi sinking roots into Mulberry Street. By some estimates there were twice as many speakeasies in New York after Prohibition as there were legitimate bars before.

A Day in the Life

The Lower East Side went by many names: the typhus ward, the suicide ward, the crooked ward, or simply Jewtown. It was the new world ghetto, an irregular rectangle of tenements and sweatshops crooked between the Bowery and the East River, an energetic Babel crammed with Russian, Polish and German Jews.

Between 1880 and 1920, more than 2 million Eastern European Jews came to the United States and over 500,000 settled in New York City, mostly on the Lower East Side. With 330,000 people per

square mile, it was the most densely populated place in the world. Sanitation was primitive; yellow fever and cholera were a constant threat, and child labor and exploitation were regarded as everyday facts of New York life. People occupied every available inch. It was not uncommon for families of six or seven to live in one small room; some lived in hallways, in basements, in alleyways – anywhere they could squeeze themselves in. And the rents they paid were extortionate.

Living and working quarters were often the same. A family slept, cooked and ate in the same room where they made their living, and from the youngest to the oldest, everyone did their part. The "needle trade" was the cornerstone of the

economy, and rooms were often cluttered with half-sewn clothes piled on the floor. The more a person produced, the more he or she was paid. As a result, the hours were long and the pace grueling. The whine of sewing machines started no later than 6am and continued into the night.

For those who toiled in the sweatshops, the situation was no better. Not only were working conditions appalling, but employees were charged for needles, thread and other supplies, billed for their lockers and chairs, and fined for material accidentally damaged at twice or three times its actual value. Wages were minimal – maybe $8 or $10 a week for a family of five or six, $14 or $15 for those getting along exceptionally well. With so little coming in, survival was often hand-to-mouth, with every penny counting.

As writer Michael Gold remembered, "On the East Side people buy their groceries a pinch at a time; three cents' worth of sugar, five cents' worth of butter, everything in penny fractions." There was no margin for any error. A family's survival could ride on a few cents. Even compassion for one's friends was given at a personal cost. "In a world based on the law of competition," Gold noted, "kindness is a form of suicide."

The Hester Street market was the central fixture of the neighborhood, and of those Jews who did not enter the needle trade many worked as pushcart vendors selling meats, fish, produce or cheap clothing. As journalist and activist Jacob Riis explained, the area was nicknamed the Pig-Market "probably in derision, for pork is the one ware that is not on sale."

Eastern European Jews placed a high value on learning and political organization, however, and among members of the community with left-wing leanings, there was a good deal of interest in the labor movement. Rudimentary unions were organized, and immigrants launched several strikes, often facing down "strike-busters" hired to intimidate them with threats and violence.

Despite the efforts of Tammany Hall to recruit their votes for the Democratic Party, East Side socialists eventually saw their candidates reach Congress. Meanwhile, organizations such as the Educational Alliance were sponsoring lectures and demanding libraries. A new Yiddish theater was blossoming on the stages of Second Avenue, and the traditional round of religious observances continued as it had in the old country. ❑

LEFT: portrait of an immigrant by Jacob Riis.

As a well-known madam is supposed to have said, "They might as well try to dry up the Atlantic with a post office blotter."

The free-spirited Twenties had its share of free-thinkers as well. Cheap rents and a certain "old quarter" atmosphere turned Greenwich Village into a hotbed of writers, artists and radicals, much to the chagrin of the Italian and Irish families that occupied the neighborhood. People like John Reed, Emma Goldman, Louise Bryant and Edna St Vincent Millay advocated everything from communism to free love. All the while Eugene O'Neill was knocking 'em back with his hoodlum buddies (the

Zora Neale Hurston, while jazz greats like Count Basie and Duke Ellington played to white audiences at the Cotton Club, Small's Paradise and other ritzy after-hours clubs.

Reigning over the festivities was the undisputed prince of Jazz-Age New York, Mayor James Walker. The wise-cracking, high-living playboy – a former Tin Pan Alley songwriter – was the perfect embodiment of the freewheeling Twenties. He was a gambler, a lady's man and a fashion plate, as loose with money as he was with Prohibition. Walker wasn't much of an administrator, though. He mostly acted as a figurehead and let the hacks at Tammany Hall

Hudson Dusters) at a speakeasy called the Hell Hole, and blowing the lid off the theater world at the Provincetown Playhouse.

The Jazz Age

Uptown, the Jazz Age was true to its name. In the early years of the century, the black community started moving out of the West 30s and into the failed developments of Harlem. In the 1920s, a blossoming of black culture known as the Harlem Renaissance produced writers like Langston Hughes and

ABOVE: Brooklyn Bridge footpath; photograph taken during the height of the Jazz Age in 1923.

take care of running the city. He played craps with reporters, hobnobbed with the stars, and flaunted his affair with a Broadway actress. When he raised his own salary by $10,000, critics attacked his extravagance. The Mayor's reply was pure Jimmy Walker: "Think what it would cost if I worked full-time."

The city may have been going to Hell in a handbasket, but most New Yorkers kept right on partying. And they kept on spending too. In the 1920s the city went on a stock-buying binge that sent the daily numbers through the roof – and it didn't look like they were ever coming down. It didn't matter that stocks were being bought on credit. It didn't matter that the city was being bilked of millions by Tammany Hall. As long as the money kept rolling in, the lights still burned on Broadway, and Jimmy Walker was still smiling, everything seemed all right. As gossip columnist and broadcaster Walter Winchell remembered, "In the 1920s the American people were hell-bent for prosperity and riches. And they wanted a politician who was hell-bent only for reelection... a man who would respect the national rush to get rich, who would accept greed, avarice and the lust for quick gain as a legitimate expression of the will of the people... Walker knew what the people wanted. And as mayor, he gave it to them."

Black Thursday

When the bottom fell out of the stock market on Black Thursday – October 24, 1929 – Walker's reign of good feelings came tumbling down with it. The Great Depression hit New York hard. Total income was slashed by more than half. Unemployment soared to 25 percent. People were robbed of their livelihoods, their homes and their dignity. Makeshift "Hoovervilles" sprang up in Central Park, and bread lines became common. As Groucho Marx put it, he knew the city was on the skids "when the pigeons started feeding the people in Central Park."

Before Walker could ride out his second term, his administration started to unravel. An investigation into city government uncovered a pile of corruption second only to the Tweed Ring. Walker was hauled up to the town of Albany where Governor Franklin D. Roosevelt reviewed the charges against him. Walker knew there was no way he was going to walk away without a political, and personal, skinning. He resigned his office in 1932, and caught the first ship to Europe.

Fiorello LaGuardia

About a year later, a new mayor moved into City Hall. Fiorello LaGuardia was a small, rather plump man with an animated face and a penchant for rumpled suits. He had none of Walker's finesse, but he was quick-witted, savvy, and determined to whip the city back into its proper shape. He could be hard-nosed, almost ruthless, but still paternalistic and warm. The same man who ordered Lucky Luciano off the streets also read out the comics over the radio every Sunday. LaGuardia had his critics, but, for a city ravaged by the Depression, he was the closest thing to a savior.

LaGuardia was elected in 1933 and immediately got on board Franklin Roosevelt's New Deal, launching massive relief and construction programs in an effort to revive the economy. His administration swung into action, building bridges, highways, housing, even finding work for artists and writers with the Works Progress Administration. At the same time, large-scale projects that had been launched in the 1920s were nearing completion. Art Deco came gloriously into its own with the opening of the Chrysler Building in 1930, the Empire State Building and Waldorf-Astoria Hotel in 1931, and Rockefeller Center in 1933.

Then, in 1941, the US entered World War II, and the city was swept into the war effort. German spies were arrested; Japanese families were locked up on Ellis Island, and blackouts were ordered – even the torch of the Statue of Liberty was turned off. In the basement of a Columbia University physics lab, Enrico Fermi and Leo Szilard were experimenting with atomic fission, laying down crucial groundwork for development of the atomic bomb, known later as the Manhattan Project. ❑

LEFT: Fiorello LaGuardia pulled the city out of the Great Depression.
RIGHT: the Empire State, a masterpiece from 1931.

NEW YORK TODAY

After surviving political chaos, near-bankruptcy and terrorist attacks,
the city seemed as determined as ever to embrace the future

With the United Nations moving into the city in 1947 and Idlewild Airport (now Kennedy) opening in 1948, New Yorkers were flush with a sense of possibilities. World peace, a healthy economy, the riches of technology – they all seemed within reach. The glass-walled UN Secretariat Building brought a relocated, and poor blacks and Hispanics flooded into the city. By the mid-1970s, New York's budget was so stressed the city teetered on the verge of bankruptcy. It seemed as if the glory days were gone for good.

The trouble started in 1946 when William O'Dwyer took over the mayor's office.

sleek look to Midtown and kicked off the 1950s with a fitting sense of modernity. A new generation of glass-box skyscrapers multiplied on Park and Madison avenues and eventually spread to the West Side and Financial District. Birdland, the be-bop nightclub named after saxophonist Charlie Parker, opened on Broadway, and Franklin National Bank issued the world's first credit card.

Goodbye to glory

As in many other northeastern cities, however, the post-war years brought an unexpected turn for the poorer in New York. The middle class began moving out to the suburbs, corporations

Although never charged with any crime, O'Dwyer presided over an administration thick with underworld connections. A change had come over Tammany Hall by this time. After Fiorello LaGuardia broke the old Democratic machine, Tammany was infiltrated by members of organized crime – "Murder Inc." as the papers called it.

The new Tammany politicos were heavily involved in gambling, prostitution and the "waterfront rackets," and they made substantial political inroads, especially at the police department, in order to protect their interests. It was clear that a major shake-up was needed.

In the 1950s, Mayor Robert Wagner oversaw

a gradual political healing, but by then a social transformation was well under way that would have repercussions for the city right up to the present day. In the late 1940s, a wave of Puerto Rican immigrants began arriving in New York and the influx continued straight through the 1950s. Some of the consequent tensions were dramatized in the 1957 musical *West Side Story*.

Attracted by war-time jobs, the black community also experienced a good deal of growth during and after World War II. Like the immigrants before them, the black and Hispanic communities faced a wall of opposition. Equality in jobs, housing, city services and education were denied them, and with the civil rights movement taking shape across the nation, they began to demand their slice of the pie.

Racial tensions

As the black power and anti-war movements gained momentum in the 1960s, the situation grew more volatile. Intended to enhance the city's international reputation, the 1964 World's Fair became a staging ground for one demonstration after another. Bitter questions were raised over the segregation of New York schools. Police were accused of brutality against minorities, and demonstrators grew more militant. One sit-in at City Hall lasted 44 days before Mayor Wagner ordered the police to haul off the protestors, setting off a minor riot.

By the summer of 1964, the black communities of Harlem and Bedford-Stuyvesant (Brooklyn) were seething with anger and energized with a new spirit of activism. When a police officer shot a young black man under questionable circumstances, Harlem erupted. Two days after the killing, on July 18, 1964, a mob of several thousand assaulted the 123rd Street Police Station. For six days rioters raged through Harlem, setting fire to white-owned buildings, looting stores that refused to hire blacks, and assaulting passers-by. All the while, Mayor Wagner tried to assure African-American New Yorkers that "Law and order are the Negro's best friend."

Wealthier whites found something to protest about, too. The demolition of Penn Station in

1965 strengthened the preservation movement. Surely not all of New York's heritage should fall so easily to the developer's dollar?

Two other significant social battles of the time involved gays and women. In 1969, the gay rights movement gained momentum when police encountered fierce resistance when they raided the Stonewall bar in Greenwich Village. The following year, the legendary McSorley's Old Ale House was forced to admit women.

Liberal Lindsay

Although the Harlem riots passed, the bitterness behind them was not resolved. In the late 1960s

and early 1970s, a liberal Republican, John Lindsay, tried to find progressive solutions to New York's problems, first as a member of the House of Representatives and then as mayor (1966–74). But, with the tax base eroding and calls on public services at an all-time high, New York City was in a financial stranglehold which constant labor disputes did nothing to ease.

By 1975, it was on the verge of bankruptcy. The banks refused to lend it any more money and, when the city came cap in hand to the Federal government, President Gerald Ford's response was summed up by the *Daily News* thus: "Ford to City: Drop Dead."

In 1976, the feisty Edward Koch was elected

LEFT: New York's largest ticker tape parade was held in 1962 for the *Apollo 11* astronauts.
RIGHT: Ed Koch, the city's flamboyant mayor from 1976 to 1988.

mayor and another effort was launched to buoy the city budget with vast borrowing – this time the Federal government provided a loan guarantee of $1.65 billion. A resurgence of corporate development injected capital into the economy, and the city began to get back on its feet. Half-empty since their opening in 1973, the 110-story twin towers of the World Trade Center sprang to life, their gravity-defying prominence being marked in 1974 when a tightrope walker strolled between them at a dizzying height. Three years later, George Willig illegally scaled one of the towers and was fined one penny per story. Close to the

vailed during a previous major blackout in 1965. In 1980, former Beatle John Lennon was shot dead outside the Dakota apartment building, where he lived, by a deranged fan, Mark Chapman. Broadway theatres began starting their shows an hour earlier to give tourists and out-of-towners a chance to get clear before the late-night muggers moved in.

The haves and have-nots

The most worrying trend was the widening gap between rich and poor. While gentrification swept through the neighborhoods, the underclass grew more entrenched. Ronald Reagan

World Trade Center in Lower Manhattan, Battery Park City and the South Street Seaport were developed. In Midtown, the Citicorp Building opened in 1977, sparking the development of One UN Plaza, the AT&T (now Sony) and IBM buildings, and many other skyscrapers.

Internationally, New York sustained its reputation as a place of excess. In 1977, Studio 54 opened, symbolizing an era of sybaritic, cocaine-driven culture, and David Berkowitz, who had terrorized the city as "Son of Sam", was arrested after killing five people. A widespread power failure the same year was accompanied by widespread looting – in marked contrast to the community spirit that had pre-

entered the White House in 1980, promising that "trickle-down" economics would ensure that the poor would benefit from concessions given to the rich. But the new wealth didn't trickle quite far enough. The legacy of homelessness was evident on almost every street corner; Aids and drug abuse pushed health-care systems beyond their capacity; and racial conflicts erupted with alarming regularity. Compounding the problems, many Manhattan businesses and middle-class workers fled to the suburbs or discovered the joys of New Jersey, thus further eroding New York's tax base.

All the while, super-rich moguls such as Donald Trump were gobbling up New York real estate as if it were squares on a Monopoly board, and the glitziness of the conspicuous consumers was celebrated in the pages of *Vanity Fair*, a long defunct magazine revived by Condé Nast in 1983. By 1987, though, the good times had turned sour, with two of Wall Street's biggest share dealers heading for jail and the market taking a record one-day drop of 508 points.

LOW CRIME

An FBI report claimed that New York had the lowest crime rate of the country's largest 25 cities.

In 1989, David Dinkins became New York City's first African-American mayor – appropriately enough since a census of the city's residents showed that whites had become a

Rudolph ("Rudy") Giuliani, an abrasive former prosecutor with the Department of Justice and a New York district attorney who promised to get tough on crime. The first Republican mayor for two decades in what is essentially a Democrat stronghold, he more than kept his promise, extending his "zero tolerance" policy towards law-breaking to encompass not only criminals and police corruption but also jaywalkers, beggars, graffiti vandals and people who didn't sort their garbage properly for recycling.

It wasn't a policy that made him loved by

minority. But his term was not a success: it saw the annual murder rate peak at 2,245 and the number of citizens on welfare reach a new high. Domestic violence was augmented by international terrorism when a car bomb exploded in the World Trade Center in 1993, killing six.

The Giuliani years

To many, the city seemed ungovernable – an attitude which partly explains the victory in the 1993 mayoral election of Brooklyn-born

LEFT: Donald Trump (here with *Playboy*'s Christie Hefner and ex-wife Ivana) symbolized the 1980s.
ABOVE: new manners for the new millennium.

liberals, but it did win him respect, especially when the crime rate began to fall dramatically, making New York one of the safest big cities in the country. By 1997, the murder rate had fallen by two-thirds from its 1990 high to an average of just 2.1 killings a day. Business Improvement Districts (BIDs) sprang up throughout the city, construction boomed, and seedy areas such as Times Square were comprehensively cleaned up. The economy, more than ever aligned with Wall Street's fortunes, rebounded wildly from a 1987–92 slump, and unemployment fell.

With much fanfare, Giuliani was elected to a second term in 1997 and began turning his attention to becoming a US senator. But his luck ran out: the combination of a prostate cancer diagnosis and a messy separation from his second wife forced him in 2000 to pull out of the contest, which was won by the high-profile Democratic candidate, Hillary Rodham Clinton. Giuliani seemed a beaten man, destined to serve out his last months as a lame-duck mayor.

Terrorism hits the Twin Towers

Then, on the morning of September 11, 2001, disaster struck. Middle Eastern terrorists hijacked two passenger planes and, in a meticulously planned suicide mission, crashed the Boeing 767s, each laden with 10,000 gallons of

near the 16-acre (6.5-hectare) disaster area, and the city's cocky self-assurance was replaced by an uncharacteristic sense of vulnerability. Such was the shared sense of trauma that, in the week after the attack, reported crimes in Manhattan were down by 59 percent.

Yet the resilience of New Yorkers soon reasserted itself, taking a cue from Mayor Giuliani, whose celebrated abrasiveness was replaced by a dignified compassion and straighttalking approach that kept hysteria at bay and earned the citizens' trust. These qualities were called on again just nine weeks later when an American Airlines Airbus crashed into the

combustible fuel, first into one of the World Trade Center's twin towers, then the other. As New Yorkers on the streets and television viewers around the world looked on in horror, both towers collapsed shortly afterwards into 1.2 million tons of twisted steel and concrete, obliterating nearly 3,000 people, including hundreds of policemen and firefighters who had raced to the scene to help.

The scale of the calamity was hard to comprehend: it took three weeks for the volcanic plume of smoke at "Ground Zero" to subside and the wreckage continued to smoulder for several more weeks. More than 20,000 New Yorkers were displaced from their apartments

REPLACING THE WORLD TRADE CENTER

In the immediate aftermath of the World Trade Center's destruction, some – such as former mayor Ed Koch – advocated rebuilding the 110-story towers as a gesture of defiance to terrorism. Others advocated that the site should become an open space, a memorial to the dead. Many architects pointed out that, despite its having become a symbol of New York's power, the center's bland giganticism had little aesthetic merit. A competition was held to decide what structure should be erected. Although there was local opposition to another soaring skyscraper, winning entries challenged the right of the Petronas Twin Towers in Malaysia to be the tallest building in the world.

Rockaway district of the borough of Queens just after taking off from Kennedy airport, provoking fears (which turned out to be unfounded) of another terrorist attack.

Such was Rudy Giuliani's popularity that he had only to endorse Michael Bloomberg as his successor to ensure that the self-made media mogul, previously trailing well behind in the mayoral race, decisively won the November election for the Republicans. The billionaire, a political ingenue who spent $41 million of his own money on the campaign, had previously been best known in

ISLAND OF COMMUTERS

Manhattan occupies just 6.8 percent of the city's land area. Only 19 percent of New Yorkers live there.

though many of New York's social services budgets had already been ruthlessly pruned. Fears of an economic recession combined with the effects of the terrorist attack swelled the ranks of the jobless.

But, as ever in New York, fresh ideas poured forth. Investment should be spread throughout the city, it was said, not just in Lower Manhattan. Transport links should be improved. The neglected waterfront should be revived. Another Rockefeller Center should be built. The future was back on the agenda.

According to a Harris Poll taken while the

Wall Street for having built a financial data empire and in the gossip columns for having escorted a series of glamorous women after his 1993 divorce.

A city of change

Bloomberg encountered a daunting set of problems. As well as the massive rebuilding program in Lower Manhattan, the city faced a projected $8.7 billion budget shortfall, even

LEFT: the remains of the World Trade Center after the terrorist attack of September 11, 2001.
ABOVE: billionaire Michael Bloomberg is elected mayor, applauded by outgoing mayor Rudy Giuliani.

twin towers still stood, New York is the place where many Americans would most like to live. A new poll would probably confirm those findings, for nowhere else can you find the same concentration of museums and theater, the same wild variety of food and shopping, the same earth-shaking business deals, stunning architecture or diversity of people. This is a city of change, struggle, joy and ambition, where anything can happen. Traffic, noise, and outrageous street life all come together in a frenzied nonstop rhythm. Whether you see this city as inhuman or superhuman, it's a sure bet that, by the time you think you understand New York, your understanding will already be obsolete. ❏

AIMING FOR THE TOP

The writer E.B. White called New York "the city
that is a goal." But only for certain people, say psychoanalysts

New Yorkers differ from one another in a multitude of ways, but so many share the same autobiographical tale that it has become almost mythic. With countless variations, the story goes something like this:

An able young man (or woman) feels the need to leave home. Perhaps he feels misunderstood and unappreciated, surrounded by what playwright Eugene O'Neill called "spiritual middle-classers." He yearns to escape these small-town minds and to be among people with broader vision. Perhaps he simply wants to reinvent himself by shedding the identities and labels of his childhood and youth. Or perhaps he has a dream, an aspiration too great to be realized at home. He feels imprisoned, be it in Iowa or the Bronx. He believes that only in a great urban center like Manhattan will he find people who can understand his strivings and applaud who he is and what he has to offer.

So he comes here, and whether or not his dreams are realized even partially, he eventually feels the city has spoiled for him any other place in the world. Despite the pressure, the pace, and the grime of New York, he has a tremendous sense of being alive.

Excellence and genius

In reality, of course, it is possible in some degree to find in other places what New York City offers. Certainly, excellence in medicine, art, the law, entertainment, business and education can be found elsewhere. But the New York striver has come to believe that nowhere else in the world is there a city with such a profusion of excellence and genius, such an abundance of alternatives and possibilities. And so for him success in New York symbolizes the success of successes.

In *From Death to Morning*, the writer

Thomas Wolfe tried to capture in print the magic of this quest: "The great vision of the city is burning your heart in all its enchanted colors just as it did when you were 12 years old and thought about it. You think that some glorious happiness of fortune, fame and triumph will be yours at any minute, that you

are about to take your place among great men and lovely women in a life more fortunate and happy than any you have ever known – that it is all here, somehow, waiting for you…"

Many New Yorkers harbor the memory of a single, vivid episode that stands out as the epitome of just what is in the city somehow waiting for them. To the psychoanalyst, such moments from the past are known as "screen memories," episodes in life that are striking because they carry a special meaning.

Take, for example, the episode recalled by Dr Gerald Fogel, for many years a training and supervising analyst at the Columbia University Psychoanalytic Center. "I grew up in Detroit and

PRECEDING PAGES: the Rockettes dance for Santa; a religious moment for Hasidic Jews.
LEFT: a top-class life – the *Wall Street Journal* and the Waldorf-Astoria.
RIGHT: New Yorkers often have high blood pressure.

came to New York the summer just after I graduated from high school," he says. "I remember the first weekend I spent in New York as a 16-year-old, with my friends. We arrived on a Sunday evening, checked into a Midtown hotel, and then went walking around town. And there, a few blocks away at a jazz club, was Dave Brubeck, playing on a Sunday night. And I could walk in off the street and see him at midnight on a Sunday. Sunday at midnight! I couldn't conceive of such a thing – it was like heaven.

"When I look at myself now, I realize my interest in jazz as an adolescent stood for other kinds of aspirations. The idea of jazz, James

Dean, Marlon Brando, and all that signified a freedom, social and sexual, from the kinds of deep inhibitions that all shy adolescents feel.

"New York meant all that. It was the place where the action was. It had all of it: the sophistication and freedom, the underside of life, the vitality. It had all the seductive allure of a place you could do things you could not do anywhere else."

It is that allure, in one form or another, that draws people to the city in what is typically a radical break from home and past. Psychiatrists say that the move away from home is a key step in psychological development. It marks the break between the person one has been as a

child and the person one will become as an adult. "The classic psychoanalytic notion is that to express your autonomy, to become your own person, you have to leave home, if only psychologically," Dr Fogel says. "Home, in this sense, stands for that part of the self that keeps you inhibited and limited. Some people have to go far away to make the break. To become someone else, they seek out people unlike members of their own family. That is why some people marry out of their religion or social class – they feel they can be sexually freer with someone who does not belong to their own group. For a person from a small town or another part of the world, New York may have that same exotic attraction."

Reinvent yourself

Dr Ethel Person, among other notable jobs, has been a director of the Columbia University Psychoanalytic Center, one of New York's principal institutions for the training of psychoanalysts. When she was a 12-year-old in Kentucky, she decided that she was meant to live in New York City even though she had never been there. "Leaving home lets you reinvent yourself," Dr Person says. "For me, the quintessential New Yorker is someone who came to Manhattan – or stays here – by choice, to do just that.

"I like to be with people who don't know who I was when I was 17 years old. In New York you have that lovely double thing: the anonymity to experiment with new identities and the chance to tie in with people who share those interests. Those people are your truer family. New York is the city *par excellence* of invented families. A lot of people leave for New York because their particular gifts or way of being in the world makes them misfits where they are.

"In my generation, which grew up in the 1950s, it was the woman who didn't want to follow the traditional role of just being a wife and homemaker, who wanted a career of her own. A more contemporary equivalent might be a woman who wants to be a mother, but who does not want to be married. That would be no picnic among people with small-town attitudes, but there would be more support for it here in the city."

But why should someone be drawn to New York rather than another city?

"Every city has its personality, its unique

style that will attract its own to it," says Dr James Hillman, a well-known Jungian analyst. In keeping with Jungian thought, which deals freely in archetype and myth, Dr Hillman sees the pull of the city in terms of a larger psychological dimension.

"Dallas, where I lived for a while, is for people in the fast lane, people concerned with consuming," Dr Hillman says. "It pulls to those who are already Dallas types. Whether they be in Illinois or Pennsylvania, they are meant for Dallas. Likewise, New York draws the cosmopolite, the person who wants to be challenged the most, who needs the most varied and rich stimulation. It is the person who is full of possibilities, but who needs New York to draw them out of him. You come to New York to find the ambience that will evoke your best. You do not necessarily know precisely what that might be, but you come to New York to discover it.

"If there were a god of New York it would be the Greeks' Hermes, the Romans' Mercury. He embodies New York qualities: the quick exchange, the fastness of language and style, craftiness, the mixing of people and crossing of borders, imagination."

The complete city

New York is the city of rampant creativity, of abundant imagination, whether you are in advertising or the theater or the stock market. They are all fields built on imagination, the spinning of ideas and creations, of fantasy becoming reality. It is everything. Any syndrome that might characterize another city is found in New York: manic energy, depression and hopelessness, the extreme excitement of the hysteric, the anger of the paranoid. Psychologically, New York is the complete city."

There are many – too many – who are drawn to the city only to end up depressed by it, hating it, even destroyed by it. But the person who fits the syndrome is, archetypally, someone who is exhilarated by the intensity of the city's challenges, who is invigorated rather than defeated by them.

"New York is a city that loves what has been called the 'Type A' personality: always feeling the press of time, aggressive and competitive,

LEFT: New York is a place to reinvent yourself.
RIGHT: the city attracts challenge-seekers.

a workaholic, dedicated to achievement," says Dr Anthony Zito, a psychiatrist engaged in stress research and who numbers among his patients many artists and performers.

"There is a common breed here who prefer that intense level of stimulation, who seek the greater challenge. For them, it's not stressful – it's the level of action they prefer. They are unhappy without it. That need is a defining quality of the New Yorker."

The Type A pattern was first identified as an indicator of susceptibility to heart disease. The original research suggested that while it might make people highly successful, it could also

kill them. Subsequent studies, however, have focused on determining what makes some people with this hard-driving pattern more hardy, and thus able to thrive under pressure that might make others more prone to coronary disease. It is important, Dr Zito observes, that people match their preferred level of activity with their environment.

"Because of its pace, this city offers more of a challenge to the person who takes it on," Dr Zito says. "He knows that if he fails, he will get plowed under. That kind of risky challenge appeals particularly to the person who seeks to define himself through his achievements."

Why come to compete in New York City

rather than settle for success in a smaller venue? In the view of those psychotherapists who are familiar with the syndrome, the intense drive to compete and succeed on the grandest scale is of primary importance. From the clinical perspective, that kind of person is a "narcissist."

The negative connotations the term holds for many people are unfortunate, psychologists say, because to some degree a streak of narcissism is essential for mental well-being and is necessary for success.

"The concept of narcissism, to put it simply, refers to self-love, or self-esteem," says Dr

Robert Michels, a chairman of the department of psychiatry at Cornell University Medical College. "Its origins are linked in early development with parental regard and approval, the desire to be the kind of person you believe your parents like and approve of. As you grow up, that becomes an internal psychological reality rather than an interpersonal one. You desire to be the kind of person you yourself hold in high regard. In its healthy form, that can lead you to many accomplishments. Take the case of someone in a small town who recognizes he has great talents. The person with a healthy dose of narcissism would seek the environment that would allow him to maximize

his potential, and so may leave for a city like New York.

"The boundary between normal and pathologic depends on whether one's pursuit of success actually leads to enhanced performance or simply is the service of a psychological hunger that can never be gratified," Dr Michels says. "People who are hungry for applause are never satisfied with the reality of their feats. They feel an ever-present yearning: the praise they receive is never enough to appease what is, unconsciously, a craving for the total approval from the infant's mother.

"Still, you have to have a bit of narcissism to succeed. To some extent healthy narcissism is one of the key motives in achievement. In order to achieve, one has to work, one has to pride oneself, to put off gratifications. All those things require a strong, healthy narcissistic pleasure in the rewards of success, and a willingness to pay the multiple prices to get it."

Driven by self-worth

As Dr Michels suggests, a related ingredient for success is the capacity to work hard. Lionel Trilling once noted how, in the past, people were thought to be driven by pleasure, while now people are more driven by a sense of self-worth, for which they will forgo pleasures. If any city epitomizes that ethic, it is New York.

From the psychoanalytic perspective, this drive for a higher satisfaction entails some degree of masochism, in the psychological meaning of the term: the taking of pleasure from painful sacrifice and intense work.

"The need for mastery requires great pain and sacrifice, but it offers another order of

THE PULITZER PRIZE

The urge to be great is unlikely to be better sated than by winning a Pulitzer Prize. The award has been given each year since 1916 by New York's Columbia University, and is funded from an endowment left by publisher Joseph Pulitzer to reward outstanding achievement in journalism, letters, drama and music. There are 14 prizes for journalism, ranging from investigative reporting to editorial cartooning, many of them won by alumni of Columbia. In 1999, on-line reporting was allowed for the first time. New York prize-winners include Norman Mailer, Neil Simon and Edith Wharton *(The Age of Innocence)*.

satisfaction, not what we ordinarily think of as pleasure," says Dr Arnold Cooper, a psychoanalyst who has written about the psycho-dynamics of this variety of behavior and how it interacts with masochism. "It is like a person who runs a marathon and feels great pleasure in the achievement afterward, while putting up with great pain during it.

"Bertrand Russell said toward the end of his life that the writing of his great treatise, the *Principia Mathematica*, had permanently damaged his brain. Whether apocryphal or not,

FAST PACED

"New York, the nation's thyroid gland," observed noted wit Christopher Morley.

satisfied just doing their work. There is another group with higher aspirations. They work much harder, push themselves a bit more. And finally there are the narcissists who really aspire to be great. Some of them really do have talent, and it makes sense for them to aim that high. But some of them actually just want people to declare them great. They have no intention of doing the hard work. That is where pathological narcissism begins."

Thus, the New York striver is usually the kind of person who is drawn to the city because

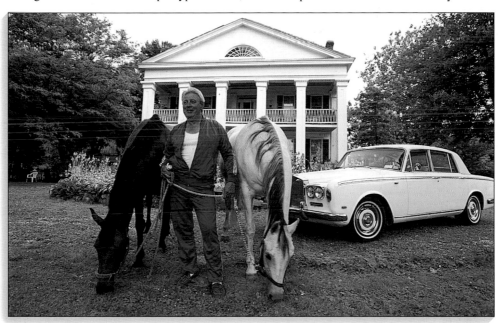

the point is that he was not at all sorry he had done it. The process was painful and excruciating, but one he and the world would say was worth it.

The urge to be great

"The urge to be great is within the spectrum of healthy narcissism. That spectrum includes those who simply do their thing well and live productive lives. They don't dream they will write the Great American Novel; they are

LEFT: facing the world head on for success.
ABOVE: hard work often produces rich rewards like this Staten Island estate.

it gives him or her the opportunity to make themselves over in terms of excellence. And then there is the school of thought that holds that city life may be good for the soul.

"I believe the city is good for the soul," says Dr Hillman, the Jungian analyst. "In fact, it is as if there were a human need to have cities to manifest the richness, including the darkness, of human nature. In nature there is no human past, no trace of man's unique stamp, of his creativity. But the city, as Lewis Mumford acutely observed, is a living work of art. It manifests the human imagination. The alive, pulsing city is the greatest artistic achievement of humankind." ❏

CITY OF IMMIGRANTS

A map of the city colored to designate nationalities would show more stripes
than on the skin of a zebra and more colors than any rainbow

Jacob Riis wrote the words printed above in the early 1900s at the very peak of the great tide of immigration that swept into the United States – and especially into New York – between 1840 and 1925. Almost a century has passed since that time, during which the city's immigrant population gradually decreased. That is, until the past few decades, when immigrants started flooding back into the city, bringing with them an exotic melange of cultures, cuisines and languages. Today, New York is once again a city of immigrants.

Averaging about 35 percent of the city's population, the percentage of foreign-born residents is only slightly less than it was at the turn of the previous century, although the total number is actually slightly higher – close to the 3 million range, possibly more, depending on one's estimate of undocumented aliens. Despite the predictable grumbling concerning more and more immigrants moving into "the old neighborhood," or new foreign workers driving down the wages, it's a situation New Yorkers seem to be remarkably comfortable with.

Minorities rule

Never closely associated with the American mainstream, New York is one of the few American cities where minorities (including American-born blacks, Hispanics and Asians) comprise the majority of the population. Multiculturalism and multiracialism have long been New York traditions. They are an integral part of the city's color, complexity and problems, and in general the people of New York have learned to be accepting, if not always enthusiastic, about the difficulties and responsibilities that a large immigrant community inevitably entails.

Public schools offer bilingual instruction. Traffic signs, advertisements and subway signs are commonly printed in two or three languages depending on the neighborhood, but most often in Spanish or Chinese, the city's unofficial second and third languages. There are at least a dozen non-English newspapers published in the city itself and countless others imported from their countries of origin. Immigrants can take driving tests in other languages, and do business at foreign banks. Even auto-

matic cash machines "talk" to users in Spanish, Chinese or French.

Although there are other cities in the US that have a high percentage of foreign-born residents, none can match the diversity of New York's ethnic communities or the cultural depth of even the smallest groups. A quick run-down of nationalities makes it quite clear that New York is the home-away-from-home for people from every continent. As demographers are fond of pointing out, there are more Greeks in New York than in any city but Athens; more Dominicans than in any city but Santo Domingo. And that only scratches the surface.

There are more Russians, Ukrainians and

LEFT: a trio of shapes, hopes, dreams and shades.
RIGHT: Korean flower vendors are everywhere.

Georgians here than anywhere outside the former Soviet republics, more Jamaicans here than anywhere outside Jamaica, and, although technically American citizens, more Puerto Ricans live here than anywhere but Puerto Rico. In fact, some people have suggested – and only half-facetiously – that there are more Puerto Ricans in the New York metropolitan area (the five boroughs, New Jersey, southern Connecticut and western Long Island) than in Puerto Rico itself. All of which is to say that the diversity of the city's immigrants is matched by the size of the

POPULATION EXPLOSION

At the turn of both the 20th and 21st centuries about 35 percent of residents were foreign born.

Irish Catholics to refugees from the former Yugoslavia – is pretty well understood, generally speaking the differences within the other groups are harder to grasp. The fact is, however, that there's as much diversity within categories as there is between them, and it's often the social and political differences within a particular group that are the most bitterly divisive.

A random sampling of Asians, for example, is as likely to turn up a Taiwanese financier or an Indian doctor as it is a Chinese immigrant smuggled in by boat. There's a similar tendency

community. One observer commented, "the city has more Ethiopian residents than several states have black people."

Planning a headache

Trying to put New York's cultural mish-mash into some kind of comprehensible order is a headache for city planners, whose standard four-part categories – white, black, Hispanic, Asian – are at best inadequate, and at worst irrelevant, to the kaleidoscope of cultures, races and nationalities that they are trying to comprehend.

While the ethnic variety of white immigrants – who include everyone from Russian Jews to

to lump foreign-born blacks together with African-Americans, which, considering that black immigrants include French-speaking Haitians, English-speaking Barbadians, Trinidadians and Jamaicans as well as a growing number of Senegalese and Ghanians, is obviously a mistaken assumption. Even Latinos, bound together by a common language, are often divided by apparently insurmountable differences.

Arguments between Argentinians and Chileans, Cubans and Puerto Ricans can be pursued with as much vigor in the city's neighborhoods as they are back home. Little wonder, then, that Latinos, numbering about 2.2 million people and easily the city's largest ethnic group, have yet to consolidate their political power into a single, unified voice.

Ellis Island

For travelers, the upshot of this ethnic mix-and-match is a sort of geographical shorthand that can turn any tour of the city into a first-hand survey of world cultures. A good place to begin is the Ellis Island Immigration Museum, in the middle of New York Harbor. The building through which millions of immigrants passed during the peak years 1898 to 1924 has been salvaged in order to tell the often heart-wrenching stories of those *en route* to new lives in the New World.

A more contemporary survey can be achieved by subway. A 20-minute subway ride through Queens, for instance, takes you from the heart of "Little Athens" in Astoria, to "Little Bogota" in Jackson Heights, to a hodge-podge of nationalities in Flushing that includes Indians, Pakistanis, Afghans, Koreans, Thais and Chinese.

In Brooklyn a similar 20-minute ride passes through the Hasidic and West Indian enclaves of Crown Heights, past the Italians and Scandinavians of Bay Ridge, to the Russian Jews of Brighton Beach, known by locals as "Little Odessa by the Sea."

The same goes for the Bronx and Manhattan, from the Irish, Puerto Ricans and Dominicans in Washington Heights to an older generation of Hungarians, Czechs and Germans still living in Yorkville on the Upper East Side to the newer Korean and Indian neighborhoods springing up in Midtown. The city's ethnic grab-bag has created any number of other odd-ball couplings: Jews, Puerto Ricans and Mexicans rub elbows on the Lower East Side; Colombians and Koreans maintain an uneasy truce in Flushing; Italians and Chinese dwell side-by-side in downtown Manhattan.

Foreigners settling into these neighborhoods hardly find themselves surrounded by mainstream America, which may be partly why the city is still such an attractive immigrant destination. Despite the hardships that come with living in New York (overcrowding, high cost of living, substandard housing, etc.), it's comforting to know that you are not alone. In a city of immigrants, no one is really an outsider. There are always other people in exactly the

LEFT: Ellis Island in lower Manhattan tells the story of the millions who passed through New York on their way to a life in the New World. Outside the museum is an immigrant wall of honor.
ABOVE: NYC: a city where the majority are minorities.

same situation, even if they come from other countries or speak different languages. In fact, it's one of the ironies of New York – and a clear testament to the city's cultural distance from the rest of the country – that an American tourist is more readily identified as an out-of-towner than an immigrant "just off the boat."

The other big attraction for immigrants, of course, is that New York remains a land of opportunity. Some variation of the American dream is still alive here, and immigrants seem eager to hop aboard. It's become a truism that once an immigrant group gets its hooks into a line of work, others follow in the same trade.

Thus, in recent years Koreans seem to dominate the grocery business, Chinese workers have flooded the garment industry, and Indian or Pakistani-owned newsstands, Greek coffee shops and Latino *bodegas* have turned into virtual New York icons.

The stereotypes are only half-true, of course, failing as they do to account for people who pursue non-typical careers and assuming that all immigrants start off at the bottom of the economic ladder. The ongoing influx of Japanese businessmen, high-rollers from Taiwan and young European professionals are hardly Emma Lazarus's "huddled masses yearning to breathe free." Most come to New York to shelter their money from the unfavorable economic climate back home, not to mention the bigger returns they can realize on American investments.

Syncretism

In the end, it doesn't matter why they come. The fact is that they are here and more are arriving every day. People have argued that New York is the least American city in the country, perhaps because the process known as the "melting pot," a melding of cultures and attitudes into a uniquely American hybrid, hasn't happened as noticeably in the city as elsewhere. New York's immigrants aren't being boiled into a homogenous cultural stew; they are hanging on to their identities and languages, and building institutions and alliances along ethnic lines.

Nor, as has been suggested by some people, is New York an example of pluralism – a multi-ethnic society where everyone has an equal say. The image of that tag is much too static. It doesn't account for the dynamism of the situation or the possibilities for powerful conflict.

The proper term for New York's cultural mix is probably syncretism, a continuous state of cultural collision, conflict, blending and overlapping, a system in which groups and individuals are continually influencing each other and creating something new. It's like a jigsaw puzzle whose pieces are constantly reshaped and put back together in novel and surprising ways.

New York is a city of immigrants. It always has been. From the very beginning, when the Dutch shared the town with English, French and Scandinavian settlers as well as with free Africans, slaves and Native Americans, it was the give-and-take – and frequently the push-and-shove – between cultures that gave the city an extraordinary, explosive vitality and a certain rough-cut worldliness.

Today, although immigrants come from much farther afield and speak languages never heard by New Yorkers 300 years ago, the same explosive energy runs through the city's ethnic communities. New York is a place that the entire world can call home.   ❑

LEFT: the clock at the aptly named Sherry Netherland Hotel is a reminder that New York City was first founded by the Dutch.
RIGHT: home thoughts from abroad.

CULTURE IN THE CITY

New York is home to legends of every possible magnitude,
using every possible definition of the word "culture"

New York is where you'll find Broadway, Radio City, Lincoln Center, Carnegie Hall and other major venues that have launched big names in theater, dance and music. Here also, on every street corner, are dreamers – talented students performing chamber music, an Ecuadorean folk band or a Caribbean musician playing Bach on steel drums, hoping for the big-time. But that leap is not easily made, as one sidewalk violinist found out: he had such a local following that he was able to raise funds for a recital in Avery Fisher Hall, where it turned out he was less popular with the critics.

Some New Yorkers stick to mainstream theater for their culture, never going below 42nd Street. Others shun Broadway's extravagance or just can't afford it. But not all New York's culture has a hefty price tag. There are operas and concerts in Central Park, as well as other parks throughout the city.

Outdoor performances of the New York Philharmonic, the Metropolitan Opera or the New York Shakespeare Festival are popular forms of free, fresh-air culture. Shakespeare in the Park means waiting in line for the tickets and, though the cast is usually star-studded, the production for some reason may not be all that it should. But, then, lines are a quintessential part of life here, as Woody Allen observed in his classic film *Annie Hall*.

Theater

Broadway, dubbed the Great White Way in 1901 for its wealth of electric street signs, is not really just one street, but takes in Seventh Avenue and several side streets. The district's heyday was before the advent of talking pictures, in 1927, and long before television. It deteriorated alarmingly in the 1970s and '80s, when the art on its stages was matched by the drugs, pornography and prostitution on the

PRECEDING PAGES: a summer night by Lincoln Center.
LEFT: an afternoon at the Museum of Modern Art.
RIGHT: waiting for the stars at the Apollo.

streets outside. Today the ever-busy Times Square area is one of New York's major tourist attractions, filled with shiny new hotels, new theaters, mega-stores and theme restaurants.

Although Broadway continues to present excellent new American (as well as imported) dramas each year, the mass of theater-goers are

flocking to musicals, many of which are aimed at a younger audiences, like *The Lion King*. Musicals also tend to have a longer life than serious plays: until surpassed by *Cats*, the longest-running musical on Broadway was *A Chorus Line*, which eventually closed after an astounding 6,137 performances.

Each of the old-time theaters has its own personality and story. The Shubert Theatre, where *A Chorus Line* played, opened in 1913 between Broadway and Eighth Avenue, separated by an alley from the Hotel Astor. Originally a private passage for the Shubert brothers, who built dozens of theaters, the thoroughfare is still famous as Shubert Alley. During the Depression

Regards to Broadway

The New York theater, like Miss Jean Brodie, has been going through a prime period for a while now. Broadway is selling more than 11 million tickets annually, earning upwards of $558 million in sales. Sir Andrew Lloyd Webber's imported musical megahits – *Phantom of the Opera*, *Cats* – dominated the box office for more than a decade. But original American dramas and comedies (often lumped together as "straight plays") are also being produced with reassuring regularity. In an average season of 35 new pro-

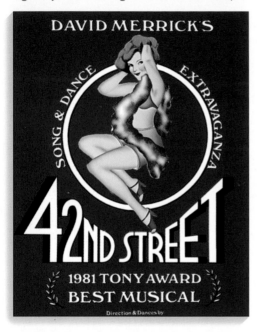

ductions, roughly half of them will be new plays.

Critics may complain that this is a far cry from the early part of the 20th century, when over 100 new plays were staged each season. Playwrights and composers such as Eugene O'Neill, Lillian Hellman, Cole Porter, Irving Berlin, Rodgers and Hart, Arthur Miller and Tennesee Williams all made their names in New York, and their work is often revived. The current crop of contemporary American playwrights, which includes David Mamet, Wendy Wasserstein, Sam Shepard and John Guare, have also seen their work resurface in recent years, both on-and off-Broadway.

Today there are 37 so-called Broadway theaters but only a handful are actually on the Great White Way itself, including the Broadway Theatre, the Palace and the Winter Garden. The rest are on the side streets around Broadway and Times Square, from 41st Street as far north as 65th Street. Roughly half of them are owned by the Shubert Organization; the Nederlander Organization is also a major owner, as is Jujamcyn Theaters.

One of the oldest theaters, as well as one of the most beautiful, is the Lyceum (1903), a neo-baroque beauty on West 45th Street, east of Times Square. The New Victory Theatre on 42nd Street is even older. Built by Oscar Hammerstein in 1890 as the Theater Republic, its name was given a patriotic boost during the 1940s. Thirty years later it was reduced to showing porno movies but now, in keeping with Times Square's resurgence, the New Victory presents an ongoing series of imaginative productions aimed at children.

Broadway may make the headlines, but off-Broadway is considered by many to be the true soul of New York theater. Occasionally a playwright who achieves fame will bypass Broadway entirely in favor of smaller venues. Off-Broadway has also, traditionally, been a cautious producer's way of staging plays that are considered to be unsuitable for the mainstream.

Off-Broadway theaters may be havens for the avant garde, but they also serve a major economic function. Plays and musicals which, in the past, might have appeared on Broadway itself cannot be mounted there today due to rising costs. A hit in an off-Broadway theater, such as Playwrights Horizons or the Public Theater, provides the confidence backers need in order to move Uptown. Those plays which have successfully made the transition from off- to on-Broadway – and subsequently the world – include *Rent*, *Bring In 'Da Noise, Bring In 'Da Funk* and *A Chorus Line*. Occasionally, however, the initial backers resist the temptation to transfer. The reasons are sound: costs are less prohibitive, runs are likely to be longer and audiences often prefer the greater sense of intimacy that a smaller house can provide.

Anyone intending to see a production should not get too obsessed with a specific show. It's better to have several options, then pick the one that offers the best ticket deal. More importantly, don't be afraid to play a hunch and try something you've never heard of. This can often be the most memorable kind of New York theater experience. ❏

LEFT: a tribute to 42nd Street: the musical *and* the street.

years, the Shubert and Booth theaters had their stage doors on the alley and during intermissions audiences could watch the cast go out for fresh air, popsicles and soda.

The evergreen Palace, on West 47th Street, had a rocky start but Sarah Bernhardt's 1913 appearance saved the house from disaster, and The Palace went on to become the world's foremost theater devoted to vaudeville from 1910 to the 1930s. Nowadays it's a prime venue for lavish musicals like *Beauty and the Beast*.

The Belasco Theatre, between Broadway and

> **TAKE A SEAT**
>
> There are some 300 off-Broadway and 600 off-off Broadway shows attracting 3 million people a year.

out Manhattan and have become both the feeding ground for Broadway stages and a strong cultural force in their own right, offering greater diversity at lower prices. Off-Broadway dates from the days following World War I, when Eugene O'Neill was presenting his early one-act plays at the Provincetown Playhouse (both the one on Cape Cod and the one downtown in Greenwich Village). It came into its own in the late 1940s and early 1950s, when Geraldine Page appeared in an unforgettable production of Tennessee Williams's *Summer and Smoke*

Sixth Avenue, was founded by flamboyant playwright-actor-director David Belasco in 1907. Belasco was known as the bishop of Broadway because he dressed like a priest – though he was said not to live like one.

After his death, actors and backstage personnel always claimed he haunted the theater, but the ghost hasn't been seen since the 1970s' production of *Oh! Calcutta*. (Apparently the show's famous and repetitive nudity was too much for "the bishop".)

Off-Broadway venues can be found through-

ABOVE: Joseph Papp's East Village Public Theater has been a godsend for off-Broadway productions.

and Jose Quintero directed a stunning production of O'Neill's *The Iceman Cometh*.

Downtown today, the Lucille Lortel and the Cherry Lane theaters, among others in Greenwich Village, are doing their bit for off-Broadway. In the East Village, the Joseph Papp Public Theater offers sometimes experimental, always quality theater, while places like P.S. 122 and LaMama are among several ultra-casual spots for intriguing off-off Broadway productions with a performance-art edge; another is the Kitchen, in Chelsea.

Not all new material is serious. Comedy clubs thrive all around town and, if you're lucky, you may catch Robin Williams or Rita

Rudner working out new material. Among the best venues are Caroline's, Stand-up New York, and the Comic Strip.

Dance

New York's dance boom began in the 1960s, with an infusion of funding and the defection of Russian superstars Rudolf Nureyev, Mikhail Baryshnikov and Natalia Makarova.

The legendary George Balanchine, one of the artistic giants of the century, created the New York City Ballet, a company of hand-picked dancers put through almost superhuman training. "Dancers are like racehorses; they need a

Opera House when the opera's not in season, originally had a more classical repertory than the New York City Ballet. Under former artistic director Mikhail Baryshnikov, however, ABT branched out from its repertory – and today it continues to offer works by contemporary choreographers, including Twyla Tharp.

Another company with both a classical and contemporary repertoire is the Dance Theater of Harlem, founded more than thirty years ago and often to be seen performing at Aaron Davis Hall at City College (in Harlem). Other venues for dance, particularly modern dance (Garth Fagan, Merce Cunningham, etc.) range from the

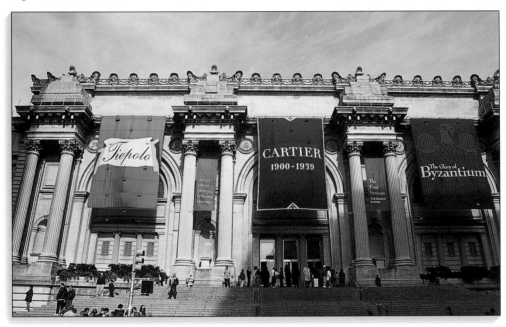

jockey on their backs," was a favorite saying of "Mr B." This mercurial genius had a widely known preference for tall ballerinas and even chose what he considered as appropriate perfumes for them. It is said he could often tell which ballerina had preceded him when he took the elevator up to his office in the morning.

Balanchine, who died in 1983, designed much of the performance space at Lincoln Center's New York State Theater (which the ballet shares with the New York City Opera), including a basket-weave dance floor to provide elasticity and minimize injury.

The American Ballet Theater (ABT), which performs at Lincoln Center's Metropolitan

Brooklyn Academy of Music to the Joyce Theater in Chelsea. Both showcase innovative troupes from around the country as well as the world.

Visual arts

Publicity about prices paid at auction houses have opened the art world to unprecedented attention. In the early 1990s a Renoir fetched $78.1 million at Sotheby's and a Van Gogh sold for $82.5 million at Christie's (Van Gogh once wrote that he wished his paintings were worth what he had spent on the paint).

At the time, art experts felt that the auction frenzy was an aberration. The sales stimulated a wider interest in local galleries, but prices there generally remained (and remain) more realistic than at auction. More recently, the major New York museums – following the example set by the Getty Museum in Los Angeles – entered the fray: the Metropolitan Museum of Art purchased Jasper Johns' *White Flag* for roughly $20 million.

"Museum Mile" along Fifth Avenue between 82nd and 104th Streets includes the Metropolitan, Guggenheim, Jewish Museum and the Frick Collection.

The Metropolitan and the Museum of Modern Art are the biggest and the best. The Frick, a once-private Fifth Avenue mansion with a courtyard, has an excellent collection of Rembrandts, Vermeers and Fragonards. Even the huge New York Public Library on 42nd Street has terrific exhibits in a majestic setting, and the grand reading room has been an "office" for many well-known writers.

If TV is your idea of art, classic episodes of *Star Trek* and *I Love Lucy* are all safely stored at the Museum of Television and Radio in Midtown, along with those of other landmark television shows. For a closer look at the workings of television, while in New York you can attend tapings of the *Late Show with David Letterman*, *Late Night with Conan O'Brien*, or a dysfunctional medley of daytime talk shows. *(See Travel Tips for details.)*

Cultural centers

When the Lincoln Center for the Performing Arts was built on the site of former tenements in the 1960s, it helped revitalize the Upper West Side. Besides being a center of dance, it is, of course, also home to great music: the Metropolitan Opera and New York City Opera, the Philharmonic, and various chamber music concerts and recitals in Avery Fisher Hall and Alice Tully Hall. Excellent theatrical productions can be seen at the Vivian Beaumont and Mitzi E. Newhouse theaters, and each September, the exciting New York Film Festival kicks off here.

Even visitors with no interest in classical music or dance should visit Lincoln Center, especially at night when the elegant fountain is lit. One of the great meeting places of New York, the fountain is controlled by a computer that adjusts the water flow according to current wind velocity, to keep people from being soaked.

Lincoln Center's cultural multiplicity is matched only by Carnegie Hall, which opened in 1891 with Tchaikovsky's American debut and since then has showcased such diverse performers and personalities as Albert Einstein, Amelia Earhart, Winston Churchill, the Beatles and Frank Sinatra. In the late 1950s, the hall was sold to developers who wanted it demolished. With violinist Isaac Stern as a spokesman, a group of outraged citizens managed to save the site from becoming an office block.

Carnegie Hall is famous for more than just music: Charles Dana Gibson drew the Gibson Girls and established the first *Life* magazine in his studio on the premises, and Isadora Duncan actually lived at the hall. The Guggenheim Foundation was established in Studio 1011–12 after the Baroness Hilla von Rebay convinced Solomon Guggenheim to aid struggling artists. Alexander Calder and Wassily Kandinsky were among the artists who received small checks for paint and supplies.

The Baroness's paintings became the nucleus of the Guggenheim Museum collection, now housed in the famous Frank Lloyd Wright building on Madison Avenue.

LEFT: the Metropolitan Museum.
ABOVE: practicing for Carnegie Hall at the Juilliard School of Music.

Live music

New York is also famous for great jazz, with many of the best clubs located Downtown, including the Blue Note and the Village Vanguard in Greenwich Village. Rock music is a more peripatetic scene, pinned down most successfully in *The Village Voice, Time Out New York*, and similar listings publications.

CBGB on the Lower East Side's Bowery started the careers of famous groups like Talking Heads and the gritty Ramones way back in the 1970s, and is still doing brisk business. The Knitting Factory in Tribeca is a good place to hear avant-garde sounds; Sounds of Brazil (SOB) in

Soho is a lively choice for world music; the Mercury Lounge is a popular venue for up-and-coming groups, and folk-rock standbys like the Bottom Line are still going strong in the Village.

Moving pictures

Once upon a time, Radio City Music Hall on Sixth Avenue was to movies what Lincoln Center is to ballet and classical music. Now it's something of a throwback – albeit a spectacular Art Deco one – and even the ladies' powder room is worth seeing. The building was designed by S.L. "Roxy" Rothafel, a showman known for the excesses of his silent film theaters, and opened as a vaudeville house in 1932.

Its concept reportedly came out of a dream Roxy had while watching the sun rise from the deck of an ocean liner.

Many of its concerts and events, such as the annual Easter and Christmas shows with the Rockettes, are of minimal interest to sophisticated New Yorkers. But even these jaded souls occasionally succumb to the pull of nostalgia (especially when entertaining young guests from out of town). And it's still an exciting place to see a film, although it mainly screens openings and special events.

Screening rooms

Space is precious in the city and many cinemas have expanded by multiplying the number and reducing the sizes of screens, which can make movie-going seem like watching television away from the comforts of home. A place that combines the best of both worlds is the Screening Room, a restaurant/movie theater in Tribeca, where old movies are served with dinner. The Angelika Film Center on West Houston Street in Soho is another good choice. Located in a Stanford White-designed building, it has six screens and an espresso bar with an atmosphere as good as the coffee.

Also on West Houston Street, the Film Forum highlights particular genres and directors, as do other venues around town, including the Museum of Modern Art and the American Museum of the Moving Image, the latter aptly located in the Kaufman Astoria film studio complex in Queens. Lincoln Center's Walter Reade Theater, in addition to hosting the New York Film Festival, shows foreign and independent features, which are also the speciality at the BAM Rose Cinemas at the Brooklyn Academy of Music, though with the added boon of Digital Surround Sound. (Established in 1861 as the country's first performing arts center, BAM is also home to year-round performances of cutting-edge theater, dance and music.)

All these places are popular, so you have to give yourself plenty of time. But movie lines that wind around the block are a common sight in Manhattan, and provide great potential for eavesdropping and people-watching. Anyway, who knows? That unobtrusive guy waiting ahead of you just could be Woody Allen. ❑

LEFT: cool sounds at a hot Village club.
RIGHT: *Brief Fling*, choreographed by Twyla Tharp.

HOLLYWOOD ON THE HUDSON

The streets of New York are made for movies and movie-makers

Ever since *The Lights of New York* was released in 1927, the city and its landmarks have been indelibly printed on the world's celluloid consciousness.The most famous image is probably King Kong atop the Empire State Building – the 1976 remake was so bad it's remarkable actress Jessica Lange's fledgling career survived the premiere. The Empire struck back when New York writer-turned-director Nora Ephron made *Sleepless in Seattle*, itself a pastiche of the 1957 three-hankie weepie *An Affair to Remember*. Director Spike Lee vividly conveyed contemporary life Uptown in *Mo Better Blues,* while Greenwich Village has featured in everything from Fonda and Redford going *Barefoot in the Park* to Scorsese's *Raging Bull* (the swimming pool by St Luke's Place). *How to Marry a Millionaire* was set in between the two areas; the classy apartment rented by those sassy dames Monroe, Grable and Bacall is 36 Sutton Place South in Midtown. Over 200 films are made each year, many at the Kaufman Astoria Studios *(see p256).* The number is rising annually; proof that Escape from New York is no longer an important feature.

KING KONG IN CHARGE ▷
Kong hit the screens in 1933, only two years after the Empire State Building was completed.

△ **NEED A TAXI, BUDDY?**
Director Martin Scorsese's *Taxi Driver (above)* and *Mean Streets,* featuring Robert de Niro as a displaced New Yorker, defined a city and a genre.

◁ **MANHATTAN**
Critic Andrew Sarris called Allen's 1979 homage to New York "a masterpiece that has become a film for the ages by not seeking to be a film of the moment."

△ **THE GODFATHER**
Things get gritty in Little Italy in Cappola's 1972 tale of the Mafia. Marlon Brando *(above)* won an Academy Award for his portrayal; the film was voted best picture.

◁ **BREAKFAST AT TIFFANY'S**
George Peppard and Audrey Hepburn's search for love, diamonds and breakfast in the 1961 comedy based on Truman Capote's better book.

▽ **SEVEN YEAR ITCH**
Marilyn Monroe's publicity shots in *that* dress were taken over *that* subway grating at 52nd and Lexington.

LOCAL HERO: WOODY ALLEN

From *Annie Hall* to *Manhattan* to *Hannah and Her Sisters*, no filmmaker has portrayed modern New York (and his own personal neuroses) with more acuity and affection than Woody Allen. Born Allen Stewart Konigsberg in Brooklyn in 1935, he started his career as a comedy writer, later became a successful stand-up comic, and segued to writer/director with *Take the Money and Run* in 1969. The city has played a pivotal role in almost all his movies since then, including *Broadway Danny Rose*, *Crimes and Misdemeanors*, *Manhattan Murder Mystery*, *Bullets over Broadway*, and *Celebrity*. Today, after a high-profile court case, he lives on the Upper East Side and plays the clarinet with the New Orleans Jazz Band on Monday nights at Cafe Carlyle where, according to *People* magazine, he recently turned down a request for an encore because he was coming down with a cold, noting: "People are always saying I'm a hypochondriac, but they're all wrong. I'm more of an alarmist."

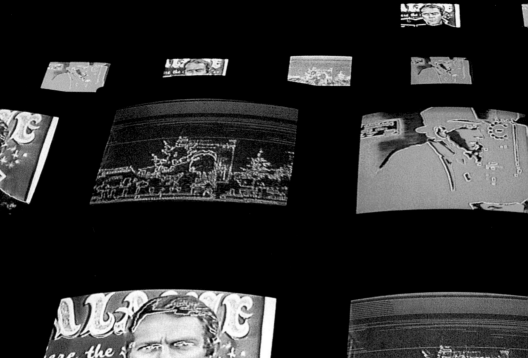

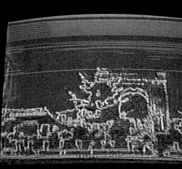

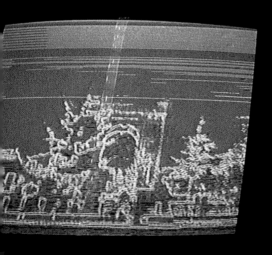

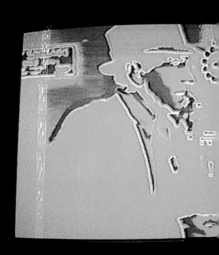

MEDIA IN MANHATTAN

Who you are is not nearly as important as what you know.

In this town, there are plenty of ways to find out

edia in New York is a physical force, not a concept, and people are driven by the sheer intensity of their addiction to information. If a savvy New Yorker wants to get ahead, knowledge is power.

"I want to wake up in a city that never sleeps…" sang Frank Sinatra, in lyrics that mask a hidden agenda: those who aren't sleeping are surfing the Net in an endless quest for information, or switching compulsively from one TV channel to another, obsessed by an appetite for stimulation.

E.B. White wrote: "No one should come to New York to live unless he is willing to be lucky." For today's New Yorker, that translates into a willingness to be bombarded by information from around 50 radio stations, more than 100 television stations, over a dozen daily and weekly newspapers, hundreds of magazines and periodicals, not to mention the World Wide Web. A logical question might be: "Is it humanly possible to process all this information?" As addicted to the Internet as a previous generation was to their newspaper and morning cup of coffee, *bona fide* media-maniacs answer back: "Yes!"

Literary layers

The traditional literary layer is made up of newspapers: New York boasts the oldest continuously published daily newspaper in the country, *The New York Post* (which was founded by Alexander Hamilton, the first Secretary of the Treasury). A voracious reader can choose from literally hundreds of local, national and international magazines and newspapers at the Eastern Newsstand in the MetLife Building above Grand Central Terminal or at Universal News on West 42nd Street, between Seventh and Eighth avenues.

Both carry everything from the *Sydney Morning Herald*, *Jerusalem Post* and assorted

British tabloids to publications that represent New York's diverse nationalities, like *The Irish Voice*, *The Jewish Weekly*, or *El Diario*.

Not to be overlooked is the national edition of *The Wall Street Journal* – much thicker than its cousin, the international edition. As every stylish man or woman knows, the Big Apple is

the fashion capital of the US, and the publication *Women's Wear Daily* proves it. For something a little more gossipy and glamorous, *WWD*'s related publication, *W*, is a glossy monthly popular with the oh-so-social set. The best all-purpose local magazines are *New York*, the *New Yorker*, *Time Out New York* and others that demonstrate a commitment to "being on top of things", as do free weekly newspapers like the *Village Voice* and *New York Press*. The pale-peach *New York Observer*, another weekly, has a loyal following; the *New York Daily News* boasts the largest circulation in the country; and, of course, there's the great "gray lady" herself (now partially in glorious color), *The New York Times*.

LEFT: perfect pictures for New Yorkers, who are only happy doing several things at once.

RIGHT: providing the papers no one can do without.

In publishing terms, it seems as if New York is where every book in the country originates – or at least the place for best-selling authors to meet with their agents for lunch at the venerable Four Seasons on East 52nd Street or one of the up-to-the-minute watering holes. Books, magazines and electronic media do quite a bit of cross-pollinating here, given that media moguls Rupert Murdoch and Si Newhouse have operations in the city. Nevertheless, an extrordinarily high number of non-conglomerate publishers continue to thrive here, too.

SPOILED FOR CHOICE

There are 50 radio and over 100 TV stations, plus 12 newspapers and hundreds of magazines.

day or night, New York radios are tuned to one of the city's commercial or non-commercial stations. It was radio that first introduced single-theme programming, a concept that now extends to cable TV and beyond.

For basic news and information on the AM dial, there's not only WINS at 1010 or WCBS at 880, but also Bloomberg Radio at 1130 AM, which airs non-stop business updates. All-sports radio is represented by WFAN (660 AM). Call-in radio shows, meanwhile, are as popular as ever, especially if the host happens to be an

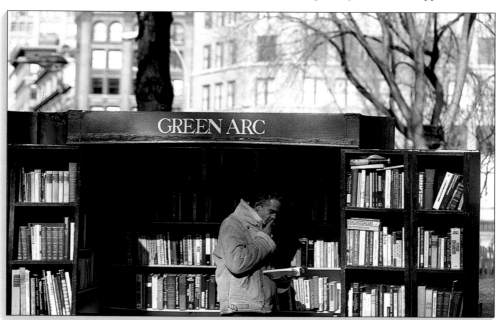

New York City has over 500 bookstores, many of them havens for kindred spirits, especially smaller venues like the cozily comfortable Gotham Book Mart on West 47th Street or such dusty, second-hand emporiums as the Strand in Greenwich Village.

Radio

Readers and radio listeners remain friendly relatives, since they both tend to be supporters of the well-turned phrase and the debate over a well-articulated opinion. Radio especially lends itself to busy city life because listeners can do more than one thing at a time, important for multi-tasking New Yorkers. At any time of the

expert in insulting his audience. This type of programming may be a reactionary trend to easy listening, but it has a large and – dare we say it – vocal following.

Classical, rock, jazz, country... these and other music genres have found a home on the FM radio dial over the years, and each corresponding notch has a permanent setting on New York car radios.

When taxicabs line up at traffic lights on Columbus Avenue early on a hot summer morning, their open windows emit the outrageous humor of "shock jock" Howard Stern or the indomitable Don Imus, between jazzy sound-bites or traffic updates.

Radio's link to TV is through sports; some New York fans are so finicky that if they don't like the TV announcer who is calling a ball game, they'll turn the sound down on the television and get the play-by-play from their preferred radio sportscaster.

The late media guru Marshall MacLuhan saw TV replacing fireplaces in the home, becoming glowing, electronic light to read by. Since then, the notion has far extended beyond merely reading – and when it comes to TV etiquette, frequent channel zapping is a necessity, not an option.

NEED A PIZZA?

At least 30 million pages on the Internet are devoted to New York City news and information.

numerologists who answer phone calls from viewers. Here is the forbidden land of cable-porn and lusty Robyn Byrd's video strip-show. It may not be art or even informative, but cable is always fascinating in a highway accident kind of way.

Mainstream appetites still get their minimum daily requirement from commercial television and its prime-time fare of national morning shows, including *Today* (beamed from the NBC Studios at Rockefeller Center), *Good Morning America* and the local *Good Day New York*, which airs on

Television

When *Late Show with David Letterman* (taped at the Ed Sullivan Theater on Broadway) goes to commercials, alternative viewing options range from NY-1, a cable television station devoted exclusively to nonstop news *only* about New York, 24 hours a day, seven days a week – to the always interesting, often wacky world of Public Access. Here are the citizen-driven, home-grown programs featuring un-telegenic astrologers or huge, big-earringed

LEFT: you're never alone with a good book.
ABOVE: serious media buffs can't get enough of the Museum of Television and Radio on West 52nd Street.

Rupert Murdoch's Fox Network, as well as from the ubiquitous evening magazine-format news programs. Local cable choices can be even more alluring. *(For how to be a member of the audience at a New York TV show, see Travel Tips.)*

Global news junkies have CNN. Insomniacs can turn to C-Span for coverage of Congressional activities and the Weather Channel to find out if it's raining in Madagascar. Nostalgia nuts can tune into TCM or AMC for movie classics. Rock fans migrate to MTV (headquartered in Times Square); and 40 years after they were originally broadcast, Nick at Night airs vintage American sitcoms for a whole new generation of fans. Some shows actually encourage doing two things at once. CNBC, for instance, simulcasts real-time stock quotes at the bottom of the screen while interviewing CEOs about corporate mergers.

Wired

Long gone is the old era of 12 television channels, when the daily newspaper and evening newscast were the limit of potential information overload. Today, the latest local news can be accessed online at *Crain's New York Business* (www.crainsnewyork.com) and by all three major daily newspapers: the *New York*

Times (www.nytimes.com), the *New York Daily News* (www.dailynews.com), and the *New York Post* (www.nypostonline.com).

Each stage of media development only confirms New York's media imprint more indelibly. Media-maniacs here are no different from others in the world, but their need to know things before anyone else does is stronger than ever. Add this need-to-know-first with the multiplication of media sources and communications tools, and there it is: the formula for obsessive-compulsive behavior. (Witness the number of city-suited, cell-phone addicts striding down the streets, informing each other of their exact locations and future plans.)

If TV built the global village, the Internet transformed it into a thriving metropolis. Currently more than 30 million online pages about New York City offer everything from where to find all-night pizza to museum hours to special events. A few of the better sites include the official visitor's website at www.nycvisit.com. Other good ones include www.ny.com; CitySearch at www.newyork.citysearch.com; and Time Out New York at www.timeoutny.com, which describes itself as "the obsessive guide to compulsive entertainment."

Customized environments

Once defined as the world of newspapers, magazines, radio and television, media now includes the ability of customized environments to provide information on demand. Increasingly, local office space and residential apartments try to entice would-be tenants with built-in communications features. A recent ad in the Sunday *New York Times* real estate section, for instance, offered apartments "pre-wired for up to nine telephone lines and high-speed Internet access, plus Direct Access Satellite TV with over 200 channels."

All this is fitting in a place where the literary Round Table of *New Yorker* editors and writers hobnobbed at the Algonquin Hotel in the 1920s, that saw the birth of national television networks in the 1940s and '50s, and introduced the world to MTV's 24-hour music television in the 1980s. With a community of website content providers and software mavens filling the airwaves from trendy offices in Union Square or Lower Manhattan (an area cyber-categorized under the designation Silicon Alley, a witty counterpoint to California's Silicon Valley), New York is poised to remain on the cutting edge of media definitions.

New Yorkers continue to fulfill what Alvin Toffler's *Future Shock* forecast decades ago: "The mass media instantly and persuasively disseminate new images, and ordinary individuals, seeking help in coping with an ever more complex social environment, attempt to keep up… Racing swiftly past our attention screen, they wash out old images and generate new ones." ❑

LEFT: business news is available online as well as on a comfortable park bench.
RIGHT: information on demand.

GREEN SPACES

Poet Frank O'Hara wrote: "One never need leave the confines of New York to see all the greenery one wishes"

Alligators may not actually be lurking in the city's subways, as the urban myth suggests, but peregrine falcons nest on ledges of certain midtown skyscrapers, a growing family of jackrabbits has settled beyond the runways at Kennedy Airport, and coyotes sometimes wander down from Westchester County into the Bronx.

From the cool ocean breezes of Battery Park, where a broke and homesick Noel Coward watched ships sail back to England in the 1920s, to the forest of oak, hemlock and tulip trees at Manhattan's northern tip, New York City is filled with unexpected wildlife and open spaces. Urban gardens bloom everywhere, from tenement rooftops and pocket parks to the Brooklyn Botanic Garden, where a grove of Japanese cherry trees explodes into clouds of riotous pink each spring. New York even has graveyards scenic enough to be considered permanent visits to the country: Green-Wood in Brooklyn, where Boss Tweed and Lola Montez are buried, and Woodlawn in the Bronx, both created in the late 1800s when the fashion for settings of rolling fields, woods and streams in which to deposit the recently deceased had reached a pastoral peak.

More than anything, however, New York has parks: over 28,000 acres (11,300 ha) of them, of which 10,000 acres (4,000 ha) or so have remained more or less in their natural state.

Springtime in New York

In 1609, when Henry Hudson sailed the *Half Moon* up the North River, later renamed the Hudson, his first mate, Robert Juett, wrote: "We found a land full of great tall oaks, with grass and flowers, as pleasant as ever has been seen." His words seem to echo when taking a stroll through Central Park, the park most people have in mind when they think of New York. To

PRECEDING PAGES: Fort Tryon Park in Manhattan's Washington Heights.
LEFT: Central Park, a "specimen of God's handiwork."
RIGHT: Isamu Noguchi Sculpture Garden, Queens.

landscape architect Frederick Law Olmsted, who designed it in the 1850s with Calvert Vaux, the purpose was simply to "supply hundreds of thousands of tired workers, who have no opportunity to spend summers in the country, a specimen of God's handiwork."

Central Park includes the largest stand of

American elms in the country (in the middle of the park, at 65th Street) as well as the North Woods, a remote overgrown forest between 102nd and 106th streets that seems to belong more in Minnesota than Manhattan. Trails run through a deep ravine here, there's a mossy loch, and a series of waterfalls tumbling between a pair of rustic stone bridges.

Past the narrow beauty of Riverside Park on the Upper West Side and the fragrant herb gardens of the Cloisters in Washington Heights' Fort Tryon Park, is Inwood Hill Park, a 196-acre (79 ha) expanse of trees and meadows that's been called one of the most isolated places on the island of Manhattan. Wolves once roamed free and Native Americans held sway in the forest here, about 100 acres (40 ha) of which remains as Manhattan's last native forest.

A family of screech owls make their home in a grove of 100-foot-high (30 metre) tulip trees. Flying squirrels have been spotted. And, according to a plaque on a rock near Inwood Hill Park's 218th Street entrance, it was here – not Fort Amsterdam in lower Manhattan – that Peter Stuyvesant negotiated the terms for leasing use of Manhattan from the Indians for sixty guilders ($24) worth of merchandise. This

ESCAPE THE CITY

"The occasional contemplation of natural scenes… is favorable to the health and vigor of men."

Beauty and the Bronx

Van Cortlandt Park is New York City's third-largest green space. Despite the fact that its 1,146 acres (which border Broadway from 240th to 263rd streets) are transversed by three major thoroughfares, parts of it feel as far removed from the rest of the city as, well, New England. One trail passes through a centuries-old hardwood forest inhabited by skunks, pheasants and racoons; another meanders along Van Cortlandt Lake and into a freshwater marsh that's home to swans, egrets and

part of the park, in fact, is known as the Shorakapok Natural Area, in honor of an Indian village that once stood between what's now 204th and 207th streets.

Manhattan ends at Spuyten Duyvil Creek, where the Harlem and the Hudson rivers meet and the Bronx begins. Several years ago, when the parks commissioner of New Hampshire complained his state's parks were starting to look like the Bronx, the outcry from officials here was loud and immediate: a quarter of the largest (and only mainland) borough, they pointed out, is made up of parks that include some of New York City's least-trammeled natural environs.

snapping turtles. The *pièce de résistance* for walkers, however, may be the route that heads north along the abandoned and overgrown tracks of the Old Putnam commuter train line.

Where the Bronx meets Long Island Sound, Pelham Bay Park's 2,764 acres (1118 ha) encompass two golf courses, a riding stable, the city's Mounted Police School and a large glacial rock where Anne Hutchinson, a religious refugee from the Massachusetts Bay Colony who settled here with a small band of freethinkers in 1642, hid whenever local Indians attacked. The Split Rock where she took refuge remains as a natural monument to an era when this was virgin forest and wetlands. The park's Split Rock trail, meanwhile, travels past Goose Creek Marsh to a wildlife sanctuary where you might spot wading herons, sandpipers and woodcocks. Beyond Orchard Beach – a popular stretch of sand created from landfill in the 1930s – the Hunter Island Marine Zoology and Geology Sanctuary offers refuge to marsh hawks, snowy egrets and tiny meadow mice. Edged by glacier rocks and boulders that are among the oldest on the northeast coast of the United States, it's part of an original land grant given to Thomas Pell, an English colonist who purchased over 9,000 acres (3642 ha) from the Siwanoy Indians in 1654 and declared himself the "Lord of Pelham Manor."

Queen of the green

Queens is known as New York's greenest borough, with more than 7,000 acres (2833 ha) of parkland and over half of the city's trees within its borders, including Kissena Park's vintage arboretum (the remains of a 19th-century nursery), Forest Park's impressive stand of native red and white oaks, and the stately Weeping Beech Tree, which was planted in 1847 and in 1966 became the first tree designated as a New York City historic landmark.

About two thirds of 324-acre (131 ha) Cunningham Park, which is wedged between the Long Island Expressway and Grand Central Parkway in northeastern Queens, is made up of natural forest, ponds and fields. Closer to the shore, Alley Pond Park borders the marshlands of Little Neck Bay and includes several parcels of woods (interrupted by highways) that total more than 600 acres (243 ha).

An overgrown stretch of the Old Vanderbilt Motor Parkway, which was built by a scion of the illustrious Vanderbilt family in 1908 so he could race his motorcars, connects the two parks. But it's the narrow dirt drive leading to the Queens County Farm Museum in Floral Park, that really feels like country. A 47-acre (19 ha) working farm, the museum includes a farmhouse that dates to 1772, a stand that sells homegrown vegetables and a farmyard filled with geese, sheep, cows and pigs.

Seasonal hayrides, nature walks, craft fairs and other events take place here throughout the year, but the highlight has to be the annual Thunderbird American Indian Midsummer Pow Wow, a two-day festival that attracts thousands of spectators to fancy-dance competitions, food stands, and demonstrations of Indian crafts.

A tree grows in Brooklyn

The oldest farmhouse in New York, as well as its first officially designated landmark, lies in Brooklyn's Flatlands district. Built in 1652 by Pieter Clacson Wyckoff, an indentured servant who rose to become one of the settlement's most prominent citizens, the small simple house was the heart of a farm carved from salt marsh originally owned by Canarsie Indians. Now a

museum, it's surrounded by a small park planted with the kind of greenery the Wyckoff family would find familiar, including a kitchen garden with vegetables and herbs, and a spring garden of daffodils and tulips.

Brooklyn's parkland includes 798-acre (323 ha) Marine Park, not far from the fishing boats of Sheepshead Bay. Mainly saltwater marshlands, where local Indians fished and early Dutch settlers harvested oysters, it's fairly unknown outside the neighborhood, although the Urban Park Rangers lead nature walks here.

Brooklyn's most famous park is 526-acre (212 ha) Prospect Park which – like Manhattan's Central Park – was designed by Frederick

LEFT: heading north alongside the Hudson, Manhattan.
RIGHT: autumn in Staten Island.

Law Olmsted and Calvert Vaux. From the entrance at Grand Army Plaza, a path leads to the Long Meadow, a vast peaceful expanse of rolling green that stretches to a dark ridge of distant trees, part of the Ravine that makes up the park's wild heart. This must be what Olmsted meant when he wrote that "the occasional contemplation of natural scenes… is favorable to the health and vigor of men."

Stately Staten Island

When he wasn't designing parks for other boroughs, Olmsted cultivated pear trees and vegetables at his farm off Hylan Boulevard on

wetlands, fields, sandy barrens and mature woodlands is also located on Staten Island, and is just one of five, mainly recreational, state parks in New York City.

Back toward the Verrazano Bridge, Great Kills Park is part of the 26,000-acre (1052 ha) Gateway National Recreation Area, a rambling patchwork of forest, beach, water and wetlands that extends from Sandy Hook in New Jersey, to the Rockaway Peninsula in Queens, and is managed by the National Park Service. Gateway's headquarters are at Floyd Bennett Field in Brooklyn, a vast expanse of meadow that, as New York's first municipal airport, was the

Staten Island. Traditionally a more rural place than other parts of New York, the borough was changed forever when the Verrazano-Narrows Bridge opened it to tri-state traffic in 1964. The commuters who whoosh by car to and through the island *en route* to Brooklyn or New Jersey, though, are missing out on the 28 miles (45 km) of trails between High Rock Park and LaTourette Park, part of the Greenbelt's 2,500 contiguous acres (1011 ha) of rocky outcrops and tangled woods that wind past housing developments, suburban ranch homes and elaborate turn-of-the-20th-century mansions.

Clay Pit Ponds State Park Preserve, a 250-acre (100 ha) wildlife refuge which includes

URBAN PARK RANGERS

The Urban Park Rangers were created to patrol New York City's parks, and to offer free environmental education programs. They also lead nature hikes through various wild areas (and places they don't recommend exploring on your own), including the Gerritsen Creek Trail in Brooklyn's Marine Park, which leads past the submerged remains of the country's first gristmill to a viewing platform where you can see herons and egrets in summer. For a schedule of walks and events, call 1-888 NY PARKS (697 2757). For general information about city parks or to report any problems, call 1-800-201-PARK.

takeoff point for record-breaking flights by such famous aviators as millionaire eccentric Howard Hughes, pilot-turned-astronaut John Glenn and "Wrongway" Corrigan (who left for Los Angeles in 1938 but ended up in Dublin). From here, National Park Rangers administer the seaswept dunes of Jacob Riis Park, the beach at Fort Tilden (a defense point since the War of 1812), and the Jamaica Bay Wildlife Refuge, a unique natural area that lies just beyond the runways of JKF International Airport.

> **OLMSTED'S DREAM**
>
> The landscape architect wanted streets planted with trees and shrubbery connecting the parks.

This 9,000-acre (3642 ha) tract of tidal wet-

with trees and shrubbery connecting all the city's parks and believed that "the object of all that is done in a park, of all the art of a park, is to influence the minds of men through their imagination."

Emerald necklace

For years the dream of conservation groups has been for an "emerald necklace" of parks and tree-lined walkways to ring Manhattan. In 1998, legislation was finally signed that created a joint city-and-state "public benefit corporation" and work is underway on creating a continuous riverfront

lands, fields, salt marsh and woods is home to a spectacular array of birdlife, and was founded partly through the efforts of Robert Moses, the city's controversial commissoner of parks from 1934 to 1960. Best-known, perhaps, for the expressways he rammed through the outer boroughs, Moses also built extensive recreational facilities like Orchard Beach, as well as scenic roads like Manhattan's Henry Hudson Parkway. In this he may have tried to emulate Frederick Law Olmsted, who envisioned streets planted

LEFT: many parks offer facilities like rowboats.
ABOVE: the 1907 Beaux Arts boathouse in Brooklyn's Prospect Park is also the park's information center.

walkway and bike path that will stretch up along the Hudson River to 59th Street. The Hudson River Park, parts of which already exist between Battery Park City and Greenwich Village, is opening up the waterfront to pedestrians for the first time in a couple of centuries.

On a brilliant sunny day, as lines of rollerbladers link hands and skate near the formerly dilapidated Christopher Street pier, and well-dressed couples gaze at glistening river currents from benches beneath shady trees, the words of the late poet and museum curator Frank O'Hara seem especially prescient: "One never need leave the confines of New York to see all the greenery one wishes." ❑

PLACES

*A detailed guide to the Midtown and Uptown areas, with
principal sites cross-referenced by number to the maps*

New York is where I *have* to be," said a character in Jack Olsen's
The Girls in the Office. "I wish I knew why." The people who
live here, and the ones who visit here, could tell her why. New
York's industrial resources are vast. So are its academic facilities. Its
cultural life is extensive – witness the fact that the Metropolitan
Museum receives over 5 million visitors a year. The city's cultural
vigor is matched, perhaps, only by its culinary awareness. Take your
choice of more than 17,000 eating establishments, from Greek coffee
shops to *bijou* bistros to worthwhile soul food at Sylvia's in Harlem.

There's a mix of freedom and foreignness in New York City which
is unsurpassed anywhere. You want to have a drink on a level with the
clouds? You want to go dancing, when the moon is high and the mood
overtakes you? You want to go in-line skating, ice skating or take in
that hot new movie? You've come to the right town.

New York City has energy to spare, along with clutter, confusion
and great charm. If there are more ways of making it here than anywhere else, there are also more ways of spending it. FAO Schwarz, on
Fifth Avenue, sells every imaginable kind of toy, while Zabar's, at
2245 Broadway, is an Upper West Side institution, each week selling thousands of pounds of cream cheese and smoked salmon.
Tiffany and Co. is where you'll find that expensive bauble of your
dreams, while the upscale stores lining Madison Avenue – Ralph
Lauren, Barneys New York – are stocked with high-ticket, high-
fashion additions to your wardrobe. Then, there's always Macy's
and Bloomingdale's.

But not all of New York comes with a hefty price tag. On sultry
summer nights free operas and concerts are held on the Great Lawn
in Central Park. Pack a picnic and take advantage of Shakespeare in
the outdoors, or even the Philharmonic Orchestra. You can visit
botanic gardens and historic buildings, Rockefeller Center or the
New York Stock Exchange, without disposing of a penny.

The best of almost everything is here for the taking. Cop an attitude
and check it out. This is, after all, New York.   ❏

PRECEDING PAGES: the bright lights of the Big Apple; the chrome and steel skyscrapers of corporate New York; Halloween in Greenwich Villlage.
LEFT: a winter welcome to some of New York City's 34 million annual visitors.

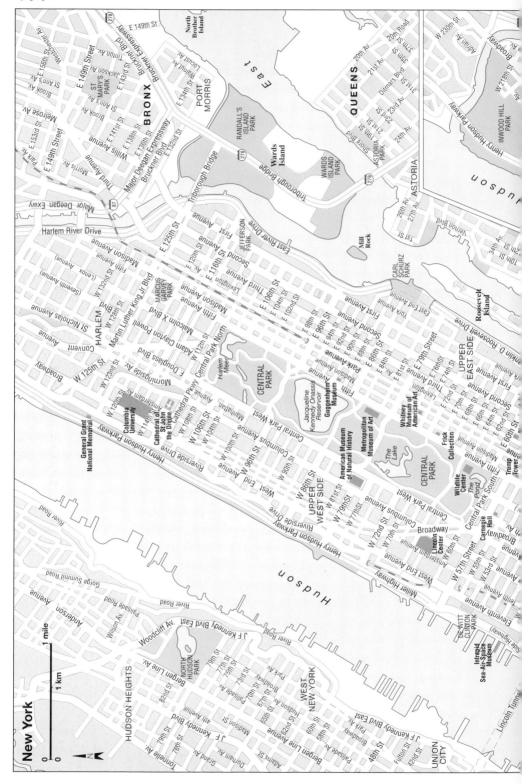

New York

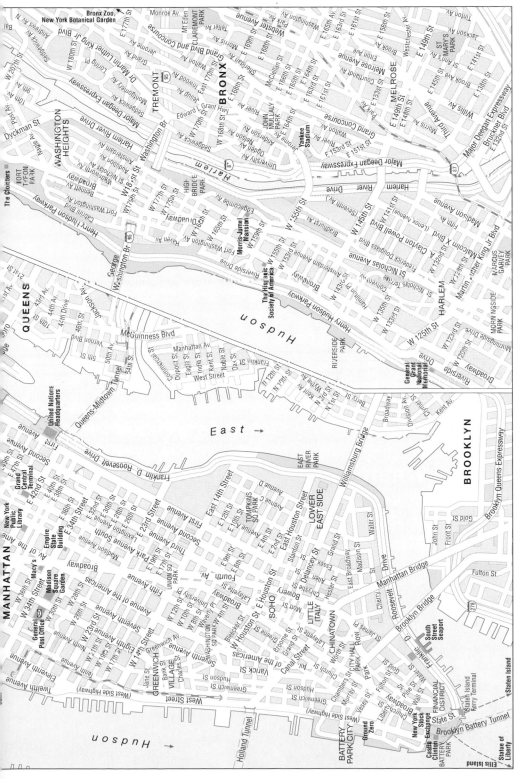

Bronx Zoo,
New York Botanical Garden

Monroe Av.

CLAREMONT PARK

BRONX

TREMONT

WASHINGTON HEIGHTS

The Cloisters

FORT TYRON PARK

Dyckman St

Henry Hudson Parkway

Washington Br

George Washington Br

MELROSE

Yankee Stadium

Grand Concourse

Major Deegan Expressway

Bruckner Blvd

HIGH BRIDGE PARK

Morris-Jumel Mansion

Harlem

HARLEM

NARCUS GARVEY PARK

MORNINGSIDE PARK

The Historic Society of America

QUEENS

Hudson

McGuinness Blvd

Manhattan Av.

West Street

RIVERSIDE PARK

General Grant National Memorial

Henry Hudson Parkway

Broadway

United Nations Headquarters

Queens-Midtown Tunnel

Franklin D. Roosevelt Drive

East →

BROOKLYN

Grand Central Terminal

New York Public Library

Empire State Building

EAST RIVER PARK

Williamsburg Bridge

Brooklyn Queens Expressway

MANHATTAN

Macy's

Madison Square Garden

General Post Office

Avenue of the Americas

Broadway

Fifth Avenue

TOMPKINS SQ PARK

East 14th Street

LOWER EAST SIDE

Fulton St

East Houston Street

Manhattan Bridge

Brooklyn Bridge

South Street Seaport

SOHO

LITTLE ITALY

CHINATOWN

CITY HALL PARK

GREENWICH VILLAGE

Varick St

West Street (West Side Highway)

Hudson

Holland Tunnel

BATTERY PARK CITY

Ground Zero

New York Stock Exchange

FINANCIAL DISTRICT

Castle Clinton

BATTERY PARK

Staten Island Ferry Terminal

Brooklyn Battery Tunnel

Statue of Liberty

Ellis Island

→Staten Island

FIFTH AVENUE

Paris has the Champs Elysées, London has
Bond Street, Rome has the Via Veneto.
And New York has Fifth Avenue

Map
on page
108

There are few streets that evoke the essence of the city as powerfully as Fifth Avenue. It's all here – the audacity of the Empire State Building, the ambition of Rockefeller Center and the old-world elegance of the Plaza Hotel. Fifth cuts through the heart of midtown Manhattan, dividing the island into East and West. This is where the rich and powerful make their moves, where New Yorkers come to celebrate, and where the city shows off to the world.

It's also a timeline, chronicling Manhattan's northward and economic growth, then pushing through an area symbolic of the city's decline. Fifth Avenue begins at Washington Square, near the crooked streets of Greenwich Village. It travels past the Flatiron Building to Madison Square Park, between 23rd and 26th streets, site of the original Madison Square Garden. The avenue marches past the Empire State Building and Rockefeller Center, hugs Central Park for 26 scenic blocks, before plunging into "Museum Mile," which plays host to some of the city's most important collections. Continuing past the mansions and embassies of the Upper East Side, Fifth runs a course through Harlem, bisecting Marcus Garvey Park, and finally comes to a halt just before the Harlem River. If there's time, you might like to consider traveling many of the 132 blocks which make up Fifth Avenue. South to north, culturally and economically, few streets in the world could offer a better overview.

LEFT: Trump Tower glitz and glitter.
BELOW: inside the Empire State.

For the short-term visitor, most of the action is on a 10-block stretch between 49th and 59th Streets, from Rockefeller Center to the Plaza Hotel. There are exceptions to this rule, however, so it makes sense to begin with the sexiest, followed by the biggest.

The **Museum of Sex** at 27th Street (233 Fifth Avenue, tel: 689 6337, closed Wed, fee) is, in the words of its executive curator, "a serious endeavor…a scholarly institution that presents sex in a very responsible manner." Fortunately, it's more fun than that implies, but you must be 18 or older to enter.

The empire strikes back

The **Empire State Building** ❶ rises like a rocket from the corner of 33rd Street *(see photograph on page 47)*. When it was completed in 1931, this was the tallest building in the world. It remains the city's tallest building – but, at 1,454 feet (443 meters) and 102 stories, it now ranks behind the Petronas Towers in Kuala Lumpur and the Sears Tower in Chicago. But when it comes to the view, it can't be beaten. On a clear day you can see as far as 80 miles (130 km). At night, Manhattan spreads out below like a floating sea of twinkling lights.

You can catch the elevator to the 86th-floor observation deck at the concourse level. From here, a second elevator goes up to the smaller observatory on the

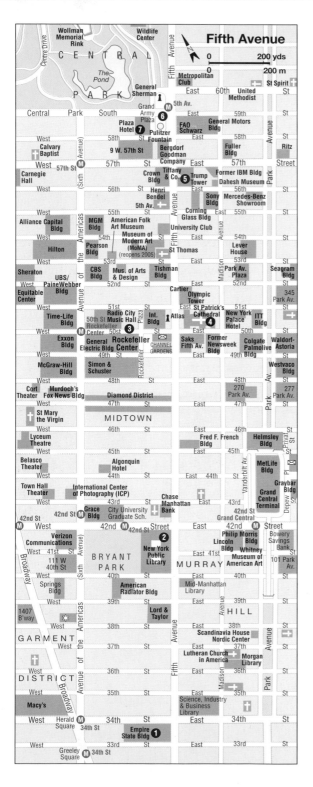

102nd floor, which is just about where Fay Wray had her fateful rendezvous with the "tallest, darkest leading man in Hollywood," a 50-foot (15 m) ape by the name of King Kong. They're not the only ones who met their fates up here. Of the 16 people who have jumped off the Empire State Building only two were wearing parachutes, and both were arrested as soon as they hit the ground. (Be aware that this second observatory may be closed, and the 86th floor the highest you can climb.)

New York Skyride (tel: 279 9777, fee) is a popular tourist attraction in the building and offers a simulated flight through and above the city (not recommended for those who suffer from motion sickness).

Lighting up

Anyone residing in New York for any length of time will notice that the Empire State Building's upper floors are illuminated at night, often by different color combinations. On St Patrick's Day the summit glows, appropriately, bright green. On Columbus Day, the national holiday for the millions of Italian-Americans who live and work in New York, it turns shades of red, white and green. After years of intensive lobbying, Manhattan's gay community finally won the right to have the lights illuminated a symbolic shade of lavender during Gay Pride Week each June.

Back on earth, in a building that once housed the B. Altman department store across the street, the **Science, Industry and Business Library** is a good place to get online if you left your laptop at home, since it's well-stocked with computers available for public use.

Five blocks north at 39th Street, **Lord & Taylor** is one of New York's most enduring department stores, and famous for its extravagant holiday displays. People have been known to line up on a cold winter day just to peer into the windows.

On the next block up, office workers and tourists can usually be found lounging in front of the main branch of the **New York Public Library ❷**, under the watchful gaze of two stone lions who flank the marble steps. Stretching between 40th and 42nd streets, this 1911 Beaux Arts monument is one of the world's finest research facilities, with some 88 miles (141 km of bookshelves and a vast archive collection that includes the first book printed in the United States, the Bay Psalm Book from 1640, and the original diaries of Virginia Woolf. In addition to a fine permanent collection of paintings, the library has a third floor space for exhibits, most but not all having to do with books. The biggest treasure of all, however, may be the main reading room, a vast, gilded gem where windows overlook adjacent **Bryant Park**. Ask inside about joining one of the twice daily tours of the entire building.

Rockefeller Center

At 49th Street, Fifth Avenue lives up to its famous legend, thanks in large part to **Rockefeller Center ❸**, one of the world's biggest business and entertainment complexes and an absolute triumph of Art Deco architecture. Rockefeller Center has been called a "city within a city," and it's got the numbers to prove it. The center's daily population (including visitors) is about 240,000 – greater than many American cities. It has over 100,000 telephones, 48,758 office windows and 388 elevators that travel a total of 2 million miles per year – that's about 40 times around the planet. Add to this a 2-mile (3.2 km) underground concourse, numerous stores and restaurants, four major subway lines, several foreign consulates and airlines, and you've got quite a little metropolis.

The **Channel Gardens** – so named because they separate La Maison Française on the left and the British Building on the right, just as their two

Map
on page
108

The New York Public Library's stone lions are called Patience and Fortitude.

BELOW:
Rockefeller's Channel Gardens at Christmas.

countries flank the English Channel – draw visitors into the center of the **Plaza**, dominated by the soaring mass of the **GE Building** which is fronted by a sunken courtyard used as an outdoor restaurant in summer and an ice skating rink in winter. The *Today* show is broadcast from the glassed-in NBC Studio here (and the NBC **Studio Experience** has lots of shops and TV exhibits).

The Channel Gardens are also where the famous Christmas tree, lit with countless bulbs, holds throngs of spectators at sway over the holidays. Visitors also pause to read the famous motto on a plaque which says: "I believe in the supreme work of the individual and in his right to life, liberty and the pursuit of happiness." The two murals in the main lobby are by Jose Maria Sert. Originally, Diego Rivera was commissioned to do the paintings, but when he refused to change a panel glorifying Vladimir Lenin, the Rockefellers – capitalists to the core – fired Rivera and destroyed the work. (Ask at the information desk for a free brochure/walking tour.)

If there was a restaurant located in heaven, it would probably look like the **Rainbow Room**, on the GE Building's 65th floor. The view of the horizon would no doubt be identical – thousands of twinkling lights stretching as far as the eye can see. With its revolving dance floor and Art Deco architecture, an evening here is a quintessential (and expensive) New York experience. The Rainbow Room has varying opening times (call 632 5000) but is only ever open for dinner or Sunday brunch. The adjacent **Rainbow Grill** serves lunch as well as dinner, costs less and comes with the same panoramic views. As both are owned by the Cipriani family of Venice (Harry's Bar), a certain decorum is encouraged, meaning jacket and tie for men, appropriate attire for ladies.

BELOW: Fifth Avenue for fashion.

Saks & St Pat's

Back on Fifth Avenue, if not real life, **Saks Fifth Avenue**, across the street from Rockefeller Center, is the department store which gave rise to Saks Fifth Avenue shops from Dallas to St Louis. On the next corner up is the **International Building**, with Lee Lawrie's massive Atlas crouching at its entrance. Although the bronze figure is over 25 feet (7.6 m) tall, it is dwarfed by **St Patrick's Cathedral** ❹ directly across the way. St Pat's is the largest Catholic church in the country.

Opened in 1879, when the city didn't extend beyond 42nd Street, the church is now one of Midtown's most formidable landmarks, its ornate Gothic facade working an intriguing counterpoint against the angular lines and smooth surfaces of the skyscrapers around it. And yet St Pat's is unmistakably New York: where else would one need tickets to attend midnight mass? Take some time for a look round the cathedral's magnificent interior, where F. Scott Fitzgerald married his southern belle Zelda, and went on to achieve fame and domestic hell. The bronze doors and stained-glass windows are particularly striking.

Beyond St Pat's, Fifth Avenue devotes itself to more worldly concerns. Namely, shopping – from Tiffany and Cartier, to Takashimaya, Fendi and Ferragamo, to Henri Bendel near 56th Street, to name a few of the stores that give the area its customary panache.

Trump card

At 57th Street, the super-rich (and those who like to pretend) can be seen bouncing between Hermès, Dior, Givenchy and the expensive shops inside soaring **Trump Tower ❺**. (You've got to hand it to realtor Donald Trump: the overall design, with its gleaming marble and a five-story waterfall may be a little self-consciously plush but it's really quite effective.)

While part of Fifth Avenue has undergone a mall-like transformation, with Coca-Cola and Disney cheek-to-jowel below 56th Street (Niketown, Levi's and Swatch are nearby), shopping is still a leisurely art form at **Bergdorf Goodman**. Located on the former site of the Cornelius Vanderbilt mansion between 57th and 58th, Bergdorf is more like a collection of small boutiques than a department store. The atmosphere is refined, the racks are filled with unique designer fashions, and the prices… well, as the saying goes, if you have to ask, you can't afford it.

On the other side of Fifth, FAO Schwarz is New York's version of toy heaven, where the latest games, puzzles, contraptions and stuffed animals attract long lines during the holiday season; sometimes the grown-ups seem to be having more fun looking around here than the kids. **Grand Army Plaza ❻** on 59th Street punctuates Fifth Avenue and marks the boundary between Midtown and the Upper East Side. Usually jammed with bright yellow taxis, limousines and hansom cabs, it borders the **Plaza Hotel ❼**, a grand, 19th-century home-away-from-home in days past for people like Mark Twain, Frank Lloyd Wright and Eleanor Roosevelt. It's still popular with celebrities today.

If you have time, stop in for a drink at the Plaza's Oak Bar, a wood-paneled salon where prices are high but worth it for the Central Park view. ❑

Map on page 108

Festivities on Fifth: famous parades include the October Columbus Day Parade, the Easter Parade and the St Patrick's Day Parade, when the center stripe is painted shamrock green. At Christmas the avenue is lit by thousands of lights.

BELOW: St Patrick's Cathedral.

MIDTOWN EAST

*Grand Central, the Chrysler Building and the
United Nations – Midtown East is an energetic
microcosm of the best of New York*

Map
on page
116

Midtown East is the part of Manhattan many people have in mind when they think of New York. This is where the city's corporate heart beats loudest, where power-lunching, power-shopping and sidewalk power-phoning is a way of life.

Like its counterpart to the west, Midtown East begins above 34th Street, and builds to a bustling climax between 42nd Street and the Queensboro (59th Street) Bridge, beyond which lies the calmer Upper East Side. Stretching east of Fifth Avenue over to the East River, it's a compact, energetic microcosm of the rest of Manhattan, encompassing glass and steel office towers, expensive shops and restaurants, historic landmarks and some very exclusive neighborhoods.

Hills and bays

If you walk along 35th Street, you'll come to the border of **Murray Hill**, a residential area in the shadow of sleek Midtown office buildings, and where cross streets are lined by brownstone relics of a more genteel era. A plaque on the south side of 35th Street and Park Avenue marks the center of an 18th-century farm owned by Robert Murray, "whose wife, Mary Lindley Murray (1726–82) rendered signal service in the Revolutionary War." Close by, on Madison Avenue, the 1864 **Church of the Incarnation** contains some attractive stained-glass windows executed by Tiffany.

The **Morgan Library ❶** (29 East 36th Street, tel: 685 0610, fee, also called the Pierpont Morgan Library) was opened to the public by financier J.P. Morgan in 1924. There are always interesting special exhibits to see here, plus a glass-enclosed garden café and a gift shop, but it's the collection of rare volumes and manuscripts that makes this a bibliophile's treasure trove. Permission is needed to visit the lovely library itself, but visitors are welcome in other areas, including the **East Room**, where ornate vaulted ceilings shelter a display that includes the Gutenberg Bible, an autographed Jane Austen manuscript and a fragment of Milton's *Paradise Lost, circa* 1605. (Open every day but Monday, tours available.)

Continuing north, past **Morgans**, a chic, streamlined hotel favored by the quietly rich, you might enjoy a quick coffee break at **Chez Laurence**, at the corner of 38th Street. Though this small café specializes in French pastries, it also serves meals and has comfortable, quiet tables perfect for enjoying a cup of cappuccino.

From here, walk back to 36th Street and east across Park and Lexington avenues, until you reach one of the city's tiniest and most charming historic districts. **Sniffen Court's** rowhouses were constructed in

PRECEDING PAGES:
defining the sky.
LEFT: looking down
on the world.
BELOW: The Beaux
Arts Grand Central
Terminal.

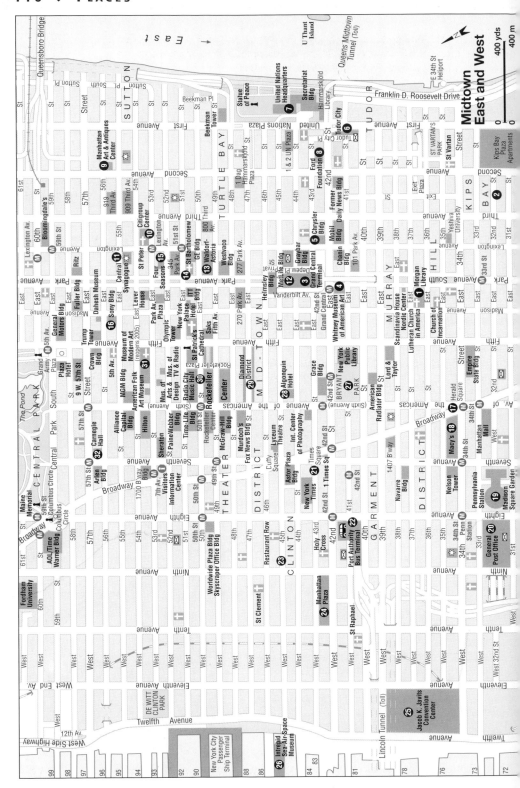

Midtown
East and West

Romanesque Revival style at the time of the American Civil War, and were originally intended as stables for Murray Hill's grander residences (now, of course, they are highly desirable and pricey real estate).

East of here is **Kips Bay** ❷, a mainly residential area of high-rise apartment buildings, medical offices, restaurants and – at 34th Street – movie theaters. The area is named for Jacob Kip, a Dutch settler whose farm overlooked a long-since filled-in bay at what is now Second Avenue and 35th Street. **St Vartan's Armenian Church**, modeled after a 5th-century house of Eastern Orthodox worship, stands at the corner of 34th and Second, and features a small collection of Armenian antiquities.

Advertising industry

Historically, **Madison Avenue** has been a metaphor for the advertising industry, especially the blocks between 42nd and 57th streets. This is one of the city's commercial hearts, where attaché-cased men and women buy their clothes at Brooks Brothers on 44th Street and stop off for cocktails at the **Yale Club** one block east on Vanderbilt Avenue, before running to catch their trains home to the suburbs from **Grand Central Terminal** ❸.

With entrances at Vanderbilt and 42nd Street, as well as Park and Lexington avenues, Grand Central is the hub in a spoke of Metro-North commuter lines reaching deep into the suburbs of Westchester County and neighboring Connecticut, and is used by almost half a million passengers each day, on over 550 trains. Unlike the old Pennsylvania Station, Grand Central was saved from demolition by the city's Landmarks Preservation Commission, and thus this 1913 Beaux Arts reminder of days when travel was a gracious experience

Map on page 116

TIP

Unless otherwise stated, all telephone numbers in this book use the 212 code. The newer codes do not apply to existing telephone numbers.

BELOW: culinary landmark – Grand Central's famous Oyster Bar.

remains almost intact. More importantly, it's undergone a $200 million restoration to renew its former glory. Advertising signs were removed, dozens of new restaurants and stores have opened, and the glorious illuminated zodiac on the vaulted ceiling of the main concourse – one of the world's largest rooms – gleams like new. Tours are available on Wednesdays (inquire at the main information booth or call the Municipal Art Society at 935 3960). Before leaving, don't miss the lower-level **Oyster Bar**, a culinary landmark in its own right.

Jewel of the skyline

Across 42nd Street, there's a Midtown branch of the **Whitney Museum of American Art** ❹ (120 Park Avenue, tel: 917-663 2453) in the lobby of the Philip Morris Building. It's open every weekday, and admission to the gallery and sculpture court is free.

Around the corner on Lexington Avenue, the famed **Chrysler Building** ❺ is one of the jewels of the Manhattan skyline. Erected by auto czar Walter Chrysler in 1930, its Art Deco spire rises 1,000 feet (305 meters) into the city air like a stainless-steel rocket ship. Stop in and admire the lobby's marble-and-bronze decor, enhanced by epic murals depicting transportation and human endeavor.

Back on 42nd Street, walk east past the glass and glitz of the **Grand Hyatt Hotel** (which adjoins Grand Central, and was built over the old Commodore Hotel), to the *Daily News* **building**, between Third and Second avenues. This Art Deco structure, though no longer home to the newspaper, looks so much like the headquarters for the fictional *Daily Planet* that they used it in the *Superman* movies. Check out the gigantic globe of the world in the lobby before continuing east toward First Avenue, past the steps leading up to **Tudor City** ❻, a pri-

The UN flags along First Avenue are those of its original member nations. In alphabetical order, the first flag is Afghanistan (48th St) while the last flag is Zimbabwe (42nd St).

BELOW: flying the flag; United Nations' Day is on October 24.

vate compound of Gothic brick high-rises dating from the 1920s when land along the East River was filled with slums and slaughterhouses (this explains why all the windows face west towards the Hudson River).

Map on page 116

The entrance to the **United Nations** building ➐ is at 46th and First, and it's well worth stopping here for a fascinating look at the workings of international diplomacy. Guided tours are offered almost every half hour from the lobby (call 963 7713), and free tickets are sometimes available for meetings of the high-level **General Assembly**. Don't miss the moon rock display just inside the entrance, the Chagall stained-glass windows, or the lower-level gift shop, which sells inexpensive handicrafts from all over the world.

On weekdays, the surprisingly inexpensive Delegates' Dining Room is occasionally open to the public. The view of the river is almost as interesting as the myriad opportunities for multi-lingual eavesdropping.

Back on 42nd Street, the lobby garden of the **Ford Foundation** ➑ (glass-enclosed, all lush trees and flowers) is considered one of the city's most beautiful institutional environments, and a small blow for visual harmony in Midtown. Nearby, UNICEF House (East 44th between First and Second) offers multi media presentations on world peace and global cooperation.

Historic districts

This part of town is also home to three of the city's classiest addresses, where the rich and famous can be spotted walking their dogs, emptying their garbage and even doing mundane things like grocery-shopping. **Turtle Bay**, for instance, is an historic district between 48th and 49th streets where 19th-century brownstones share a common garden hidden from the public. Among the privacy-

BELOW: the UN's symbol of peace.

THE UNITED NATIONS

The name "United Nations" was devised by US President Franklin D. Roosevelt, and was first used in the "Declaration by United Nations" of January 1, 1942, during World War II, when representatives of 26 nations pledged their governments to continue fighting the war in Europe together. The UN Charter was drawn up in 1945 during a conference in San Francisco and signed by dignitaries from 50 countries; half a century later membership had grown to 185. The institution has won many Nobel Peace Prizes.

Four-fifths of the work done by the UN is spent helping developing countries build the capacity to help themselves, while major events like the first "Earth Summit" held in Rio de Janeiro in 1992 – the largest intergovernmental gathering in history – highlight issues of a global nature. Concerned with establishing human rights and facilitating the free flow of information and its balanced dissemination, the aims of the United Nations are hampered by serious cash problems. According to one source at the UN's Department of Public Information, the budget for the core functions of the United Nations is about 4 percent of New York City's annual budget, and nearly a billion dollars less than the yearly cost of Tokyo's Fire Department.

loving celebs who've lived here have been actress Mary Martin, conductor Leopold Stokowsky and, more recently, actress Katharine Hepburn and author Kurt Vonnegut.

At **Beekman Tower**, an Art Deco apartment hotel at 50th and First, you can admire the view from the Top of the Tower bar before exploring **Beekman Place** itself, an enclave of elegant townhouses set along the East River.

Named for a wealthy Dutchman who sailed to the New World with Peter Stuyvesant, the area has housed magnates, movie stars, diplomats and members of the exiled Iranian royal family, at one time or another. History was made too, as the plaque on the corner of 51st and First explains. This was the site of William Beekman's original mansion, which served as British headquarters during the Revolutionary War. American patriot Nathan Hale was imprisoned here, and on the gallows in a nearby orchard supposedly spoke the immortal words, "I regret I have but one life to give for my country."

Life of luxury

Sutton Place, an oft-used synonym for luxury in books and movies, starts above 54th Street, its dowager-and-poodle-filled high-rises stretching north for five blocks, visual relief provided by the occasional quaint cul-de-sac of town-houses, gardens and promontories offering expensive views of the river.

You can find food for every occasion in this part of town. Sample the cozy, old-world neighborhood ambience of **Billy's** on First Avenue and 52nd Street or the pricey meat and potatoes at steakhouses like the **Palm**, a former speakeasy on Second Avenue, between 44th and 45th streets. The sidewalk outside the popular **Sparks Steakhouse,** around the corner at 210 East 46th Street, is where

BELOW: homeless people are less visible, but still around the city.

mobster Paul Castellano met an abrupt end (which had nothing to do with cholesterol). If your palate's more delicate, and your pocketbook can afford it, just four blocks north, on East 50th Street, **Lutece** is considered one of the city's best French restaurants.

From 48th Street up, Second Avenue is home to one of the liveliest collection of Irish bars this side of Dublin, culminating with **Eamonn Doran**, at 54th, where the Guinness is perpetually on tap. The oldest and most colorful drinking establishment around is **P.J. Clarke's**, on Third Avenue and East 55th Street, known simply as Clarke's to generations of drinkers and diners (there's a reasonable restaurant in the back). Part of *The Lost Weekend*, Billy Wilder's 1945 movie classic about alcoholism, was filmed here.

You'll find more than enough shopping opportunities nearby, starting with the **Manhattan Art and Antiques Center ❾** on Second Avenue between 55th and 56th streets. Over 100 small shops sell everything from antique clocks to jewelry. On the lower level, you'll find that ever-rare NY commodity, public restrooms. Or stop in the **Citigroup Center ❿**, on 54th Street between Third and Lexington avenues. Its slanted roof makes this a skyline standout, while the indoor atrium lined by shops (including a branch of Barnes & Noble) make it a pleasant stopping place.

Before exiting onto Lexington Avenue, drop by the adjoining **St Peter's Church**, which includes a chapel designed by artist Louise Nevelson. St Peter's is famous for its weekly jazz eucharists; it also has frequent concerts. The York Theater, where plays by authors both known and unknown are presented, is located on the church's lower level.

Map
on page
116

Walking north, note the landmark, Moorish-style **Central Synagogue ⓫**, at the corner of 55th Street. Built in 1872, it adds a note of exotic grace to an otherwise ordinary block; severely damaged by fire in 1998, it was rebuilt and reopened in September 2001.

There are boutiques and galleries in both directions on 57th Street, and they generally grow pricier the closer you get to Fifth Avenue. Toward Third, however, expensive gadgets galore are displayed at **Hammacher Schlemmer**; right next door is Le Colonial, a stylish, retro Indochinese-style bar and restaurant with fine French-Vietnamese cuisine.

A Borders Book and Music store is at the corner of Park Avenue, while a little further south **T. Anthony** sells up-market leather goods. Continuing west on 57th, you'll find such fashion fortresses as Turnbull & Asser, Chanel, Hermès, and Burberry. Along the way to these stores, be sure to note the elegant, *circa* 1929 **Fuller Building** (41 E. 57th), home to numerous art galleries where exhibits are open to the public.

The MetLife Building was constructed in 1963. Grand Central was built in 1913.

Above Grand Central

The view down Park Avenue stops abruptly at the **MetLife Building ⓬** (formerly the Pan-Am Building), which was plonked on top of Grand Central Terminal in the early 1960s. But this part of the avenue still retains some of its original glamour. The **Waldorf-Astoria ⓭**, between 49th and 50th, is one of the

BELOW: the Duke and Duchess of Windsor lived here.

Map on page 116

city's grandest hotels, and has attracted guests of the royal and presidential variety since it opened here in 1931. The Duke and Duchess of Windsor and Cole Porter were only some of the "permanent residents" who lived in the hotel's exclusive towers. The original Waldorf Hotel, on Fifth Avenue, was torn down to make way for the Empire State Building.

St Bartholomew's Church ⓮ opened its doors on Park and 50th Street in 1919 and is a fine example of neo-Byzantine architecture. One block west, on Madison, the opulent **New York Palace Hotel** incorporates as part of its public rooms two of the **Villard Houses**, 19th-century mansions once used as offices by the Archdiocese of New York. Built in 1884 by the architectural firm McKim, Mead & White, these half-dozen houses were originally constructed to look like one large Italian palazzo. The owner was the noted publisher Henry Villard, after whom the houses are named.

Almost 100 years later, when two of the mansions were sold to provide a lavish interior for the Palace, several New York historians took exception to the sale. Today, the hotel serves afternoon tea beneath a vaulted ceiling designed by Stanford White; it's also home to Le Cirque 2000, a popular dining spot for well-heeled New York society types.

Picasso for a season

You'll see lines of limos waiting in front of the **Four Seasons** ⓯, on East 52nd Street between Park and Lexington, a restaurant so important that its interior has been declared an historic landmark. The world's largest Picasso can be found inside, as can notable figures from the worlds of politics and publishing. The restaurant is located inside the distinctive **Seagram Building**. The tycoon Samuel Bronfman, head of Seagram Distillers, had planned to erect an ordinary office block until his architect daughter introduced him to Mies van der Rohe. The result is one of the best of the Modernist constructions of the 1950s period.

In the 1980s, some of the city's biggest corporations created public spaces that vastly improved the quality of Midtown life. One of the first was tiny little **Paley Park**, at 3 East 53rd Street, built on the site where the glamorous Stork Club once stood. A short walk away Philip Johnson's mammoth and impressive **Sony Building** ⓰ (originally built for AT&T), on Madison Avenue between 55th and 56th streets, includes a public arcade squeezed between shops displaying the latest Sony equipment and gear. Drop into the adjacent four-story **Sony Wonder Technology Lab** to see how all this super high-tech stuff works (tel: 833 8100, closed Mon).

On the corner of 56th Street is the former IBM building, a sharply angled tower designed by Bauhaus-inspired architect Edward Larrabee Barnes. The below-ground concourse houses exhibitions, while on the upper three floors is the **Dahesh Museum of Art** (tel: 759 0606, fee), with a fine collection of 19th-century academic European art. Alternatively, head for the atrium (casual dining on the mezzanine) and relax for a while before heading back into the adrenalin-pumping Midtown madness outside. ❑

BELOW AND RIGHT: the Chrysler Building; the distinctive spire weighs 30 tons and was designed in secret by architect William Van Alen. It was lifted into place as a solid piece in a operation that was swift and efficient.

MIDTOWN WEST

*With spruced-up Times Square as its hub, the
West Side has world-class art and the
world's biggest department store*

Map
on page
116

The West Side shines as brightly as the east, at least in terms of sheer neon wattage, and what Midtown West lacks in finesse it makes up in tenacity. This is where billboards vie with world-class art, and where, as the old saying goes, there's a broken heart for every light on Broadway.

At the center of it all, Times Square has donned new neon baubles like an aging beauty queen with a facelift. The flash and frenzy dazzle the eye. Even Broadway – the glamorous Great White Way – has been rejuvenated. But then, that's the story in Midtown West. It's been bruised, but it's never gone down for the count. The lights that burn on Broadway, and a bevy of new hotels, restaurants and other businesses here, assure that the West Side is alive and booming.

Starting down at 34th Street, the transition from East to West sides begins at **Herald Square** , where Broadway intersects Sixth Avenue. Named for the *New York Herald* newspaper, whose headquarters once stood here, today this chaotic intersection is best known for shopping.

Macy's

Immediately south of Herald Square is the **Manhattan Mall**, where nine floors are occupied by some 20 eateries and 90 retailers. The big draw, however, is **Macy's**, a New York institution for more than a century. Like the sign says, Macy's is the biggest department store in the world, and it's worth seeing for its size alone. In the past, Macy's was a staple for middle-class shoppers, but these days it's filled with panache and designer labels. In any event, don't expect to find the same bargains your grandmother came here for. And don't dare leave without visiting the "Cellar," a gourmet emporium with every culinary doodad a creative chef could desire.

Exiting Macy's on Seventh Avenue puts you right in the middle of the **Garment District**, a jangly, soot-covered workhorse that still turns out a lion's share of American fashion. There's not much to do or see here, although dedicated bargain-hunters have been known to walk away with some first-class deals from the factory floor. Showrooms, too, dot the area, where you can find the latest, if not always the greatest, fashions, although you may have to shop around a bit, both for the bargains and the showrooms themselves.

If you really want to get a feel for the Garment District, your best bet is to have lunch at one of the coffee shops on Seventh Avenue, where you'll find fashion buyers cutting deals and garment workers gobbling down a bite to eat. Check out the diners between 35th and 39th streets; they're lively, crowded and filled with chatter. One word of warning while you're snooping around, though: keep an eye out for

PRECEDING PAGES:
NY's boys in blue.
LEFT: the Algonquin
welcomes *literati*.
BELOW: Macy's
Thanksgiving Day
parade.

the young men pushing clothing racks through the streets. They're definitely not looking out for you. The only things worth noting are on the southern end of the Garment District, which is dominated by the fur and flower industries, two distinct entities that do most of their business south of 30th Street.

The shapeless, sprawling structure at Seventh Avenue and 33rd Street is **Madison Square Garden** ⑲, disliked by purists not only for its functional, clumsy design but also for replacing McKim, Mead & White's magnificent **Pennsylvania Station**, which was demolished in 1963. The "new" Penn Station is now some 50 feet (15 metres) beneath it, where it shuttles a quarter-million commuters daily to Long Island and elsewhere. Once located between Madison and Fifth avenues – that is, Madison Square itself – Madison Square Garden is one of America's biggest entertainment arenas, where rock shows, ice hockey, basketball games, tennis matches and even circuses are held, and it attracts fans from all over the world. Whatever your feelings about the building, there's no denying it fulfils its function, and then some.

If you're a Glenn Miller fan, you may want to check out the venerable **Hotel Pennsylvania**, across Seventh Avenue at 33rd Street. This used to be one of the Big Band era's hottest tickets, immortalized by Miller's hit *Pennsylvania 6-5000* – still the hotel's phone number *(see Travel Tips)*.

Directly behind the Garden on Eighth Avenue, the **General Post Office** ⑳ is hardly a tourist attraction, although it's impressive, with a monumental Corinthian design that makes your average Greek temple look like a tiki hut. There are plans to re-develop the building so that the US Postal Service shares space with AMTRAK's rail service. There's also that terrific slogan inscribed on the frieze: "Neither snow nor rain nor heat nor gloom of night stays these couriers from the swift completion of their appointed rounds." The inspirational motto was actually stolen from Herodotus, who obviously never mailed a letter in Manhattan.

Heading back to Herald Square, Broadway slices through the Midtown grid to 42nd Street. This is the Downtown end of Times Square, the garish heart of Midtown West, and one of the city's most dramatic success stories.

Times Square

Stretching along Broadway all the way up to 48th Street, with the Theater District sprawled loosely on either side, the highly publicized, multi-billion dollar renovation of **Times Square** ㉑ has made this once again the "crossroads of the world" *(see page 134)*. Whether you're here for a show or not, be sure to take a stroll down **Shubert Alley**, a busy walkway that runs behind the Booth and Shubert theaters, from 45th to 44th Street. **Sardi's**, a '40s-era restaurant still favored by show-business biggies, is across the way at 234 West 44th Street. Nostalgia-buffs can also indulge themselves at the **Lyceum Theatre**, a block east on 45th Street, which is one of the oldest on Broadway and – with its elaborate baroque facade and dramatic mansard roof – probably the most beautiful.

The walk-in **Times Square Visitors Center** (open daily 8am–8pm) is located in the landmark **Embassy**

Be on the lookout for advertised sales in the Garment District showrooms around Seventh Avenue.

BELOW: be alert; these Seventh Avenue fellas with their garment racks move *very fast.*

Theater between 46th and 47th streets, across from the half-price TKTS **booth**. The Embassy was an early bastion of feminism: the theater's original manager, a woman, hired only females for everything from running the projectors to playing in the orchestra. The square is changing all the time: recent attractions include the **Ford Center for the Performing Arts** and the **E-Walk** entertainment complex. At the corner of 44th Street is the Viacom building, where MTV's **Times Square Studio** is located. Despite the square's transformation, however, there's an old-fashioned sleaze-factor seeping over from the few remaining sex shops on Eighth Avenue, where the cleaned-up **Port Authority Bus Terminal** ㉒ (between 40th and 42nd) is a major commuter hub.

Hell's Kitchen

Heading north on Eighth or Ninth avenues, things get interesting in the old **Hell's Kitchen** neighborhood, now known as **Clinton** ㉓. At the start of the 20th century, Hell's Kitchen was one of the most notorious slums in the country. Immigrants were crammed into unsafe and insanitary tenements, and Irish gangs like the Hudson Dusters and Battle Row Annie's Ladies Social and Athletic Club governed the streets like petty overlords. Even the police were afraid to venture into the neighborhood alone.

There's still a certain gut-level edginess to the neighborhood and a new generation of immigrants, but there's also artists and actors, as well as some trendy shops and restaurants. During the annual **Ninth Avenue Food Festival** (May), thousands of New Yorkers come here to gorge themselves on an endless variety of ethnic delicacies. If you love to eat, it's an event that shouldn't be missed.

There's also an active off-Broadway theater scene on 42nd Street between

Map
on page
116

BELOW: hot town, summer in the city.

TIP

The walk-in NYC & Company information center is located at 810 Seventh Avenue between 52nd and 53rd streets. It's open Mon-Fri 8.30am–6pm; Sat, Sun from 9am–5pm. Telephone 212-484 1222 for more details.

BELOW: the Jacob K. Javits Convention Center.

Ninth and Tenth avenues, where the block of small, experimental or low-budget venues here are known collectively as **Theatre Row**. Directly across the street, a residential high-rise called **Manhattan Plaza**  offers housing to performing artists for a percentage of their income rather than a flat rent.

West, the main attraction is the **Jacob K. Javits Convention Center** ㉕. Located at Twelfth Avenue and 34th Street, this is the country's largest exhibition space – and home to the National Boat Show and other events. Unless you're here for one of them, you may want to continue heading uptown. At 43rd Street, the popular **Circle Line** boats depart on cruises around Manhattan from Pier 83. At Pier 86, the *USS Intrepid* is a huge, decommissioned World War II aircraft carrier that's now the **Intrepid Sea-Air-Space Museum** ㉖ (West 46th Street and Twelfth Avenue, tel: 245 0072, fee), where fighter jets are strewn across a deck the size of a few football fields. It's open Wednesday to Sunday, with the last admission at 4 pm. Beyond here, the Hudson piers serve as docking berths for cruise ships and the few remaining transatlantic liners, such as the *Queen Elizabeth II*.

For an alternate tour of Midtown West, you can always walk east from Times Square to Sixth Avenue, instead of west. The street signs will say it is called the **Avenue of the Americas**, but don't be fooled. To New Yorkers, Sixth Avenue is **Sixth Avenue**, no matter how many flags hang from the lampposts. At the corner of 42nd Street is **Bryant Park** ㉗, where fashion shows and summer concerts take place (and sometimes outdoor movies). The next corner up is where you'll find the **International Center of Photography** (1133 Sixth Avenue, tel: 768 4682, closed Mon, fee).

Clubbable atmosphere

A right turn at 44th Street puts you in the neighborhood of the **Algonquin Hotel** ㉘, where Dorothy Parker, Robert Benchley and other distinguished *literati* hobnobbed at the famous Round Table. West 44th Street has quite a clubbable atmosphere in fact. No. 27 is the premises of the **Harvard Club**, whose interior can more easily be observed by peering into a back window, rather than shelling out for four years' education; No. 37 houses the distinguished **New York Yacht Club**, whose 1899 facade sports Beaux Arts details with a nautical flair; and at No. 44 is the **Hotel Royalton**. The Royalton only feels like a club; it is, in fact, a chic and ultra-modern hotel created by Ian Schrager and the late Steve Rubell who also created Studio 54. The restaurant here is the place to be seen for Midtown power lunches.

Another right leads to the **Diamond District** ㉙, a block-long enclave at 47th Street where close to $500 million in gems is traded every day. Most of the diamond merchants are Hasidic Jews, who wear black suits, wide-brimmed hats and long beards. Booklovers should also stop in at the **Gotham Book Mart**, where the late Frances Stelloff held court over a comfortable clutter of books while lending a helping hand to writers like Eugene O'Neill, Tennessee Williams and James Joyce, at whose censorship trial she defended *Ulysses*.

At 47th Street, Sixth Avenue really starts flexing its corporate muscle. This is actually Rockefeller Center's backyard. The four monumental office buildings between 47th and 50th Streets make up the **Rockefeller Center Extension**, which kicked off Sixth Avenue's march of corporate monoliths with the Time-Life Building in the 1950s. The buildings feature broad plazas, hidden courtyards and several fine works of art, but they lack the human scale of the original development and are often battered by chilly updrafts.

Map on page 116

Radio City

The exception to this buttoned-down modernism is **Radio City Music Hall** ③ which graces the corner of Sixth and 50th Street. Radio City is the world's largest indoor theater and Rockefeller Center's crowning glory. The outside is being refurbished and the interior is absolutely magnificent; well worth seeing on one of the guided tours (inquire at the box office or call 307 7171). From the 2-ton chandeliers in the Grand Lobby to the plush scallop-shaped auditorium, the Music Hall is the last word in Art Deco extravagance. Even the restrooms are custom designed. In fact, the Stuart Davis mural that once graced the men's smoking lounge has since been installed at the Museum of Modern Art.

The Museum of Television and Radio (25 West 52nd Street, tel: 621 6600, fee) is designed for serious couch potatoes. Founded by CBS magnate William S. Paley, it's also a valuable resource for media buffs, comprising gallery space, two theaters, a screening room that shows retrospectives of your favorite directors, and a vast archive of vintage radio and TV programs which can be hired for an hour at a time. It's the perfect rainy day activity, except for Mondays, when the museum is closed.

BELOW: the home of the Rockettes opened in 1932.

MoMA

The **Museum of Modern Art** ❸ (tel: 708 9400, fee), known to culture vultures as MoMA, has one of the most exciting collections in the city. Not content with owning the best late 19th- and 20th-century art in the country, the gallery – which doubled its exhibition space in 1984 – has embarked on another multi-million dollar expansion that's expected to be completed in 2005. Until then the museum's temporary home is at 33rd Street and Queens Boulevard, Long Island City in the borough of Queens *(see page 256)*, in a space known as MoMa QNS. For the next couple of years the superb pieces and paintings will have to be rotated, as MoMa QNS is much smaller, but by the middle of the decade MoMa at 53rd Street will not only be back on course, but thriving in its state-of-the-art galleries, where every space will either be new or redesigned and equipped with the latest technology, in every way better for us to savor the wonderful Picassos, Monets, Matisses and Pollocks.

In the same block as "old" MoMA, the **American Folk Art Museum** (45 West 53rd Street, tel: 595 9533, closed Mon, fee) is home to traditional art from the 18th and 19th centuries. The museum has also retained its small, Lincoln Center branch *(see page 159)*. The **Museum of Arts and Design** (40 West 53rd Street, tel: 956 3535, open daily, fee) exhibits works in clay, glass and even paper. If you're hungry after all that culture, try the **Carnegie Deli** on Seventh Avenue near 55th Street. Sample the pastrami, the corned beef, the rich French toast, or an old standby, bagels, cream cheese and lox (and don't take off the onion).

From Seventh Avenue and 55th Street, you're two blocks away from the Carnegie Deli's namesake – **Carnegie Hall** ❷ – which is located at the corner of 57th Street. As every New Yorker knows, there's only one way to get to

BELOW: hello 2005; vast, captivating MoMA is expanding its exhibition space for the second time.

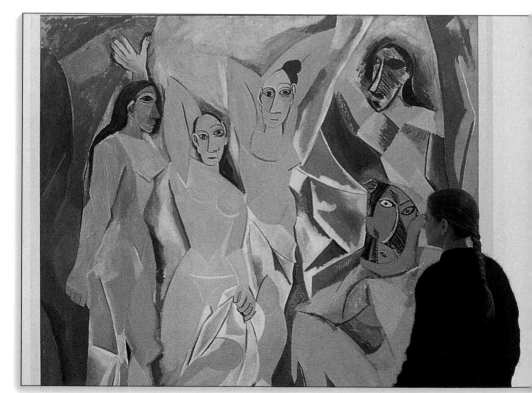

Carnegie Hall – practice, practice. The joke is about as old as the hall itself, which was built in 1891 by super-industrialist Andrew Carnegie. Ever since Tchaikovsky conducted at the opening gala, Carnegie Hall has attracted the world's finest performers including Rachmaninov, Toscanini and Sinatra; it would be nice if the hall's architecture was as inspiring as its history or acoustics.

Map on page 116

Rock and Russians

57th Street, heading east, has a dense concentration of art galleries, including George Adams (41 West 57th) and PaceWildenstein (32 West 57th). This part of town is also the center of a lively theme-restaurant scene. Between Sixth and Seventh avenues is the **Jekyll & Hyde Club**; between Broadway and Seventh Avenue, there's the **Brooklyn Diner** (an ersatz "authentic" '50s diner), not to mention the **Hard Rock Café**, one of the first eateries to start the trend.

For traditionalists, there has always been the **Russian Tea Room**, at 150 West 57th (back between Sixth and Seventh, near Carnegie Hall). Founded by members of the Russian Corps de Ballet, over the years the Tea Room has attracted its share of Broadway stars and Hollywood luminaries. Recently, though, the Tea Room's fortunes have changed, and in 2002 it closed its doors. Whatever happens in the future is anyone's guess, but for many New Yorkers the Tea Room remains a landmark – the sophisticated home of a classic urban treat.

Midtown West wraps itself up with a sophisticated flourish just two blocks away on **Central Park South**, famed for luxury hotels and lines of sleek limousines. It's also a good place to catch one of the city's **horse-drawn carriages** that clip-clop around the park. A half-hour ride is expensive but well worth it – especially in December, when Midtown glistens with holiday lights. ❏

The Hard Rock between Broadway and Seventh was one of the first of the theme-food cafés.

BELOW: Carnegie Hall.

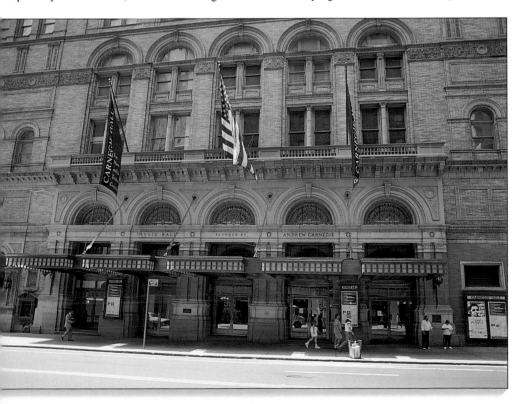

TIMES SQUARE THEN AND NOW

How long does it take for a Times Square light bulb to burn out? 2½ years. For more about the "Crossroads of the World," read on...

Times Square
42 Street Station
Ⓐ Ⓒ Ⓔ Ⓝ Ⓡ Ⓢ
① ② ③ ⑨ ⑦

In the late 1800s, the harness shops and stables around 42nd and Broadway began to give way to an entertainment district which came to be known as Times Square. Theaters sprouted up all around the area, and hotels and restaurants soon followed. During the Golden Age of the Theater District in the 1920s, big-name producers like the Shubert Brothers and song-and-dance man George M. Cohan staged as many as 250 shows a year. That same decade, Prohibition brought speakeasies, gangsters and Damon Runyon stories to the square.

The 1930s saw the premier of such classic plays as *Our Town*, although many of the old vaudeville theaters were by this time being replaced by burlesque or movie emporiums. In 1945, more than two million people crowded into the square to celebrated VJ Day. Twenty years later, Times Square was in the midst of a decline that lasted another couple of decades, its image indelibly linked with sleaze, crime and porn.

In one of the great revival stories of the 20th century, in the 1990s a combined public and non-profit private sector effort transformed the area into a tourist mecca once again, with hotels, restaurants and enter- tainment offerings that attract more than 20 million visitors a year. The big draw continues to be the plays and musicals presented in the theaters; while ticket prices can be high, the TKTS Booth at Broadway and 47th Street offers half-price relief. *For more about tickets, see Travel Tips*

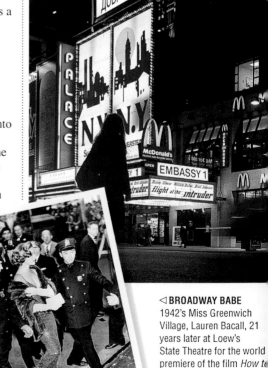

◁ **BROADWAY BABE**
1942's Miss Greenwich Village, Lauren Bacall, 21 years later at Loew's State Theatre for the world premiere of the film *How to Marry a Millionaire*.

◁ THE GREAT WHITE WAY
Free walking tours of the area depart from the Times Square Visitors Center at 1560 Broadway between 46th and 47th streets. The center, in the historic Embassy Theater, is open daily 8am–8pm.

△ CRIME AND PUNISHMENT
Times Square may have been cleaned up, but pickpockets still operate on the side streets. Be alert!

△ BREADLINES ON BROADWAY
During the Great Depression in the 1930s, a city news-paper opened a relief kitchen in the square to feed the poor.

MANHATTAN VICE
Times Square reached a low point in the 1980s, when 56 people in NY were robbed every 24 hours. Now officials claim it is the safest of the 25 largest US cities.

▷ 21ST CENTURY
To celebrate the "new" Times Square and the new millennium, the New Year's Eve ball from 1907 was replaced by a Waterford Crystal-designed ball.

THE NEW YORK TIMES

Times Square takes its name from *The New York Times*, which used to be headquartered at the Times Tower at the intersection of 42nd Street and Seventh Avenue, now called One Times Square. Founded in 1851 as *The New-York Daily Times*, in 1896 the paper was purchased by Tennessee newspaperman Adolph S. Ochs, who in 1904 moved its offices from downtown Manhattan to what was then known as Longacre Square. (The poster detail above is *circa* 1900.) In 1913 it relocated around the corner to 229 West 43rd Street where today, headed by publisher Arthur Sulzberger, Jr, Ochs' great-grandson, the paper continues to follow its mandate as "an independent newspaper... devoted to the public welfare" under the slogan: "All the News That's Fit to Print." *The New York Times* currently has a weekday circulation of around 1.1 million (around 1.6 million on weekends) and has received the most awards for journalistic exce-llence of any other newspaper in the world, including almost 80 Pulitzer Prizes.

CENTRAL PARK

*Central Park is New York's year-round backyard,
where Manhattan's tired and huddled masses
kick off their work shoes and relax*

Map
on page
138

A t least 20 million people use Central Park every year, yet there's always a quiet spot to get away from the sounds of the city. Bordered by **Central Park West** (i.e, Eighth Avenue) and Fifth Avenue, this 843-acre (340 ha) urban oasis stretches for over 2 miles (3.2 km), all the way from **Central Park South** (59th Street) to **Central Park North** (110th Street). Besides recreational facilities which include 21 playgrounds, 26 baseball diamonds, 30 tennis courts, miles and miles of bridle paths and jogging track, Central Park is also the city's premier place for people-watching and street entertainment.

Most impressive of all is the look of the park itself. Hills, meadows, woods and lakes combine to offer city dwellers the illusion of real country – albeit one surrounded by a multi-story wall of highrises. No small accomplishment, considering this was originally an unsavory expanse of granite quarries and swamp occupied by illegal distilleries, pig farms and wild dogs.

LEFT: looking west over Central Park. **BELOW:** the main information booth is in The Dairy.

People's park

By the 1850s, New York City was already the biggest metropolis in the United States, with over 700,000 citizens crammed into a growing urban sprawl. Despite street plans that called for a regular series of small parks, there was little (or no) space for relaxation. It was poet-turned-editor William Cullen Bryant who first made an impassioned plea for a city park; he was soon joined by journalists and civic figures. The New York State Legislature eventually approved the purchase of a large tract of land – then open countryside – and appointed Frederick Law Olmsted as superintendent.

A Connecticut-born farmer, engineer and journalist, the 35-year-old Olmsted was greatly influenced by the egalitarian People's Park in Birkenhead, England, which he had visited a few years earlier. When the city held a park design contest in 1857, it was his Greensward Plan, created with the help of English architect Calvert Vaux, which won.

While Vaux contributed a formal mall, fountain and ornamental bridges, Olmsted was determined to make the new park as natural as possible, keeping intact the rocky outcrops that once characterized the rest of the island, designing sunken crossroads to keep traffic from intruding and creating meandering pathways to draw pedestrians deeper into his carefully engineered wilderness. The object of all this, he wrote at the time, was not only to give New Yorkers "the most agreeable contrast to the confinement, bustle and monotonous street division of the city," but also to "supply hundreds of thousands of tired workers, who have no opportunity to spend summers in the country, with a specimen of God's handiwork."

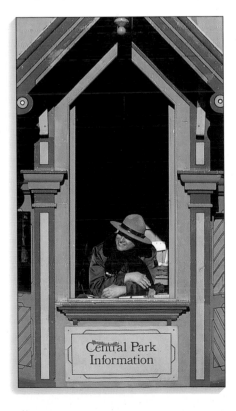

Central Park
Information

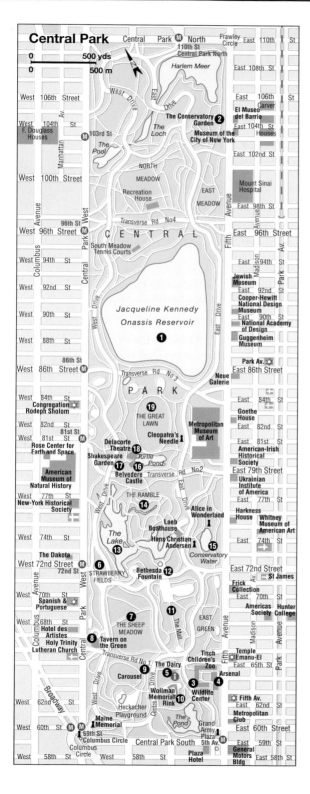

Central Park

Central Park North

Frawley Circle

110th St

Central Park North

Harlem Meer

It took 16 years, more than $14 million, 21,000 barrels of dynamite, the planting of 17,000 trees and shrubs – plus a constant battle with a hostile Tammany Hall – to transform this wilderness into the world's first major public park. And though the "father of American landscape architecture" went on to create more than 100 parks stretching from Maine to California, Central Park is considered his crowning achievement.

20,000 tulips

Roughly divided into a north and south end – with the **Reservoir** ❶ (around which the city's fleet of joggers make their rounds and named after Jacqueline Kennedy Onassis) in the middle – the park has entrances at regular intervals around the periphery. The least visited area, at least by out-of-towners, is the northern end above 96th Street. A shame, seeing as this is where the beautiful **Conservatory Garden** ❷, the park's only formal horticultural showcase, is located. Benches from the 1939 World's Fair line pathways, and in spring more than 20,000 tulips burst into bloom. (To get here, walk through the elegant **Vanderbilt Gate** at Fifth Avenue and 105th Street.)

Most visitors tend to stick to the park's southern end, entering through the **Maine Memorial** at Columbus Circle or at **Grand Army Plaza**, adjacent to the Plaza Hotel at 59th Street.

Go past the statue of General William Sherman astride his trusty horse and follow the path to get to the **Central Park Wildlife Center** ❸ (tel: 861 6030, open daily, fee) known to locals as the Central Park Zoo. The polar bears here have one of the best swimming pools in town. Exhibits include recreations of Temperate, Tropic and Polar Zone environments – and the emphasis is on education, with classes and programs offered regularly.

Stop to admire the **Delacorte Clock** (with its orchestra of carved animals that dance in a circle every half hour), just past the red-brick **Arsenal** ❹.

Once the home of Civil War weaponry and later the Museum of Natural History, the Arsenal is now headquarters for the city's Department of Parks and Recreation. Nearby, the **Tisch Children's Zoo** is designed expressly for the under-six set, and can also be entered from Fifth Avenue at 64th Street.

Farther into the park, **The Dairy ❺** (also reached via the 65th Street Transverse or up the East Drive from Grand Army Plaza) used to be where milkmaids served fresh milk to city kids. It now serves as Central Park's **Visitor Center** (tel: 794 6564, closed Mon), and is the place to go for maps and directions to places like **Strawberry Fields ❻**, Yoko Ono's memorial to the murdered John Lennon. There are also special exhibits on the park's history as well as information about daily walking tours, led by the Urban Park Rangers.

Sheep and handcarved horses

To the west, **Sheep Meadow ❼** is a 22-acre quiet zone popular with picnickers and sunbathers. The sheep that grazed here in the 1800s are long gone, but nearby is the upscale, somewhat touristy **Tavern on the Green ❽** restaurant. There's a **carousel ❾** with over 50 handcarved horses and the **Wollman Rink ❿** for ice skating in the winter. (You can rent skates, too.) From here, follow paths north to **The Mall ⓫**, Central Park's only formal promenade. This leafy expanse is lined by the country's finest stand of stately elm trees, one of which was planted by the Prince of Wales in 1919. The avenue now comes to a halt at ornate **Bethesda Fountain ⓬**, designed with the surrounding Terrace to be the park's architectural centerpiece. From here, there's a wonderful view of **The Lake ⓭**; the Loeb Boathouse has rowboats for rent beginning in March. (There's also a bicycle concession and a restaurant with outdoor dining).

Map on page 138

The Tavern on the Green opened in 1934, and is still going strong.

BELOW: Bethesda Fountain, the park's centerpiece.

Map on page 138

In 1927, the sale of peanuts was banned from Central Park to stem what had become a rising tide of peanut shells.

BELOW: Belvedere Castle is a trick of perspective.
RIGHT: Hans Christian Andersen and friend.

Castles and concerts

Northeast of the Lake, the **Ramble ⓮** is the wild heart of the park. Its 38 acres of twisting paths and rocky cliffs are a favorite with local birdwatchers in search of the more than 250 migratory species that stop off here; it's also popular with gay couples and the occasional mugger. (Despite its reputation, Central Park actually has one of the city's lowest crime rates, but it is always advisable to explore the more secluded areas with a friend or two.)

A short walk east brings you to the **Conservatory Water ⓯**, home of model boat races in warm weather and the occasional free-form ice-skating in winter. (The nearby statue of Hans Christian Andersen is the site of summer morning storytelling for children, sponsored by the New York Public Library.)

Above the 79th Street Transverse, **Belvedere Castle ⓰** sits like a Gothic folly atop **Vista Rock** and serves as a US weather bureau station. Today, it is also a children's environmental education facility and information center – and the best place to go for that quintessential view of the park and surrounding city. The castle is a trick of perspective. It was deliberately built on a small scale because the designers wanted visitors at Bethesda Fountain to think it was farther away than it actually is.

A particularly pleasant walk is to wander through the overgrown delights of the **Shakespeare Garden ⓱**, planted with trees and flowers mentioned in the playwright's work. At dusk, you can peer through the glass at the illuminated Temple of Dendur, inside the Metropolitan Museum of Art. The Bard's plays are presented free of charge during the New York Shakespeare Festival, held every June through August at the open-air **Delacorte Theatre ⓲**. Not far away is the **Swedish Marionette Theater** for children, and the **Great Lawn ⓳**, where music lovers spread their blankets for free evening performances (twice each during June and July) performed by the Metropolitan Opera and the New York Philharmonic Orchestra. Another open-air event is the annual Summerstage festival, where concerts and dance performances are staged at the **Rumsey Playfield**, near the 72nd Street entrance on Fifth.

No traffic

On summer weekends, traffic is forbidden, making a stroll, a bike ride or even a carriage ride a particularly pleasant Manhattan experience. You can hire a carriage from the Tavern on the Green, at Fifth Avenue and 59th Street, and along Central Park South. Each ride lasts half an hour. Although there's a fixed price, you could always try negotiating, especially if trade isn't particularly brisk. But no matter what day of the week, or what time of the year, New Yorkers come to Central Park to find a brief respite from the on-going stress of city living.

Despite a constant battle against overuse, litter and erosion, despite the well-meaning but characterless facilities added by subsequent park administrations, despite the occasional sensationalized crime, Central Park endures as Olmsted envisioned: a place where "the mind may be more or less lifted out of the moods and habits into which it is, under the ordinary conditions of life in the city, likely to fall." ❑

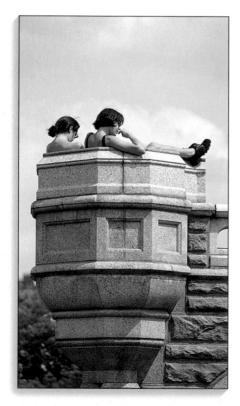

UPPER EAST SIDE

*When New Yorkers think of the Upper
East Side, one word springs to
mind: money. And lots of it*

Map
on page
146

The Upper East Side's romance with wealth began in the late 1800s, when the famous Four Hundred – so-called because a contemporary social arbiter had decreed that in all of New York there were only 400 families that mattered – moved into Fifth Avenue to set down roots alongside Central Park. The homes they built were the most luxurious the city had seen – mansions and townhouses decked out like European palaces and filled with priceless art.

Since then, the Carnegies, Fricks and Astors have moved to greener pastures, but the Upper East Side has never lost its taste for the good life. Today, Fifth, Madison and Park avenues are still home to the privileged few, people who know the high cost of luxury and make no bones about paying for it. Even the areas east of **Lexington Avenue ❶** are starting to put on airs. Now that gentrification has set in, the old blue-collar neighborhoods once occupied by German, Czech and Hungarian immigrants have become smart and upscale.

Millionaires' Row

As always, the air of wealth is most intoxicating on **Fifth Avenue ❷**, known to old-time New Yorkers as Millionaires' Row. The name doesn't get used much now, but there are still plenty of millionaires – although, unlike the extravagant Four Hundred, they tend to keep a low profile. In fact, most of the newer apartment buildings are understated to the point of boredom. There are a few eye-poppers left over from the glory days, however, and if you happen to be passing by, take a look.

Standing at the corner of 60th Street, for example, is J.P. Morgan's stately **Metropolitan Club ❸**, founded in 1892 after one of the financier's *nouveau riche* buddies was denied membership at the Union Club. Oddly, the **Knickerbocker Club**, located in a landmark building at 62nd Street, was established 20 years earlier to protest a perceived laxness in overall club membership standards.

The enormous **Temple Emanu-El ❹** cuts a brooding, Moorish figure at the corner of 65th Street, where 2,500 worshippers can gather under one roof, making this cavernous temple one of the largest reform synagogues in the world.

Up in the 70s there are several splendid old mansions including the **Harkness House ❺** (1 East 75th Street), the château-style **Duke mansion** (1 East 78th Street), which houses the New York University Institute of Fine Arts, and Payne Whitney's Renaissance-style *palazzo*, now serving as a branch of the **French Embassy** (972 Fifth Avenue).

International relations are the order of the day on the Upper East Side: the former Stuyvesant mansion at 79th and Fifth is the **Ukrainian Institute ❻**; and

PRECEDING PAGES:
retail therapy center.
LEFT: young Ms
Upper East Sider.
BELOW: from the
Met Museum's
collection.

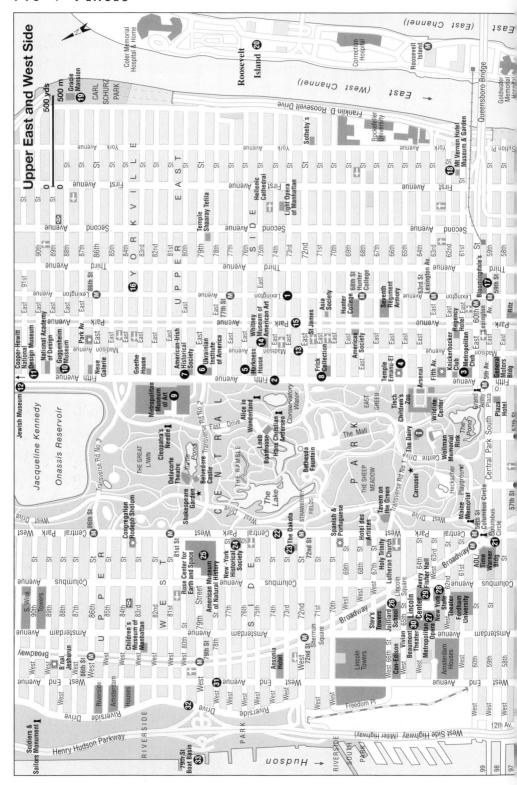

Upper East and West Side

Soldiers & Sailors Monument

Jacqueline Kennedy Onassis Reservoir

THE GREAT LAWN

Cleopatra's Needle

Metropolitan Museum of Art ⑨

Cooper-Hewitt National Design Museum ⑫

Jewish Museum ⑫

National Academy of Design ⑪

Guggenheim Museum ⑩

Neue Galerie

Goethe House

American-Irish Historical Society ⑦

Ukrainian Institute of America ⑥

Harkness House ⑤

Whitney Museum of American Art ⑭

St James ⑮

⑯

①

Asia Society

Hunter College

Seventh Regiment Armory

Frick Collection ⑧

Americas Society

Temple Emanu-El

Knickerbocker Club

Metropolitan Club ③

Regency Hotel

Bloomingdale's

⑰

General Motors Bldg

Arsenal

Wildlife Center

Tisch Children's Zoo

The Dairy

Wollman Memorial Rink

The Pond

Plaza Hotel

Carousel

Columbus Circle

AOL/ Time Warner Bldg ㉑

Maine Memorial

Heckscher Playground

THE SHEEP MEADOW

Tavern on the Green

Holy Trinity Lutheran Church

Hotel des Artistes

Spanish & Portuguese

The Dakota ㉓

STRAWBERRY FIELDS

THE RAMBLE

The Lake

Bethesda Fountain

Loeb Boathouse

Hans Christian Andersen

Alice in Wonderland

Conservatory Water

Belvedere Castle

Delacorte Theatre

Turtle Pond

Shakespeare Garden

Congregation Rodeph Sholom

New-York Historical Society ㉔

Rose Center for Earth and Space ㉕

American Museum of Natural History ㉕

Children's Museum of Manhattan

B'nai Jeshurun

S. Wise Towers

Ansonia Hotel

Stev's Towers

Con-Edison

Lincoln Towers

Juilliard School ㉖

Vivian Beaumont Theater

New York State Theater ㉗

Metropolitan Opera House ㉚

Lincoln Center

Fisher Hall ㉙

Avery

Fordham University

Amsterdam Houses

㉛

㉜

79th St Boat Basin ㉝

Riverside Houses

Freedom Pl

Lincoln Square

Carl Schurz Park

Gracie Mansion ⑲

Coler Memorial Hospital & Home

Roosevelt Island ⑳

Correction Hospital

Roosevelt Island

Queensboro Bridge

Goldwater Memorial Hospital

Sotheby's

Rockefeller University

Franklin D. Roosevelt Drive

Mt Vernon Hotel Museum & Garden ⑱

Hellenic Cathedral

Light Opera of Manhattan

Temple Shaaray Tefila

Sutton Pl

Ritz

500 yds

500 m

East (East Channel)

East (West Channel)

Hudson

RIVERSIDE PARK

Henry Hudson Parkway

West Side Highway (Miller Highway) 12th Av.

CENTRAL PARK

the **American-Irish Historical Society** ❼ is further up the street at No. 991. Between 68th and 70th streets, the classic McKim, Mead and White building at 680 Park Avenue is home to the **Americas Society**, while the Georgian-style house at No. 686 is the **Italian Cultural Institute**.

At the corner of Fifth Avenue and 70th Street, the **Frick Collection** ❽ (1 East 70th Street, tel: 288 0700, fee) is showcased inside the former home of steel magnate Henry Clay Frick, a man whose passion for art was surpassed only by his ruthlessness in business. The collection, which is made up almost entirely of European works from the 16th to 19th centuries, represents one of the city's most successful combinations of art and ambience – a bit stuffy perhaps, but filled with gracious touches like a tranquil courtyard and soft chairs to sink into when your feet get tired. (Open Tues through Sat, and Sun afternoon.)

The magnificent Met

Opened in 1874 the **Metropolitan Museum of Art** ❾ (82nd Street, tel: 535 7710, fee) is a sprawling Gothic behemoth containing the largest art collection in the United States. In a word, it's awesome – covering everything from an Egyptian temple to modern art. The holdings are so vast that it's not really a single museum at all, but dozens of distinct collections housed in a maze of galleries, gardens and period rooms; there's even a "hidden" sculpture garden on the roof, boasting stellar views of Central Park. Half the fun is getting lost, wondering what treasures you'll bump into next. Be sure to give yourself plenty of time and, whatever you do, don't try to tackle the whole thing in one day. It's much too good to rush through (and it's open every day but Monday).

If pressed for time, look out for these highlights in the American wing. The

Map on page 146

Mother and Children by *Pierre Auguste Renoir, a highlight of the Frick Collection.*

BELOW: the Metropolitan Museum of Art.

The museum of the National Academy of Design, one of the places worth visiting on Museum Mile.

Frank Lloyd Wright Room is in gallery 127 on the first floor. Also on the first floor, Charles Engelhard Court contains the *Grapevine* stained-glass window by Louis Comfort Tiffany and staircases from the Chicago Stock Exchange of 1893 by Louis Sullivan. Galleries 217–224 on the second floor include *George Washington* by Gilbert Stuart and *Snap the Whip* by Winslow Homer.

Walk four blocks past the Met, and you've hit upon yet another New York classic, the **Solomon R. Guggenheim Museum ➓** (1071 Fifth Avenue, tel: 423 3500, closed Thur, fee). Located at the corner of 88th Street, the white spiral-shaped structure built to a design by Frank Lloyd Wright is an architectural masterpiece, and was one of the first to achieve the cachet now afforded to the Guggenheim museum in Las Vegas (opened in conjunction with Russia's Hermitage museum), the Frank Gehry-designed building in Bilbao, Spain, and others in Berlin and Venice. This Guggenheim was given landmark status by the New York City Landmarks Preservation Commission, one of the youngest buildings ever awarded the honor. Take the elevator to the top floor and slowly make your way down the circular ramp. Although exhibitions change often, they are likely to include works by Renoir, Van Gogh, Toulouse-Lautrec, Kandinsky, Klee and Picasso. A 10-story tower, opened in 1992, doubled the museum's exhibition space, but another major expansion was called off in 2003.

Museums all in a row

After the Guggenheim, Fifth Avenue runs into a barrage of museums between 89th and 104th streets, including the **National Academy of Design** (1083 Fifth Avenue, tel: 369 4880, closed Mon and Tues, fee); the **Cooper-Hewitt National Design Museum ➊➊** (2 East 91st Street, tel: 849 8300, closed Mon, fee); the

Jewish Museum ⓬ (1109 Fifth Avenue, tel: 423 3200, closed Fri and Sat, fee); the **Museum of the City of New York**, (Fifth Avenue at 103rd Street, tel: 534 1672, closed Mon and Tues, fee); and **El Museo del Barrio** (1230 Fifth Avenue, tel: 831 7272, closed Mon and Tues, fee). All are fine institutions, but of varying interest depending on the quality of the changing exhibits. *(For the location of the latter two museums, see map on page 166; also see page 151).*

Map on page 146

Ritz and glitz

Geographically, Fifth is only one block away from **Madison Avenue** ⓭, but in spirit they're worlds apart. You can kiss "prim and proper" goodbye, because Madison is the land of "ritz and glitz" – a slick marketplace tailor-made for the hyperactive consumer. It's a bit mellower in the pleasant low-90s neighborhood of **Carnegie Hill** than it is in the 60s, but even if you cross over from the top of Museum Mile you'll still find plenty of boutiques and art galleries worth exploring. Tiny Bistro du Nord, at 93rd Street, is a good place to stop for lunch before continuing back downtown, since Madison's fashion profile doesn't really get started until about 81st Street, where Agnès b is at 1063 and Betsy Johnson is across the street at 1060.

You'll find Missoni at 78th Street and Carolina Herrera at 75th Street, along the way passing the more casual – and affordable – elegance of Eileen Fisher (1039 Madison). A block away, Lanciani has fanciful costume jewelry, Edith Weber specializes in estate pieces, and several small neighboring galleries display modern European and American art, including David Findlay. However, if you're running late, or your watch has stopped, just below 76th Street, is **Time Will Tell**, a terrific little place filled with vintage timepieces.

BELOW: two views of the Guggenheim; when the museum opened in 1959, many people hated it.

The wheels of capitalism slow down a bit at 75th Street, where the **Whitney Museum of American Art**  (945 Madison Avenue, tel: 570 3676, fee except Thurs 6–8pm) is located. You can hardly miss it. Marcel Breuer's oddly cantilevered structure is a work of art in its own right, second only to the Guggenheim as one of the area's boldest architectural statements. The Whitney collection was founded in 1930 by Gertrude Vanderbilt Whitney, whose taste ran to the works of American realists like Edward Hopper and George Bellows. Since then, the museum has employed a policy of acquiring pieces that represent the full range of 20th-century American art, including the works of Georgia O'Keefe, Willem de Kooning, Jackson Pollock and Jasper Johns. Every other year, the museum mounts the Whitney Biennial, a survey of the most provocative American art of the previous two years. The museum is closed Monday and Tuesday.

Stop in at the 3 Guys Restaurant across the street if you haven't eaten: not only does this tidy establishment have a traditional lunch counter with stools, but the food is decent and relatively inexpensive. But for a first class dessert and coffee, go to Sant Ambroeus, a stylish *pasticceria* just north of 77th Street. The *gelato*, in over a dozen flavors, is inspired.

Shop till you drop

From the Whitney Museum to 59th Street, Madison turns into a veritable orgy of conspicuous consumption. The names on the storefronts read like a roster of the fashion elite: Ralph Lauren, Yves Saint Laurent, Kenzo, Giorgio Armani, Prada, Emmanuel Ungaro, Calvin Klein. Needless to say, unless you're packing a king-size bankroll, most of these stores are more for browsing than serious and prolonged buying. One of New York's quintessential shopping scenes is **Barneys New York**, at 61st Street, which also has a chic lower-level restaurant.

Skipping crosstown to **Park Avenue** , the scene again changes dramatically. Compared to the flashy indulgence of Madison, Park seems rather bland. One exception is the **Regency Hotel**, a favorite with big-wheel media-types for power breakfasts, where the library bar serves afternoon tea. Another is the **Colony Club**, a block up at 62nd Street, which has a stately redbrick facade, appropriately reflecting the stately demeanor of the society women who belong to it. There are also two nearby cultural sites: the **Museum of American Illustration** (128 East 63rd Street, tel: 838 2560, closed Sun and Mon) and the **China Institute** (125 East 65th Street, tel: 744 8181, closed Sun, fee). Both are between Park and Lexington and offer, respectively, exhibits about the history of illustration and by contemporary Chinese artists.

Continuing north, you can't miss the **Seventh Regiment Armory** at Park and 66th Street, a medieval castle look-alike that was built in the 1870s and serves as an exhibition hall for major art and antiques shows.

A few blocks up at 70th Street, the **Asia Society** (725 Park Avenue, tel: 517 ASIA, closed Mon, fee) houses the Rockefellers' fine collection of Asian art. It also features a performance hall, lecture theater and cinema for shows and events dealing with Asian culture. East of Park Avenue, the Upper East Side falls a

BELOW: ladies who lunch do so at Barneys New York.

few notches in the prestige department, but makes up for it with a healthy dash of self-indulgence. Once dominated by East European immigrants, much of the area is now heavily gentrified, although remnants of the old German, Hungarian and Czechoslovakian quarters remain in the area called **Yorkville ⓰**, which runs approximately between 79th and 98th streets.

Map
on page
146

Food for the famous

You'll find mouth-watering German specialties at the cozy Heidelberg Restaurant, at 1648 Second Avenue between 85th and 86th streets, which serves huge mounds of rib-sticking German food. A few blocks further south, Mocca Hungarian (1588 Second Avenue) is the place to go for inexpensive goulash. In fact, there are a slew of eateries to choose from around here. Many are on the upscale side; a few – like J.G. Melon at Third Avenue and 74th Street – are neighborhood standbys that have outlasted trendier competition.

Artist Andy Warhol lived at 57 East 66th Street. The house was recently declared a historic cultural site in a ceremony that lasted 15 minutes.

Two very different establishments that should be mentioned are Elaine's (Second Avenue between 88th and 89th streets) and Papaya King (86th Street and Third Avenue). Elaine's is the quintessential show-biz restaurant made famous by all those Woody Allen movies. The crowd tends to be exclusive, and the food is famously mediocre, so unless you've got a friend who's got a friend who knows Elaine, you might want to think twice about giving it a try.

Papaya King falls into an altogether different category. It's not a restaurant so much as a hot dog stand. But this place doesn't serve just any old wiener. No indeed. Papaya King hot dogs are among the tastiest in the city. And as if that weren't enough, you can wash them down with a luscious assortment of tropical juices. Keep in mind, however, that this is not the place for a sit-down meal. In

BELOW: smoked salmon display at Barneys.

MUSEUM MILE

The Upper East Side's Museum Mile begins with the Frick Collection on 70th Street and ends up in Harlem with El Museo del Barrio on 105th Street. In between are seven other prestigious museums, which, together with the city's lesser-known establishments *(see page 210)* confirm New York City's status as America's cultural capital. So dazzling are these major museums, however, that visitors tend to overlook the smaller places on Museum Mile. The Cooper-Hewitt National Design Museum, for example, is housed in a mansion built by steel tycoon Andrew Carnegie. The Museum of the City of New York – far from being just a musty historical institute – has a fine collection of doll houses that children will love. The Jewish Museum is one of the largest in the US devoted to the history and culture of the Jewish people, and includes prehistoric artifacts and rare manuscripts. Culture, however, is all in the eye of the beholder, especially one with a sense of humor. On being informed he was required to check in his walking stick at the cloakroom of the Metropolitan Museum, Mark Twain exclaimed: "Leave my cane! Leave my cane! Then how do you expect me to poke holes through the oil paintings?"

true New York fashion, Papaya King supplies about two or three stools. Everybody else has to eat on their feet. As far as shopping goes, this half of the Upper East Side is scatter-shot with all sorts of specialty stores, antique dealers and galleries. Your best bet is to peruse Lexington Avenue, especially in the mid-60s and 70s. Basically, it's Madison without the froufrou.

Presidents and mayors

Serious shoppers may want to head straight for one of the city's retail queens: **Bloomingdale's** 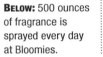 at 59th Street – a minor institution that most dyed-in-the-wool New Yorkers could not live without. Style and quality are keynotes at Bloomies. The shop is almost always crowded – it can be oppressively so during holidays and sale times – but if you only go to one department store in New York City, this should probably be it. (Entrances are located on both Third and Lexington avenues.)

Between First and York Avenues, the **Mount Vernon Hotel Museum and Garden** ⓲ (421 East 61st Street, tel: 838 6878, closed Mon and all of Aug), is one of the few 18th-century buildings still standing in Manhattan. It's a wonder that it has survived, as it sits under the busy 59th Street Bridge (also known as Queensborough Bridge). The museum has been meticulously furnished with period antiques redolent of its later incarnation as a hotel, and gives a good indication of what life was like in the early to mid-19th century. **Sotheby's**, the high-stakes auction house favored by art collectors, is about 10 blocks away, near the corner of York Avenue and 72nd Street.

BELOW: 500 ounces of fragrance is sprayed every day at Bloomies.

Still farther up, at 88th Street and East End Avenue, **Gracie Mansion** ⓳ is the mayor's official residence and another fortunate survivor of the 18th century.

It was built by Scots-born Archibald Gracie as a summer home and in 1942 was first used by Mayor Fiorello LaGuardia. Before that the house served as the Museum of the City of New York. Tours can be arranged by appointment; tel: 570 4751 for details.

Gracie Mansion is located in **Carl Schurz Park**, a pleasant patch of green overlooking the treacherous currents of Hell Gate, where the waters of the East River and the Harlem River flow together. If time allows, hitch a ride on the Roosevelt Island Tramway at Second Avenue and 60th Street. The riverfront views are quite spectacular, especially at sunset.

Roosevelt Island

Across the water, **Roosevelt Island ⓴** is a 147-acre (60 ha) respite from heavy urban living. Lying only 4 minutes by tram from the East Side, this tiny (2-mile/3.2 km), tranquil, cigar-shaped island contains one main street, one church, one supermarket, a few restaurants, and one of New York City's more recent subway extensions. This annexation to the B&Q lines made Roosevelt a desirable residential neighborhood – witness the highly luxurious apartment complex, **Manhattan Park**, which would not look out of place on the other side of the river. As an added bonus, facilities include an indoor swimming pool, several playgrounds and five small parks – plus an active community center based in the ecumenical Chapel of the Good Shepherd, a landmark Victorian stone-and-brick structure that dates back to 1899. From the specially built walkways edging the shoreline, there are panoramic views of the Upper East Side. You can also walk to a small park at the northern end and admire a stone lighthouse built in 1872. Madison Avenue seems a long way away. ❑

An extension of the city subway line has made Roosevelt Island a desirable place to live.

BELOW: East Side slumber party.

UPPER WEST SIDE

*Geographically, the Upper West Side is laid out like a
hot pepper sandwich: it looks tempting on the
outside, but it's spicy in the middle*

Map
on page
146

The spicy bits of the Upper West Side are Broadway, Columbus and Amsterdam Avenues, a sort of 24-hour circus squeezed between the dignified calm of Riverside Drive and Central Park West. In the 1980s, this became the yuppie capital of New York City – the "Yupper" West Side as local wags put it. But it hasn't always been brunch and boutiques; before the yuppie invasion, the Upper West Side was infested with crime, and even the well-heeled residents of Central Park West were cautious when leaving their apartments at night. Although the area is now pretty thoroughly gentrified, there are still some scruffy streets amid the wealth.

The entrance to all this is **Columbus Circle ㉑**, a tangle of cars and pedestrians zipping around a statue of Christopher Columbus, who looks a bit frazzled by all the commotion. Other than the **Trump International Tower and Hotel**, located on the northern end of the Circle, there's not much of interest here, although the gateway to Central Park is usually thronged with people eating lunch, passing through or just plain hanging around.

Apartment architecture

Central Park West ㉒ branches off Columbus Circle and heads up into the area's most affluent residential section. The apartment houses overlooking the park are among the most lavish in the city, and the cross streets, especially 74th, 75th and 76th, are lined with equally splendid brownstones. Among the most spectacular buildings are Art Deco masterpieces like the **Century** at No. 25 and **Majestic Apartments** at No. 115, and the classical inspired, twin-towered **San Remo Apartments**, Nos.145–146. At the corner of West 67th Street, the **Hotel des Artistes** has counted Valentino, Isadora Duncan, Noel Coward and Norman Rockwell among its tenants, and is still home to the **Café des Artistes**, an exquisite hide-away on the ground floor which is perfect for a romantic rendezvous.

The most famous apartment building on this stretch is **The Dakota ㉓** (1 West 72nd Street), built in 1884 by Henry Hardenbergh, who also designed the Plaza Hotel. At the time, people joked that it was so far outside the city, "it might as well be in the Dakota Territory," which explains the name and the Indian's head above the main entrance. Urban streets caught up with it soon enough, and over the years the Dakota has remained the grandest residence on Central Park West, attracting tenants like Boris Karloff, Leonard Bernstein and Lauren Bacall. Strawberry Fields, a quiet knoll dedicated to the memory of John Lennon, who lived at the Dakota and was shot outside in 1980, is located across the street a few steps into Central Park.

PRECEDING PAGES:
zillions of people
shop at Zabar's.
LEFT: the American
Museum of
Natural History.
BELOW: The Dakota.

Columbus Circle is a quick way to enter Central Park – if you don't get run over by all the traffic.

BELOW: Juilliard ballet student and potential new star.

From 72nd Street, it's a short walk uptown, past the somber facades of the Universalist Church and the **New-York Historical Society ㉔** (2 West 77th Street, tel: 873 3400, closed Mon, fee), to the 79th Street entrance of the lumbering **American Museum of Natural History ㉕** (tel: 769 5100, suggested fee), a lumpy giant that sprawls over four city blocks, and is open daily.

Tallest dinosaur in the world

Guarded by an equestrian statue of Theodore Roosevelt, the museum's main entrance is actually one of the many additions built around the original structure. The old facade – a stately Romanesque arcade with two ornate towers – was built in 1892 and is visible from 77th Street.

If you're traveling with children, visiting the museum is an absolute must, though with 40 exhibition halls housed in 23 buildings, there's plenty for grown-ups to see, too, not the least of which is a 34-ton meteorite, the largest blue sapphire in the world, a full-scale model of a blue whale and a renowned anthropological collection. The famous dinosaur exhibits, installed in six renovated halls, offer an astounding look at life on earth over many millennia. There's even an interactive computer system for visitors for whom gigantic skeletal remains aren't enough. The world's tallest dinosaur – the 50-foot-high (15m) Barosaurus – can be found in the Theodore Roosevelt Rotunda, off of which a Hall of Biodiversity includes a stunning recreation of an African rainforest.

The museum also includes the **Naturemax Theater** where films are presented on a screen four stories high and 66 feet (20 meters) wide. As if that weren't enough, the **Rose Center for Earth and Space** includes a **planetarium** and other cool stuff. But don't even think about doing the whole place in one shot, especially if you're on a schedule.

Returning back down to Columbus Circle, Broadway swerves west toward Columbus Avenue and just nicks the corner of the Lincoln Center, flanked on one side by Juilliard and on the other by **Fordham University**. Even to be accepted at the **Juilliard School of Music ㉖** is an honor, as the school's highly selective enrollment practice and small classrooms draw some of the most talented students in America. They no doubt attract inspiration from neighboring Lincoln Center, which is worth a visit even if you're not attending a performance. Guided tours of the complex are given every hour on the hour between 10am and 5pm, but it's just as well to save time and money by exploring on your own.

The **Lincoln Center for the Performing Arts** began construction in 1959 as part of a massive redevelopment plan intended to clean up the slum that used to occupy the site. More than 180 buildings were demolished and 1,600 families relocated in order to make room for the complex, inflaming social critics who saw it as nothing more than a playground for the elite. Architectural critics gave it a beating too, citing a general lack of gravity and an overdose of ornamentation. Despite all this, Lincoln Center has become one of the city's most popular outlets for the performing arts, with attendance now running at about 5 million people a year.

Standing at the black marble fountain in the middle of the plaza, you are surrounded by the glass and white marble facades of Lincoln Center's three main structures. The **Metropolitan Opera** ㉗ is directly in front with two large murals by Marc Chagall hanging behind the glass wall – *Le Triomphe de la Musique* to the left, *Les Sources de la Musique* to the right. The Met is home to the Metropolitan Opera Company from September to April and the American Ballet Theater from May to July. Although marvelous, its lavish productions and big-name performers carry a hefty price tag.

To the left of the central fountain, the **New York State Theater** ㉘ is shared by the New York City Opera and the New York City Ballet – both more adventurous than the Met and less expensive. If the doors are open, look at the Jasper Johns painting on the ground floor and the two controversial marble statues by Elie Nadelman in the upstairs foyer.

Map on page 146

Mostly Mozart

The third side of the main plaza is occupied by **Avery Fisher Hall** ㉙, home of the New York Philharmonic and the Mostly Mozart series held in the summer. For years the hall was plagued with bad acoustics, and after several renovations failed to correct the problem the auditorium was gutted and rebuilt. Peek in for a look at Richard Lippold's *Orpheus and Apollo*, a hanging metal sculpture that dominates the foyer. Two secondary courtyards flank the Met on either side. To the right, the **Vivian Beaumont Theater** ㉚ is fronted by a shady plaza and reflecting pool where office workers gather for lunch. The oxidized bronze sculpture in the center of the pool is by Henry Moore. A spindly steel sculpture by Alexander Calder is near the entrance to the **Library of the Performing Arts**. The Bandshell in **Damrosch Park** is used for free concerts during the summer, usually around lunchtime although occasionally in the early evening as well. When you've finished gazing around Lincoln Center, cross Columbus Avenue for a quick look at the **American Folk Art Museum** (2 Lincoln Square, tel: 595 9533), which is free, open daily and has a great little gift shop *(see page 132)*. Then head uptown for some high-grade browsing.

Like Madison Avenue on the opposite side of Central Park, Columbus is committed to the art of mass consumption, although fortunately most of the shops and restaurants don't take themselves as seriously as their East Side counterparts. As usual, there are far too many places to list by name, but those that deserve a special mention are north of 68th Street.

Picking up the trail in the 70s, there's outrageous fashion at Betsy Johnson (248 Columbus), upscale women's wear at Eileen Fisher (341 Columbus) and equally upscale men's wear at Frank Stella (440 Columbus). A few doors further up puts you at the entrance to Penny Whistle Toys, which offers an intriguing assortment of old-fashioned games, stuffed animals and other items designed to delight all those childish hearts. There's also a wide selection of funky vintage wear (and wares) for sale at the flea market held every Sunday between 76th and 77th streets.

Skipping west to Amsterdam Avenue, the scene is

BELOW: Lincoln Center. Its popular outdoor fountain is computer controlled to wind velocity so people do not get hit by the spray.

slightly different, with trendy boutiques and twenty-something bars scattered amidst a few remaining Latino-flavored groceries and other traditional neighborhood shops. You'll also find some good restaurants, which tend to be more casual in price and atmosphere than the eateries on Columbus Avenue.

Home cooking

If you're into home cooking, be sure to check out Sarabeth's Kitchen, a cozy little nook on Amsterdam between 80th and 81st streets that serves hearty American-style breakfasts until 3:30 pm (and is a favorite spot for Saturday and Sunday brunch.) At the corner of 83rd Street, a more typical urban scene can be found at the sprawling Hi-Life Bar and Grill, where the eclectic cuisine plays second fiddle to the lively young crowd that hangs out here after work. If neither one suits your fancy, there are plenty others to choose from, including Barney Greengrass, Manhattan's mecca for smoked salmon, bagels and cream cheese, which has been serving customers from its locale at 541 Amsterdam, just north of 86th Street, since 1929.

Three blocks north, the **Claremont Riding Academy** (175 West 89th Street), has been in business for more than a century. At the time the Claremont was built, this part of town contained many stables; now it's the only one left on the island. But if you want the experience of riding through Central Park with your horse's nostrils flaring and mane flying, the Claremont is the place to come.

This part of town is also where the Upper West Side really gets down and dirty – and where Broadway becomes a round-the-clock stage, with all the incongruities of the Upper West Side flowing clamorously together. Here, boutique-hoppers, stockbrokers and carriage-pushing mothers mingle with street vendors, artists and panhandlers, and while the shopping isn't generally as rich as it is on Columbus Avenue, a few places are practically institutions.

At 80th and Broadway, **Zabar's** is the gourmet shop against which all gourmet shops are measured. The people at Balducci's downtown in the Village may not agree, but take a look around and judge for yourself. Even if you're not in the mood for buying, it takes kick elbowing your way up to the counter for a free taste of all the cholesterol-soaked goodies. It's worth visiting for the glorious smells alone.

A stone's throw from Zabar's is a busy branch of Barnes & Noble, where a veritable beehive of books attracts browsers of all kinds (and the sociable Mezzanine Cafe serves excellent coffee). Should you find yourself in dire need of another bagel smothered in cream cheese, H&H Bagel – located just down the street – makes over 60,000 every day. Around the corner, at 212 West 83rd Street, the amusing **Children's Museum of Manhattan** (tel: 721 1223, fee) is a multi-level kiddy kingdom featuring interactive exhibits and special events. They're open for business Wednesday through Sunday; the noise level is high, so bring along ear plugs.

In recent years, new meaning has been added to the term "off-Broadway", with a burgeoning Upper West Side theater scene that includes performances and literary readings at **Symphony Space**, on Broadway

BELOW: the Claremont has been in business for more than a century.

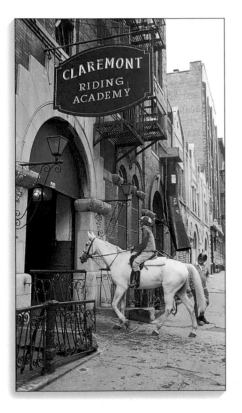

Map on page 146

between 94th and 95th streets, and hits produced at the **Promenade Theater** between 76th and 77th streets. Meanwhile, the **Beacon Theater** (2124 Broadway at 74th Street) is a popular music venue where you might catch Judy Collins one night and a gospel group the next.

Occupying the entire block between 73rd and 74th streets is the **Ansonia Hotel**, and while it's a bit worn around the edges, this is still the *grande dame* of West Side apartment buildings, with a resident guest list that over the years has included the likes of Enrico Caruso, Igor Stravinsky, Arturo Toscanini and Theodore Dreiser. Although retailers now dominate the ground floor, the Ansonia's mansard roof, corner towers and terracotta detailing still add up to a Beaux Arts fantasy that captures the gaze and refuses to let go.

Down by the Riverside

From here you can wrap up the tour by going west on 72nd Street to **West End Avenue ③** and then on to Riverside Drive. North of 72nd Street, West End is affluent and strictly residential; it's a great street to live on, but not very exciting. Humphrey Bogart lived for a while in Pomander Walk, an English-style mews between 94th and 95th streets, bordered by West End Avenue and Broadway. All the drama has been stolen by **Riverside Drive ㉜**, which winds along the edge of Frederick Law Olmsted's **Riverside Park**; the 72nd Street entrance is marked by a stately bronze sculpture of Eleanor Roosevelt, one of only four statues of real-life women gracing New York City's parks. This is one of the most picturesque corners of Manhattan, with exceptional architecture and sweeping views of the Hudson River. Be sure to get a look at the houseboats at the **79th Street Boat Basin ㉝**, where a few hardy Manhattanites brave the elements year-round. ❑

The Beaux Arts Ansonia Hotel. Caruso, Stravinsky and Toscanini all lived here.

BELOW: Riverside Park café.

AROUND HARLEM

Fidel Castro and The Beatles couldn't wait to visit. Famous both then and now, Harlem has the highest name recognition factor of any neighborhood in the state of New York

Map
on page
166

An Alabama-born, African-American professor remembers being in Europe at the age of 18 in the late 1950s. He was asked repeatedly about Harlem, a place where he'd never been in his life. His inquisitors didn't want to hear this. The man was black, he lived in the United States; therefore he had to be from Harlem. What they didn't know was that the only thing he "knew," based on the same stereotypes shared by the Europeans, was that Harlem was a destination full of naughty nightlife which featured devilish dancing, mind-blowing music, dangerous dudes and wicked women. Harlem was and is much more than that. As well as its well-documented attractions, artists have recently discovered Harlem's handsome buildings and inexpensive rents, and the next few years sees the area poised for change.

Geographically there is an **East Harlem** (Madison Avenue to the East River), sometimes called **Spanish Harlem**; a **Central Harlem** (Fifth Avenue to St Nicholas Avenue), whose citizens are overwhelmingly African-American; and a **West Harlem**, which extends to Riverside Drive. In general, West Harlem has a larger population of white residents than the others and includes the neighborhoods of **Morningside Heights** and **Hamilton Heights**. Farther up (*see map on page 104*), **Washington Heights** is close to Manhattan's northern tip and is an ethnically-mixed area with cultural treasures.

Going Dutch

Originally the home of Native Americans, Harlem was settled by the Dutch in 1658 as Nieuw Haarlem, after the city in the Netherlands. In 1664, it fell to the British, who tried to change its name to Lancaster.

Serious protest prevented this from occurring, but Haarlem was anglicized by dropping one "a". Which raises the question, would Harlem be the same if it had been called Lancaster? It's hard to imagine watching the Boys Choir of Lancaster, or attending performances by the Ballet Theater of Lancaster. Maybe names do make a difference.

Basically still farmland in the early 1800s, Harlem became New York City's first upscale suburb when Alexander Hamilton, the country's Secretary of the Treasury, built a country home called Hamilton Grange (It still stands today, though not in its original spot.) This exclusivity changed in 1837 with the opening of the Harlem River Railroad, followed by Harlem's 1873 annexation to New York City, the extension of the elevated rapid transit lines in 1880, and in 1904 by the building of the IRT Lenox Avenue subway. All of this made Harlem more accessible, which in turn led to an influx of immigrants. In the early 1900s, black people began moving into homes on 135th Street, west of Lenox Avenue. From then on, Harlem became a place

LEFT: Richie.
BELOW: the Studio Museum is a major cultural center.

*A highlight of
Harlem Week held
each year in August
is the Jazz and Music
Festival, which takes
place at major
venues around the
neighborhood.*

where Americans of African descent made their presence felt. Poet Langston Hughes and writer Zora Neale Hurston, along with musicians Duke Ellington, Louis Armstrong and Bessie Smith, all launched their careers here in the 1920s and '30s, during what was termed the Harlem Renaissance.

It was this Harlem that gained an international reputation as a playground for thrill-seekers. According to the late Charles Buchanan, who was general manager of the Savoy Ballroom from its opening in 1936 to its closing in 1958, eager Europeans would check into their hotels, and then make mad dashes to the Savoy to savor its dazzling dancers and never-ending music. Later, Harlem, or more precisely, a restaurant called Sherman's Barbeque on 151st Street and Amsterdam Avenue, was where the all-girl singing group the Ronettes brought the Beatles in 1964. It was the Fab Four's first American tour in 1964, and their Midtown hotel, the Plaza, was surrounded by hysterical fans. It was only by sneaking out a side door and escaping up to Sherman's that the Beatles were able to breathe easy, play the jukebox, and relax with like-minded musicians.

Bad press

That Harlem no longer exists; neither does the Harlem historically portrayed in the press as a place where every other resident is a drug pusher. What does exist is a diverse community where Irish, Italian, Dominican, Haitian, Puerto Rican, West African and other residents sometimes live side by side, and where ongoing renovations are attracting increasing numbers of middle-class African-American and white professionals and artists. Nevertheless, there are some areas tourists should avoid. To best experience this part of the city, take a tour or contact the Harlem Visitors and Convention Association.

BELOW: street
scene, *circa* 1930s.

Central Harlem

A good place to begin a tour is **125th Street** ❶, Harlem's famous main drag. It's Fifth Avenue and Times Square compressed into one river-to-river street, a street where every north-south Manhattan subway stops and several north-south buses cross over. A main shopping area, it's vibrantly alive with throngs of people and music blasting from nearby record stores. If you're interested in what some call "street art," make an attempt to be on 125th Street in the morning so you can see the colorful and imaginative paintings of **Franco the Artist** on the metal roll-down gates that cover storefronts before they open.

Several of Central Harlem's most important attractions are located on 125th Street, most notably the **Apollo Theater** ❷, between Adam Clayton Powell Jr Boulevard and Frederick Douglass Boulevard. This is where the presence of such great singers of yesteryear as Billie Holiday, Mahalia Jackson, Dinah Washington and Ella Fitzgerald can still be felt, especially during the Apollo's weekly Amateur Night. (Among other stars whose careers have been launched here are Michael Jackson and Boyz ll Men.) For visitors, this event is often a highlight of their trip to New York; the experience of seeing and hearing rising young talent, while at the same time being a part of the highly responsive, often appreciative and sometimes harshly critical Apollo audience, is not to be missed. For information about tours or current shows, call 749 5838.

The Studio Museum in Harlem ❸ (144 West 125th Street, tel: 864 4500, fee) is one block east and where you'll find changing exhibitions as well as a permanent collection of contemporary paintings and sculpture by artists of the African diaspora. It also has extensive archives, including the work of James Van Der Zee, who photographed Harlem's heyday of the 1920s, 1930s and 1940s.

Map on page 166

As word gets out about Harlem, the area becomes more and more popular; professionals and artists are moving in fast. Notable among them is Bill Clinton, the former president, who established an office on 125th St.

BELOW: doing the jitterbug in Harlem *circa* 1940s.

Besides exhibitions, the Studio Museum holds lectures, films, readings and workshops. (Open Wednesday to Friday and weekend afternoons.) The arts are well catered for in the area: a short distance away, at 2035 Fifth Avenue, the **National Black Theatre** is a 288-seat performing arts complex that offers innovative works of drama and music.

There has been talk of moving Hamilton Grange, the home of the first US Secretary of the Treasury, from Convent Avenue and West 141st Street to Central Harlem's St Nicholas Park.

Retail art reaches its zenith with an enormous five-story mall development called **Harlem USA** ❹ on 125th Street between Frederick Douglass Boulevard and St Nicholas Avenue. Among the tenants are a huge Disney Store, a Loews-movie theater, an HMV music store, a fitness center and several smaller boutiques, as well as a jazz club. Harlem USA's nightspots are joining the clubs and restaurants already in the 125th Street area, like **Showman's Café** and **The Cotton Club** ❺, both of which offer visitors the chance to meet Harlemites in their favorite hang-outs.

Name change

From 125th Street in Central Harlem, walk up one of the neighborhood's north-south streets, like **Malcolm X Boulevard** (Lenox Avenue) ❻ or **Adam Clayton Powell Jr Boulevard** (Seventh Avenue) ❼. Malcolm X Boulevard is probably Central Harlem's best known street after 125th Street – which itself is officially known as Martin Luther King Boulevard.

Several landmarks are located along here, including **Sylvia's Restaurant**, a family-owned eatery between 126th and 127th streets, where the Southern-inspired food is justly world-famous; the **Liberation Bookstore** at 131st Street, for those interested in reading about the experiences of people of African descent; and the **Schomburg Center for Research in Black Culture** ❽ at

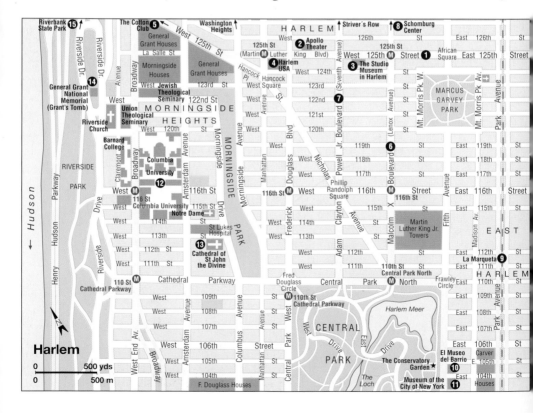

135th Street (tel: 491 2200), one of the top institutions of its kind. The library is a gold mine of books, magazines, records, films and photos about black Americans in general and Harlem in particular, and is where writer Alex Haley did much of the research for his book *Roots*.

On the other side of Adam Clayton Powell Jr Boulevard, a recently dedicated **Walk of Fame** honors such famous black Americans as Langston Hughes, Duke Ellington and former New York City mayor David Dinkins. From here it's not far to the **St Nicholas Historic District**: four rows of 19th-century townhouses between 137th and 139th streets, known as **Striver's Row** in honor of the prominent professionals who moved here in the 1920s.

Fidel's hotel

On the corner of Adam Clayton Powell Jr Boulevard and 125th Street, the former Theresa Hotel, now an office tower, was *the* place for VIPs to stay in the 1930s, 1940s and 1950s, since most downtown hotels barred black visitors. One of the Theresa's most famous guests was Fidel Castro, who moved in after a dispute with a downtown hotel in 1960. World leaders like Nikita Khruschev came to visit him here, and every evening Castro would step out onto his room's small balcony and wave to the enthusiastic throngs gathered below. The Theresa's last major claim to fame was as the site of the office of the Organization of Afro-American Unity, which was founded by Malcolm X in 1964, a year before he was assassinated.

If you happen to be in Central Harlem on a Sunday morning, make an effort to attend services at a local church. The fervor of the singing and the response of the congregations is stirring; it's a spiritual experience that is hard to get

The Walk of Fame is part of the Striver's Center Development Project that also includes Striver's Garden, where a Jazz Hall of Fame has been proposed.

BELOW:
streetwise,
Harlem-style.

East (Spanish) Harlem is from Madison Avenue to the East River.

BELOW: Sunday at the Abyssinian Baptist Church.

back home. (Judging by the number of people who show up at the **Canaan Baptist Church** on 116th Street every Sunday morning, visitors from all over the world are aware of this already.) Harlem churches play a significant role in the political, economic and cultural life of the community. In addition to the Canaan Baptist Church, other religious sites like the **Abyssinian Baptist Church**, **St Philip's Episcopal Church** and **Mother AME Zion Church** have all played a role since the early 1900s.

East Harlem

Traditionally, this is considered **Spanish Harlem**, its residents by and large having close ties with Puerto Rico. But East Harlem also includes a strong Haitian presence, as well as the remnants of an old Italian section along First and Pleasant avenues, above 114th Street. Frank Sinatra liked the pizzas at **Patsy's**, 2287 First Avenue between 117th and 118th streets, so much that he used to have them flown to his mansion in California.

The most colorful place to visit is **La Marqueta ❾**, located under the elevated train lines on Park Avenue from 111th to 116th streets. You can find mangos, papayas, cassavas, tamarinds, exotic herbs and other imported tropical staples here, along with fresh-grown regional produce. Fridays and Saturdays are the best time to come and shop – or just stroll around and enjoy the type of market experience usually found in Latino and African countries. Another East Harlem attraction is **El Museo del Barrio ❿** (tel: 831 7272, fee) at Fifth Avenue and 104th Street. Open Wednesday to Sunday, this is the only museum in the city devoted to Latin-American art; the same building contains the **Heckscher Theater**. One block south at 103rd Street, the **Museum of the City of New**

York **⓫** (tel: 534 1672, open Wed to Sun, fee) displays old maps, ship models, doll houses and other souvenirs from New York's 300 years of history. *(These are part of New York's Museum Mile, so also see page 148 and page 151.)*

Map on page 166

West Harlem

West Harlem extends from around Amsterdam Avenue to Riverside Drive, taking in the Convent Avenue and Sugar Hill areas, along with Hamilton and Morningside Heights. Many of Harlem's white residents live in this district, which includes **Columbia University ⓬** and **Barnard College** (for women) as well as the Jewish Theological and Union Theological seminaries, all located on or near upper Broadway.

At 112th Street and Amsterdam Avenue, the impressive **Cathedral of St John the Divine ⓭** is home to the city's largest Episcopal congregation; it's also the world's second-largest Gothic cathedral (and still under construction). Not far away, at Riverside Drive and 120th Street, the non-denominational **Riverside Church** has the world's largest bell carillon atop its 22-story tower. Both churches feature special cultural events throughout the year.

At 122nd Street, **Grant's Tomb ⓮** is the final resting place of former president and Civil War general Ulysses S. Grant and his wife, Julia; it was dedicated in 1897 as a national park site and said to be inspired by the Invalides, Napoleon's final resting place. Further north on Riverside Drive, Manhattan's only state park opened in 1993 on the 28-acre (11 ha) roof of a former sewage treatment plant that stretches along the Hudson River between 137th and 145th streets. Today, the swimming pools, skating rink and spectacular views of **Riverbank State Park ⓯** are enjoyed by an estimated 3 million people every year.

BELOW: Columbia University, where numerous Pulitzer Prize winners were educated.

West Harlem has numerous other historical attractions, including the lovely **Morris-Jumel Mansion** (65 Jumel Terrace at 160th Street, east of St Nicholas Avenue, tel: 923 8008, closed Mon and Tues, fee). One of George Washington's headquarters during the American Revolution, the Palladian-style home was visited by Queen Elizabeth and Prince Philip during the American Bicentennial of 1976. Adjacent to the mansion, **Jumel Terrace** is a series of 20 beautifully presented row houses built around the turn of the 19th century; the famous singer and activist Paul Robeson lived nearby at 7 Sylvan Terrace.

Audubon Terrace, back on Broadway between West 155th and 156th streets, is lined by stately neoclassical buildings built between 1905 and 1923 as a cultural complex. Among them is the **American Academy and Institute of Arts and Letter**s, whose members have included everyone from Mark Twain to Toni Morrison; the **American Numismatic Society** (tel: 234 3130), which has exhibits of old money; and the **Hispanic Society of America** (tel: 926 2234), with a collection that includes works by El Greco and Goya. The latter two are open Tuesday to Saturday, and Sunday afternoons; admission is free.

Met Museum Uptown

Once mainly Irish, today the far-northern **Washington Heights** area is ethnically mixed, with Dominicans, Puerto Ricans, Haitians, Irish and others claiming it for their own. (The largest Jewish educational institution in the city, **Yeshiva University**, is located on West 185th Street.) On West 192nd Street, 62-acre (25 ha) **Fort Tryon Park** was designed by Frederick Law Olmsted and contains **The Cloisters**, a branch of the **Metropolitan Museum of Art** which is open from Tuesday to Sunday (tel: 923 3700, fee). French and Spanish monastic

BELOW: the Morris-Jumel Mansion, built in 1765, is the city's oldest residential structure.

cloisters, a 12th-century chapter house, the Fuentaduena Chapel and both a Gothic and a Romanesque chapel were imported and reassembled here, stone by stone. The prize of the medieval collection is the Unicorn Tapestries, six hand-woven tapestries from the 15th century. The Cloisters is a beautiful, inspiring spot. Farther north, at 204th Street and Broadway in **Inwood**, the **Dyckman Farmhouse Museum** (tel: 304 9422, closed Mon, fee) is a two-story Dutch colonial dwelling built in 1785 and restored in 1915 *(see photo, page 210)*.

Annual Events

Back down in Central Harlem, the neighborhood around 125th Street is the best place for annual events that highlight Harlem's cultural richness. These include the **Black World Championship Rodeo,** held every spring, which brings the role of African-Americans in the history of the American West to wider public attention; the **Jazzmobile concerts**, presented outdoors throughout the summer; and the **African-American Day Parade**, held in early September.

For serious fans of basketball, the **Rucker Tournament** attracts NBA pros and members of the Harlem GlobeTrotters during the week between Christmas and New Year. In the summer months, there's the **Golden Hoops Tournament**, featuring high school basketball players from around the country.

The largest annual event, however, is **Harlem Week**, which began as a one-day celebration in 1975 and is now held during the first three weeks of August. With a multitude of cultural activities taking place throughout the neighborhood, Harlem Week is not only one of the city's best summer attractions but also, according to the Greater Harlem Chamber of Commerce, the third-largest summer festival in the entire country. ❏

Map on page 104

TIP

The best way to find out about local events and attractions is by contacting the Harlem Visitors and Convention Association at 219 West 135th Street, tel: 212-862 8497.

BELOW: the medieval Cloisters is worth a trip to Washington Heights.

DOWNTOWN

*A guide to Manhattan's lower half and the Outer Boroughs,
with principal sites cross-referenced by number to the maps*

Downtown and uptown New York are two very different places.
Uptown, where life can scream with a neon fury and adrena-
lin is high, passions run hot and furious. Downtown's attitude
is cooler – if you don't count the frenzy of the Stock Market at closing time. Some of the oldest sites in the city are located here, but
some of New York's newer destinations are, too.

Downtown is where nightclubs spring up with energizing regularity, and close again quicker than you can change your dancing
shoes. Restaurants, too, are fashionable and then scorned, at a pace
which only *cognoscenti* with a keen sense of direction can follow.
Downtown is Alphabet City. There's Avenues A, B, C and D, plus
NoHo, NoLita and SoFi: a large-scale map of Downtown looks like
a kidnapper's ransom note. The latter three are among New York's
newer neighborhoods – expect, in a few years for the letters to be all
the same size: familiarity breeds regularity, as in the case of the
neighborhoods formerly written in this book as SoHo (South of
Houston) and TriBeCa (Triangle Below Canal). An amorphous section North of Houston Street, known locally as NoHo, began appear-
ing in that guise in the early 1990s. SoFi (South of Flatiron) has also
gained credence. The latest designation, NoLita, refers to a few
streets north of Little Italy (and east of Soho). As the city continues
to change, there will be more neighborhoods; watch this space.

Lately, Downtown has attracted some of the city's small but thriving new-media companies, which tend to stretch from the Flatiron
District above Union Square to Soho and Lower Manhattan (skirting
Chinatown and the Villages), under the cyber-designation Silicon
Alley. The southern portion of Downtown is the traditional center of
financial New York, where Wall Street banks keep tabs on everybody's money and South Street Seaport takes it away again with a
series of shops and seafood restaurants. Battery Park City is a residential complex whose scenic riverside walkways helped inspire the
development of the Hudson River Park, a welcome green space that
is expected in a few years' time to stretch north from the tip of Manhattan at Battery Park all the way up to 59th Street.

A brief description of the Outer Boroughs – Brooklyn, Queens,
Staten Island and the Bronx – are included here, too. This is where
the hot dog was born and where museums, sculpture gardens, historic
houses, wildlife refuges and even boatyards attract increasing numbers of visitors from all over the world.

"The Bronx? No thonx," said poet Ogden Nash. Be surprised. ❏

PRECEDING PAGES: they plan to wake up in the city that never sleeps.
LEFT: an example of Downtown's distinctive architecture.

GRAMERCY PARK, UNION SQUARE AND CHELSEA

These changing neighborhoods straddle Midtown and Downtown and share characteristics with both; there's also a genteel, old-fashioned park

Map on page 178

The area from Madison Park to Union Square – loosely referred to as the Flatiron District – is home to writers, photographers, ad agencies, publishers, new restaurants and new-media firms. Chelsea has a flourishing art gallery scene, a flourishing gay scene along Eighth Avenue, as well as a riverside sports and entertainment development that attracts an estimated 8,000 visitors a day. Only Gramercy Park maintains its usual well-heeled reserve.

LEFT: the Flatiron Building of the Flatiron District.
BELOW: the infamous Chelsea Hotel.

Gramercy Park

On the East Side between 20th and 21st streets, **Gramercy Park ❶** is a 2-acre (0.8 ha) square that punctuates Lexington Avenue and Irving Place with a welcome leafy greenery. This is Manhattan's only private park, established in the 1830s by a wealthy lawyer named Samuel Ruggles. Only residents of the surrounding townhouses have keys, although guests at the **Gramercy Park Hotel**, a shabby-genteel hostelry at 2 Lexington Avenue, are allowed in too.

On the park's southern perimeter, note the elaborate 19th-century facades of the **National Arts Club**, home to the Poetry Society of America, and the next-door **Players Club**, where members have included leading American theater actors, as well as Mark Twain, Winston Churchill and Frank Sinatra.

Irving Place, which Samuel Ruggles named for his friend Washington Irving, runs south from Gramercy Park to 14th Street, and is lined by pretty brownstones that continue with particular charm along East 19th Street. At 18th Street, **Pete's Tavern** is a dark, historic bar where the atmosphere reeks of speakeasies and spilled beer. Short-story scribe O. Henry is said to have written *The Gift of the Magi* here.

More civilized fare is available on the next block, where the Verbena restaurant is tucked beneath the **Inn at Irving Place** (56 Irving Place) which offers afternoon tea and expensive, countrified accommodation. Down at 15th Street, **Irving Plaza** is one of the city's best small venues for rock music performances.

Drifting northward, the often overlooked green space wedged between Madison Avenue and Broadway from 23rd to 26th streets is **Madison Square Park ❷**. A century ago, this was one of the city's cultural hearts – and until 1925, home to the original Madison Square Garden. The Beaux-Arts **Appellate Division Courthouse**, which has stood at Madison Avenue and 25th Street since 1900, was used as a locale for the Milos Forman's 1981 film *Ragtime*. A block south, the 54-story **Metropolitan Life Insurance Tower ❸**, completed in 1909, was briefly considered

*Gramercy Park is
New York's only
private park. A farm
in the 18th century,
its name comes from
the Dutch for
"crooked little
swamp" (Krom
Moersje).*

the world's tallest building. Until its recent incarnation as a place to meet and greet like-minded fashion and media types in a number of watering holes, however, the Madison Park area was noted mainly for its proximity to one of Manhattan's favorite architectural whimsies, which rises from the corner where Broadway crosses Fifth Avenue, just below 23rd Street.

Flatiron District

The triangular **Flatiron Building ❹**, 285 feet high, raised eyebrows and hope for a bright future when it was erected in 1902. It soon became known as the Flatiron Building (original name: Fuller Building) because of its distinctive shape. The neighborhood below it has been dubbed **SoFi**, which stands, of course, for **So**uth of **Fi**atiron.

From here, Broadway follows the old "Ladies Mile," a shopping route that during the latter part of the 19th century, ranged along Broadway and what was then plain old Sixth Avenue, from 23rd Street down to 9th Street. Among the notable emporiums were Siegel-Cooper Dry Goods, which opened in 1898 to a crowd reported at 150,000; Arnold Constable at Broadway and 19th, purveyor of luxury silks and brocades; and Lord & Taylor, which began as a small shop Downtown on Catherine Street and opened on the southwest corner of Broadway and 20th Street in 1872 (10,000 customers used its elevator in the first three days). The store moved Uptown to 38th and Fifth in 1914, where its fashionable doors are still open. At the **Theodore Roosevelt Birthplace ❺** (28 East 20th Street, tel: 260 1616, closed Mon and Tues, fee), the late president's toys and collection of mounted lion heads are on display, along with various other memorabilia dating from the days when Ladies Mile was thriving *(see page 199)*.

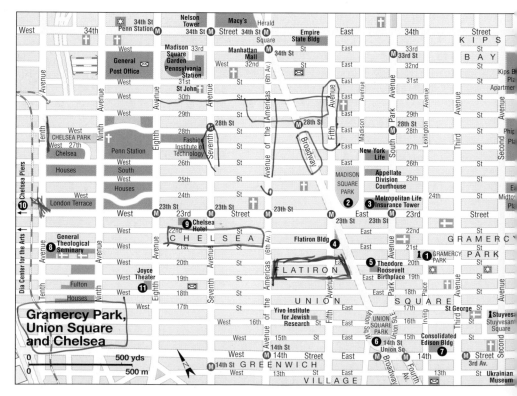

Union Square

Named for the convergence of Broadway and Fourth Avenue, **Union Square ⑥** sits comfortably between 17th and 14th streets. A stylish prospect in the mid-1850s, by the turn of the century it was more or less deserted by genteel residents and became a thriving theater center.

Eventually the theaters moved north to Midtown and the square became best known for political meetings: in the years preceding World War I, anarchists and socialists regularly addressed sympathizers here. The highlight came in 1927, when a huge crowd gathered to protest the execution of Sacco and Vanzetti, anarchists widely believed to have been wrongly accused of murder.

Rallies continued to draw crowds throughout the 1930s, but finally even radicalism dwindled, and the area went into a decline that lasted until the 1980s. Today, Union Square bustles with life, a resurgence that might be attributed to the **Greenmarket**, which brings farmers and their produce to the northern edge of the square four days a week. While there are other Greenmarkets in other parts of the city, this is the biggest and the best, and a great place to wander around on a Saturday morning. An outdoor café operates on the nearby plaza in warm weather, and there are a number of popular adjacent restaurants. For something comfortably funky there's **Chat n' Chew** on 16th Street. Or try the deservedly fashionable **Union Square Cafe**, at 21 East 15th Street, or the ultra chic **W Hotel** at Union Square at 17th and Park Avenue South.

Food for the soul can be found at the **Union Square Theatre**, 100 East 17th Street (between Park Avenue South and Irving Place), an historically appropriate locale considering that the **Consolidated Edison Building ⑦**, at 4 Irving Place, stands on the site of the old Academy of Music, featured in the opening

Map on page 178

BELOW:
Union Square's Greenmarket is the biggest and the best in the city.

scene of Martin Scorsese's 1993 movie adaptation of Edith Wharton's *The Age of Innocence*. Con Ed's headquarters dominated the skyline hereabouts until the 1980s, when the adjacent Zeckendorf Towers development stole its thunder. This, in turn, has been eclipsed, at least on street level, by a gargantuan movie complex and a **Virgin Megastore**, both on 14th Street. The ultimate sports clothing and sundries shop in the city, **Paragon**, is at Union Square's north end.

BELOW: put together your own look from the Chelsea flea market.

Chelsea

West of Fifth Avenue to the Hudson River, from 14th up to about 30th Street, Chelsea borders the midtown Garment District and includes the **Flower District**, wedged between 28th and 30th along the Avenue of the Americas, more usually known as Sixth Avenue. In the spring and summer, these short blocks are crowded with leafy vegetation and bathed in a sweet loamy odor.

Fifth Avenue between 14th and 23rd streets has stores like Banana Republic, Emporio Armani and Paul Smith (interspersed by art supply and stationery stores), while **Sixth Avenue** is lined by modern chains that have moved into the historic Ladies Mile buildings, many of which boast Corinthian columns.

One of Chelsea's most popular shopping arenas is the **flea market** held on Sixth between 25th and 27th streets, where you can find everything from antique clothing to jewelry and furniture. It's only open weekends, so if you have a yen for vintage stuff during the week, try the **Chelsea Antiques Building** at 110 West 25th between Sixth and Seventh, open daily; more booths are located inside a former parking garage next door.

In 1750, a large piece of land along the Hudson was acquired by Captain Thomas Clarke. In 1813, the land was inherited by his grandson, Clement Clark

Moore, a Greek and Hebrew scholar best known for writing *A Visit from Saint Nicholas*. Faced with the onslaught of the northward-creeping city, Moore divided it into lots that were sold off with certain restrictions: "undesirable" uses, like stables, were prohibited, and all houses had to be set back from the street. Today, these make up the **Chelsea Historic District,** in the gentrified blocks between Eigth and Tenth avenues from 19th to 23rd Streets – attracting gays, young moderns and others with a sense of history and a flair for style.

Clement Clark Moore also contributed land to the **General Theological Seminary** ❽, which opened on Ninth Avenue between 20th and 21st streets in the mid-19th century. Among the best buildings are the **Chapel of the Good Shepherd**, with its massive bronze doors and 161-foot (49 metre) bell tower, and the St Mark's Library, which boasts an impressive collection of religious books. The Seminary's peaceful, tree-lined quadrangle can be visited on weekday afternoons via the main entrance at 175 Ninth Avenue.

A walk west on long, busy 23rd Street (or better yet, a ride on the M23 crosstown bus) takes you past the gothic-looking **Chelsea Hotel** ❾, which rises almost halfway between Seventh and Eigth avenues. One of the city's most famous residential hotels, the list of artists who've lived here since 1909 includes Thomas Wolfe, Arthur Miller, Jack Kerouac, Bren

Map
on page
178

dan Behan and Virgil Thompson. This is where Andy Warhol filmed *Chelsea Girls* in 1967 and also where punk-rocker Sid Vicious murdered his girlfriend before dying of a drug overdose several weeks later. If you can appreciate the weirdness, it's a reasonable place to stay. Cool downstairs basement bar, too. By all means have a look at the unusual artwork in the lobby (done by guests and changed at a whim), or stop in for a drink or a meal at the adjacent Spanish restaurant, El Quijote.

Between Eighth and Ninth avenues, Chelsea Bistro and Bar is another popular neighborhood restaurant, with French cuisine and ambience.

Piering into the distance

The last stop for crosstown buses is **Pier 62**, the start of the **Chelsea Piers Sports and Entertainment Complex ⑩** that sprawls south along the Hudson River from 23rd to 17th Street. In addition to Pier 62, site of two outdoor roller rinks and a public "pier park", the 30-acre (12 ha) development includes **Pier 61**, with two 24-hour ice skating rinks and a riverside restaurant; **Pier 60**, home to a lavish fitness club (day passes for non-members are available but pricey); and **Pier 59**, where a four-story golf driving range and a brewery pub/restaurant overlooking the water help complete the picture of ersatz suburbia. (So does the 80,000-square-foot (7,430 metre sq) Field House, back toward Pier 62, which has indoor, turf-covered areas for soccer and lacrosse.)

The transformation of these formerly dilapidated piers – which served the White Star and Cunard lines until 1930 – has given New Yorkers new recreational access to the Hudson River. Private yachts like *Forbes* magazine's *Highlander* are moored at the marina here, but the public can book passage on

BELOW: all-night ice skating is only one of the sports on offer at Chelsea's piers.

Map on page 178

passenger boats that embark on day and evening cruises, and even go on speed-boat rides. They can also stroll along the walkway that weaves through and around the piers for over a mile, and enjoy the refreshing vistas of water and sky. For more information about Chelsea Piers, call 336 6666.

Chelsea Culture

In the earliest days of moving pictures, the Famous Players Film Studio was located on West 26th Street; today, the **Silver Screen Studios** at Chelsea Piers are where such popular television shows as *Law and Order* are filmed. Chelsea's gallery scene flourishes nearby, particularly along 22nd Street between Tenth and Eleventh avenues. In 1987, the **Dia Center for the Arts** opened at 548 West 22nd Street, eventually followed by the Matthew Marks Gallery (522) and other refugees from Soho's congested art scene, including Pat Hearn (530) and Paula Cooper (534).

People from the arts, media and fashion come here.

In what some see as an alarmingly Soho-ish development, designer stores like Comme des Garçons, as well as a few model-friendly restaurants, have opened in the converted garages and warehouses of this relatively desolate area. There are still a few original pioneers, too, including the **Empire Diner** on the corner of Tenth Avenue and 22nd Street. It looks like an old-time aluminium-sided diner on the outside, but inside it's an Art Deco fantasy. The clientele is predictably hip, the prices are inflated, but it's open 24 hours and thus popular with diehards after a long night of partying.

BELOW: the Empire Diner is open 24 hours a day.
RIGHT: romantic view of the skyline.

Walking east on 20th Street from Tenth Avenue brings you to one of the Chelsea Historic District's most scenic stretches of Greek Revival and Anglo-Italianate townhouses. A block farther south, between Tenth and Eleventh, the

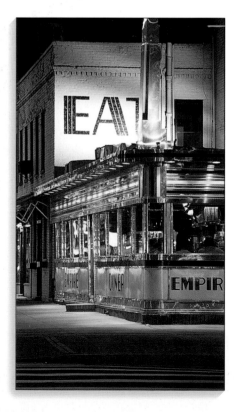

Kitchen (512 West 19th Street) is a long-standing experimental arts center where video, dance and performance art are staple fare. The **Joyce Theater** ⓫ (175 Eighth Avenue at 19th Street) presents some of the city's most innovative dance performances, from Spanish Gypsy flamenco artists to Native American troupes. Other interesting performances can be viewed at the **Dance Theater Workshop** (219 West 19th Street) between Seventh and Eighth. Nearby restaurants that cater to these venues' discerning audience include Mary Ann's, which stands on Eighth Avenue near the corner of 16th Street and specializes in hearty cuisine with a Tex-Mex-Cajun twist. A little farther away, El Cid (322 West 15th Street), is a friendly Spanish restaurant between Eighth and Ninth.

Around here, the neighborhood starts melding into the West Village – or, more accurately, the gritty meat-packing district that stretches west along 14th Street to the Hudson. Before heading elsewhere, however, stop in at **Chelsea Market**, 75 Ninth Avenue between 15th and 16th streets. An ambitious renovation in 1996 transformed what were 18 individual buildings erected between 1883 and 1930 into a single whole-sale food market, with a waterfall, sculpture and more than 20 outlets selling produce, meat, vegetables, farm-fresh milk and baked goods. There are usually people waiting in line for the daily special at Hale and Hearty Soups; if you're hungry, join them.

GREENWICH VILLAGE

Greenwich Village was the country's first true bohemian neighborhood, a place where Mark Twain, Walt Whitman, Dylan Thomas and Bob Dylan found inspiration

Map on page 188

Writers and poets, radicals and runaway socialites, artists and others seeking freedom from conventional lifestyles have long flocked to Greenwich Village, epitomized in recent history by the poets and musicians of the 1950s and '60s. Today, as other neighborhoods set the scene and come up with the trends, some New Yorkers consider "The Village" just one big tourist attraction. Untrue. Though a commercial element certainly exists, many of the streets are as quietly residential as they were in the late 18th and early 19th centuries, when the village of Greenwich was first settled by New Yorkers fleeing a series of epidemics at the tip of the island.

As in other Manhattan areas, spiraling real estate prices have forced out all but the most successful (or lucky holders of rent controlled leases), but the Village is still where many people would prefer to live – and barring that possibility, where they go to walk and shop and enjoy the variety of street life.

Here you can find cobblestone alleys, graceful architecture, Italian bakeries, gourmet markets, theaters and the oldest gay community in New York. In addition, there's a remarkable array of restaurants, bars, and jazz clubs. Bordered by 14th Street to the north, the Hudson River to the west and Broadway to the east (where the East Village begins), it's where the off-beat is the norm, and where the annual Halloween Parade has to be one of the world's best spectacles.

PRECEDING PAGES: Village architecture. **LEFT:** young lovers love Washington Arch. **BELOW:** the *Village Voice* started in the 1950s.

Squares and arches

Manhattanites who dwell Downtown are fond of saying they never go above 14th Street, which stretches from the 1940s high-rise apartment towers of Stuyvesant Town to the meat-packing district by the Hudson River. Encompassing everything from New York University dorms to art galleries and gay clubs, 14th Street also edges near to historic Union Square – once fashionable, later radical, still-later derelict, and now surrounded by thriving restaurants, stores and movie theaters.

Walk south down Fifth Avenue and you'll see **Washington Arch** rising in the distance. First designed in wood by Stanford White to memorialize the 1889 centennial of the first president's inauguration, this imposing marble version, completed in 1918, stands at the entrance to **Washington Square ❶**, the geographic and spiritual heart of Greenwich Village.

Before continuing, walk east to Broadway and you come to the **Strand bookstore**, one of the last survivors of what was once known as "Booksellers' Row." Located at the corner of 12th Street, the Strand offers "eight miles" of used books, and the stalwart searcher may just discover that rare first edition he or she has been trying to find. Just down the street,

Protestors, mime artists, jugglers, students, musicians, mothers and chess players migrate to Washington Square.

Grace Church ② is one of the city's loveliest ecclesiastical structures. Built in 1846, its exterior white marble, now a muted gray, was mined by convicts at the infamous Sing Sing prison in upstate New York.

Turn right at 10th, walk west towards Fifth Avenue, crossing **University Place**, which runs parallel to Fifth from 14th to Eighth Street. On West 12th Street, the **New School for Social Research** offers classes in everything from Arabic to screenwriting. Around the corner, the **Forbes Magazine Galleries ③** (62 Fifth Avenue. tel: 206 5548; closed Mon, Wed, Sun) hold the late Malcolm Forbes's collection of tin soldiers and Fabergé eggs. The nearby **Salmagundi Club**, at 47 Fifth Avenue, is the country's oldest artists' club, and was founded in 1870. Take a stroll west along 9th and 10th streets, two of the most picturesque in the city. Lined by stately brick and brownstone houses, these desirable residential byways have been home to numerous artists and writers (Mark Twain lived at 14 West 10th). The **Church of the Ascension ④**, on the corner of 5th and 10th Street, was designed by architect Richard Upjohn in 1840, and features a marble altar relief by sculptor Augustus Saint-Gaudens.

Positively 8th Street

If 14th Street forms downtown Manhattan's northern border, then **8th Street** is the bridge between the east and the west. East of Fifth is one of the city's most outrageous clothing stores, **Patricia Field** (10 East 8th Street), where fashions like vinyl *bustiers*, heavy metal jewelry and formidable hats and wigs have been displayed with tongue-in-chic irony for years. The designer hit the big time when her show-off creations for TV's *Sex and the City* attracted major interest from several countries. West 8th, on the other hand, is a no-excuses-

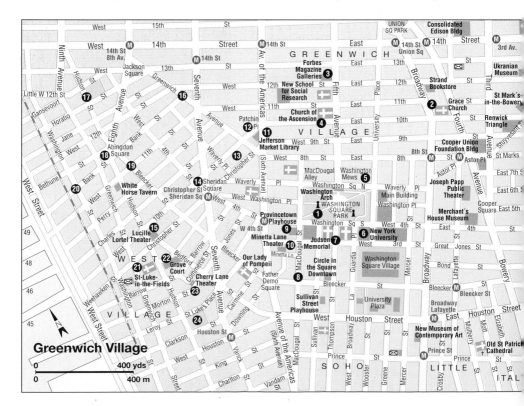

Greenwich Village

0 ____ 400 yds
0 ____ 400 m

needed commercial strip of discount shoe shops and chain boutiques. It's a far cry from the 1950s, when it was lined by bookstores and music clubs, or even from the 1930s, when Gertrude Vanderbilt Whitney opened the prototype for the Whitney Museum of American Art here, in what's now the New York Studio School of Drawing, Painting and Sculpture.

Edward Hopper and Henry James

Tucked away just above Washington Arch are two tiny dead-end streets that look just like stage sets. **Washington Mews ❺** lies just south of **One Fifth Avenue** (a stately building that houses an ever-changing bar and restaurant), situated between Fifth and Washington Square North, an extension of Waverly Place. Originally built as stables for the townhouses along Washington Square North (where the artist Edward Hopper lived), the pretty rowhouses here and along nearby **MacDougal Alley** are now highly sought-after residences.

All of this could distract you from **Washington Square** itself. Originally a potter's field, where the poor and unknown were buried, it later became a parade ground, and still later a residential park. Although it's lost the cachet it knew in the days of Henry James — who was inspired to write his novel by the same name while living nearby – on weekend afternoons the park is filled with musicians, mime artists, jugglers and other street performers playing to appreciative crowds of New York University students, mothers with babies in strollers, Japanese camera crews, chess hustlers, passers-by and pot dealers.

With its two blocks of Greek Revival townhouses, **Washington Square North** retains a 19th-century elegance at odds with the monolithic **New York University ❻** buildings that adjoin the park. The enormous gray building on

Map on page 188

BELOW: Washington Square, once a potter's field, is the geographic and spiritual heart of the Village.

Washington Square East claims to be the Washington Square College of Arts and Sciences, but is actually NYU's main building. Inside you'll find the **Grey Art Gallery** (tel: 998 6780; closed Sun, Mon; fee suggested), showcasing some of the savviest contemporary and historical art exhibits in town.

Continue on Washington Place to NYU's **Brown Building**, built on the foundations of the 1900 Asch Building, a garment factory that in 1911 was the site of the Triangle Factory Fire, where 146 young women workers lost their lives in a tragedy that was to instigate wide-reaching labor reform laws. Past NYU's Loeb Student Center, Library and Catholic Center (all on Washington Square South), you come to **Judson Memorial Church** ❼. Designed in 1890 by the ubiquitous Stanford White in Romanesque Revival-style, the church has been for decades a cultural as well as a religious center.

Beatnik heaven

Turn left off Washington Square South onto **MacDougal Street** ❽, and you're in the heart of what was once beatnik heaven, where world-weary poets sipped coffee and discussed the meaning of life late into the night. These days, it's a mecca for out-of-towners, drawn by the bevy of ersatz crafts shops and "authentic" ethnic restaurants. A stroll around here offers the added pleasure of a pilgrimage to past grooviness; some nights you swear you could see the shadow of the young Bob Dylan hovering over the intersection of Bleecker and MacDougal streets. Many of Eugene O'Neill's plays were first produced at the **Provincetown Playhouse** ❾ on MacDougal, which is now owned by NYU.

Stop in at the **Minetta Tavern** where Ernest Hemingway hoisted a beer or two, or **Caffé Reggio** (119 MacDougal) one of the old-time coffee houses made famous in the 1940s and '50s. Another is **Le Figaro** on Bleecker, which offers maximum sidewalk people-watching opportunities, along with first-rate espresso and cappuccino.

BELOW: the Jefferson Market Library was built in 1877 as a courthouse.

Nearby entertainment opportunities include performances by the world's jazz greats at the **Blue Note** (West 3rd Street between MacDougal Street and Avenue of the Americas); excellent contemporary theater at the **Minetta Lane Theater** ❿; and the eternally-running production of *The Fantasticks*, which has been entertaining audiences at the **Sullivan Street Playhouse** (118 Sullivan Street) since 1959.

Besides a profusion of juice bars, shoe stores and souvenir shops, every other door around here seems to lead to a restaurant, and the smell of Indian, Spanish, Japanese and Italian cuisines spills out onto the sidewalk in a miasma of olfactory overkill. The Village excels in restaurants both old and new. If you're in the mood for old-world atmosphere and service walk down to Bleecker Street and back over to MacDougal: a few doors down on the right, at No. 69 **Villa Mosconi** is a Village classic: a friendly, family-run eatery where the welcome is expansive, the portions are huge and the atmosphere unabashedly Southern Italian. Heading toward the West Village is **Blue Hill** (75 Washington Place), a modern, upmarket venue that regularly receives raves for it inventive, American-style haute cuisine.

The West Village

The area west of the Avenue of the Americas (Sixth Avenue) and a few blocks north is the Village that hosts the annual Halloween Parade, witnessed the gay-rights riots at the Stonewall Inn in the late 1960s, and has pretty streets that wind confusingly between the major avenues.

Map on page 188

A good place to start is the striking, Gothic **Jefferson Market Library** ⓫ at 10th Street and the Avenue of the Americas, just up the road from the famous **Balducci's** gourmet market, a mecca for food enthusiasts. Originally part of a complex that included the old Women's House of Detention, it was built as a courthouse in 1877 and is where Harry Thaw went on trial for shooting Stanford White, in 1906. Next door is a pretty community garden which is occasionally open to the public.

Walk west on 10th Street, past **Patchin Place** ⓬ – a mews where Eugene O'Neill, the journalist John Reed and the poet e. e. cummings lived – to Greenwich Avenue, and you reach the city's most unusual pet shop, **Urban Bird**. A sign on the sidewalk advises that your visit can last no more than ten minutes. Exotic birds fly free inside, to the delight of browsers.

From here, continue west on **Christopher Street** ⓭, symbolic center of the gay community and a main cross-street that slants across the heart of the West Village to a renovated pier, walkway and bike path that, on a sunny day, make New York seem like a brand-new city. (At night, however, it's still the haunt of homeless kids and hustlers.)

You can find a wide selection of books with gay themes at the Oscar Wilde Memorial Bookshop (15 Christopher Street), just beyond a series of stores called Amalgamated which offer unusual housewares and decorative items.

The Lucille Lortel Theater at 121 Christopher Street has a Hollywood-style Walk of Fame that awards shiny bronze stars to playwrights whose work has been shown off Broadway.

BELOW: if pigs could fly…

A CITY OF SAINTS AND FIRSTS

Everyone in New York likes to think things happen here first. And, of course, they do. New York City can claim America's first 24-hour bank, first algebra book, first automobile accident, first speeding ticket, and its first saint – Mother Cabrini, who came from Italy and now has a shrine in Washington Heights, above Harlem. The first saint born in America was Elizabeth Ann Seton, who hailed from Lower Manhattan and later converted to Catholicism in Little Italy's Old St Patrick's Cathedral. To complete the holy trinity, Pierre Touissant, an 18th-century Haitian slave who is buried in the same church, may soon become the country's first ever black saint.

The first flea circus ("an extraordinary exhibition of industrious fleas") held its opening night at 187 Broadway in January 1835. The first elephant to step ashore in the New World landed here on April 13, 1796. Now the city's exotic wildlife includes the elephants that march through the Queens Midtown Tunnel when the Ringling Brothers Circus comes to town; the alligators which persistent folklorists claim roam the city's sewers (untrue, it seems); and a mysterious colony of ants that was spotted on top of the Empire State Building, nearly 1,500 feet (480 m) above street level. No one knows how the ants got there, or why.

Just past **Waverly Place** with its curved row of small Federal houses is the **Northern Dispensary**. A non-profit health clinic from 1831 until fairly recently, it's one of the oldest public buildings in the city. A few doors up and some three decades ago, the modern gay rights movement got its spontaneous start one night in 1969 at the Stonewall Inn (51 Christopher Street), a gay bar whose habitués got tired of being rousted by police. Today, there's a bar with the same name operating next door. Just across the street, tiny fenced-in **Christopher Park** features a statue of the Civil War general Philip Sheridan. In the traditional spirit of Village confusion, **Sheridan Square** ⑭ is actually a few steps away, at the triangular junction where Grove, Christopher and West Fourth Streets meet in a tangle of city non-planning.

White horses and onion soup

More shopping opportunities await on the other side of Seventh Avenue South – including McNulty's Tea & Coffee Company at 109 Christopher; at 121 Christopher Street is the playwright's friend, the **Lucille Lortel Theater** ⑮. If it's music rather than theatre that gives you a cultural *frisson*, this is the neighborhood for you: the tiny, historic **Village Vanguard** (178 Seventh Avenue South) has been in business for more than half a century.

BELOW: Dylan Thomas drank here. He later expired at nearby St Vincent's Hospital after too much of the White Horse's hospitality.

Greenwich Avenue ⑯ angles past Jackson Square to the heart of Manhattan's wholesale meat district, an area populated by galleries, gay clubs and transsexual hookers. **White Columns**, a gallery founded in 1969, is located at 320 West 13th Street, between West Fourth and Hudson streets. **Florent**, a small restaurant at 69 Gansevoort Street, between Greenwich and Washington streets, has the best onion soup in town (and one of the strangest mix of patrons, especially in the early morning).

Hudson Street ⑰ runs south from 14th Street and includes Myers of Keswick (No. 634), a British specialty shop where Keith Richards, Elton John and Princess Margaret have stocked up on delicacies like homemade pork pies; and the **White Horse Tavern**, serving drinks from the corner of 11th Street since 1880. This is where Dylan Thomas had one too many before expiring at nearby St Vincent's Hospital.

Above the White Horse, **Abingdon Square** ⑱ leads to the start of **Bleecker Street** ⑲, which at this end is lined by pleasant stores like the Biography Bookshop and Susan Parrish Antiques (No. 390), a good source of American folk art. It's also bisected by some of the village's prettiest thoroughfares.

For example, at the corner of Charles Street and Greenwich Street is an urban anomaly: a white wooden house surrounded by a fence and a yard, which looks like it belongs in a country village, rather than leaning up against a city tenement. (It was actually moved to 121 Greenwich Street from the Upper East Side in 1967.) **Bank Street** ⑳ is particularly scenic, with its cobblestones and pastel houses, and lies in the center of the **Greenwich Village Historic District**'s finest 19th-century architecture. Not that it's all historic houses around here. Years ago, Automatic Slim's, on the corner of Bank and Washington, was named the best bar in the West Village. (It's still going strong.)

**Map
on page
188**

Toward the end of Bank Street, **Westbeth** is a sprawling, government-funded artists' enclave that looks out over the Hudson River. A combination of subsidized apartments and theater complex, it was once home to Bell Laboratories, and the development of sound production as well as early television took place on the premises. Today it contains galleries and performance spaces, as well as rehearsal studios often used for Broadway and off-Broadway productions, and is one of Downtown's most interesting off-the-beaten-track venues.

Byways and speakeasys

It's only a short walk from here to **St-Luke-in-the-Fields ㉑**, the city's third oldest church and built in 1821 when this area was still pretty much open countryside. Easily reached by continuing down Hudson, you can also get there by walking west on **Grove Street** from Seventh Avenue South, a route which takes you through a rabbit-warren of lanes and byways that cross themselves or change names without warning.

Detail from the Blue Note club logo.

Number **17 Grove Street**, built in 1822, is another wooden relic of days gone by, as is **Grove Court ㉒**, an alleyway with a cluster of white-brick houses hidden inside. Grove Street intersects **Bedford Street**, one of the oldest Village byways. If you turn right here, you'll discover the original "Twin Peaks" (102 Bedford Street), built as an artists' residence in 1830. As its name suggests, the gabled roof comes to two peaks, not just one.

A left, however, takes you to **Chumley's**, a former speakeasy turned bar and restaurant at 86 Bedford where novelist John Steinbeck was a regular; there's a secret entrance around the corner on **Barrow Street**, one of the quietest, quaintest streets around, which intersects Bedford at **Commerce Street**, an equally pleasant lane.

BELOW: end the day at a Village jazz club; some have been around for half a century.

Tiny, well-known poet Edna St Vincent Millay was once a tenant at nearby **75 Bedford Street**, Manhattan's narrowest house at just over 9 feet wide. Another tenant of the same premises, some years later, was larger-than-life John Barrymore, of the theatrical Barrymore family. More recently, a pre stardom Barbra Streisand worked as an usher at the **Cherry Lane Theater ㉓** on Commerce, which was originally a farm silo and later a box factory before it was eventually converted into a theater.

Back toward Barrow Street, the **Grange Hall** is a popular local restaurant and bar that dates back to the Prohibition days of the 1930s, when it was known as the Blue Mill Tavern. From the corner of Barrow and Hudson, you can see the grounds of St Luke's, which include a small hidden garden. A two-block walk south takes you to the corner of St Luke's Place, where **Anglers and Writers Cafe** is a fine spot to stop for a cup of tea.

St Luke's Place ㉔ itself is lined by gracious Italianate rowhouses. One of New York's mayors, Jimmy Walker, lived at No. 6, and two lamps – a sign of mayoral honor – are still at the foot of the steps. At Seventh Avenue South, St Luke's turns into Leroy Street before coming to a stop at Bleecker, where **Our Lady of Pompeii Church** is a signal you've reached the South Village, an old Italian neighborhood. ❑

ESTABLISHED 1892

OVER 90 YRS

NO ARTIFICIAL INGREDIENTS

MOZZARELLE FRESH 4.29 lb VERY DRY 4.59 lb RICOTTA $2.28 lb 3 lb TIN $5.99

HOMEMADE PESTO SAUCE $3.80 EACH

CACIOCAVALLO 6.99 LB.

CACIOTTA

CROTONESE CHEESE $4.99 lb

FRESH PEPATO $5.99 lb

PROSCIUTTO BREAD $2.49 EACH

RICE BALLS $1.49 EACH

FRESH HOMEMADE SPINACH BREADS BROCCOLI BREADS $3.79 EACH

STROM BRE $4

MASCARPONE GORGONZOLA WITH BASIL

GORGONZOLA 7.89

PORTED VOLETTE 5.99 lb

HOMEMADE TOMATO SAUCE $3.95 EACH

STRACCHINO $8.39 lb

MASCARPONE $3.79 AND $6.99

HOMEMADE TIRAMI SU $3.25 EACH

NO SALT

SMOKED MOZZARELLE + PEPPERONI $4.59 lb

MOZZARE + PROSCIU $5.29

EAST VILLAGE TO CHINATOWN

Map on page 198

Old churches and new boutiques, Jewish delis, Chinese temples and Italian restaurants characterize these highly individual neighborhoods

Bordered by 14th Street to the north and Houston Street to the south, roughly centered between Third Avenue and Avenue B, the **East Village** is a place that stays up late, where fashions and politics are historically more radical than elsewhere in the city, and residents have included everyone from Beat icons like Allen Ginsberg and William Burroughs to Yippies and Hell's Angels.

Beneath its scruffy avant-garde surface, the East Village is also a neighborhood of immigrants, with Ukrainian and Puerto Rican social clubs next to offbeat boutiques, and free health clinics not far from expensive co-op buildings. Like other Downtown neighborhoods, old and new are juxtaposed here in an ever-changing mosaic.

St Mark's-in-the-Bowery ❶, at Second Avenue and 10th Street, is the second-oldest church building in Manhattan – and a good place to start exploring. Built in 1799 on a *bouwerie* (farm) belonging to Dutch governor Peter Stuyvesant, St Mark's has a long history of liberal religious thought, a reflection of the neighborhood that manifests itself in such long-standing community programs as the Poetry Project. The red-brick Anglo-Italianate houses across from the church on East 10th Street and on Stuyvesant Street, which veers off at an angle from Second Avenue, form the heart of the **St Mark's Historic District**. Number 21 is the **Stuyvesant Fish House**, a national historic landmark built by Peter Stuyvesant's great grandson.

Poor man, rich man

Keep walking on Stuyvesant Street to Third Avenue, where the **St Mark's Bookshop** is well-stocked with obscure new fiction and political tomes. It's a short walk from here to **Astor Place ❷**, named for John Jacob Astor, who arrived in New York in 1784 as a penniless immigrant and was the richest man in town by the time he died 36 years later. Today the area's most notable landmark, besides the **subway kiosk** nearby, is the giant rotating black cube by Tony Rosenthal called *The Alamo*. One of the first abstract sculptures installed on city property, it has stood at the intersection of Astor Place, St Mark's Place and Lafayette Street since 1967.

The brown Italianate **Cooper Union Foundation Building ❸** between Third and Fourth avenues opened in 1859 as one of the country's earliest centers of free education. Famous as an art school, it's also where Abraham Lincoln gave the speech said to have launched his presidential campaign. A statue of founder-philanthropist Peter Cooper by Augustus Saint-Gaudens, who studied here, stands behind Cooper Union at **Cooper Square**, where Third and Fourth converge to create the Bowery.

Colonnade Row on Lafayette Street, which runs

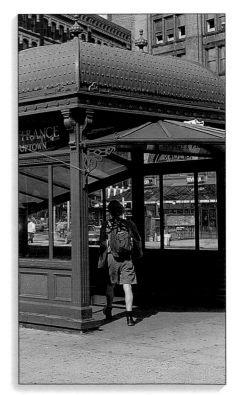

East Village,
Chinatown,
Soho and Tribeca

0   500 yds

0   500 m

Map on page 198

south from Astor Place, was originally a group of nine columned homes built in 1833, when this was one of the city's most elegant neighborhoods. Only four of the houses still stand, with current occupants including the perennially stylish Indochine, a restaurant at No. 430 and the **Astor Place Theater** (No. 434). Across the street, the **Joseph Papp Public Theater** ❹ (actually a complex of five theaters) was originally the Astor Library. This was John Jacob Astor's only public legacy, which he envisioned as a center of learning for the common man. (The fact that it was only open during working hours didn't strike him as a problem.) Since 1967, the building has been home to the city's Shakespeare Festival as well as contemporary productions (from *Hair* and *A Chorus Line* to *Bring In 'Da Noise, Bring In 'Da Funk*) that have gone on to Broadway.

A block further down you can drop in and see the city as it used to be at the **Merchant's House Museum** (29 East 4th Street, tel: 777 1089), a small Greek Revival-style brick townhouse built in 1832. The same family lived here for generations and their furnishings and personal effects are on display Sunday through Thursday afternoons, for a small admission fee.

Past to present

At the beginning of the 20th century, lower Broadway around 9th Street was part of the "Ladies Mile" of fashionable retailing that stretched north to 23rd Street. Later it was just a dingy pause before Soho (when it was still known as SoHo), but all that changed when Tower Records and other young consumer centers moved in. Officially known as **NoHo** ❺ (an abbreviation for North of Houston), the area includes Broadway from Astor Place down to Houston Street, an area now crowded with stores and shoppers.

Several interesting furniture and antiques emporia are also located on Lafayette Street, where the **Time Cafe** (380 Lafayette, at Great Jones Street) has a nice outdoor terrace, as well as a popular basement jazz club. At the corner of Astor Place and Broadway, a large, busy K-mart reflects the changing times; a few steps away, the **Astor Place Hair Designers** is a Downtown institution where the latest "do" is yours for the asking – cutting time: 10 minutes.

St Mark's Place ❻, a continuation of 8th Street between Third Avenue and Avenue A, is the East Village version of main street. In the 1960s, this was the East Coast's counter-culture center. The Dom (a former Polish social club where Andy Warhol presented Velvet Underground "happenings" and, later, barefoot freaks tripped out at the Electric Circus) is now a **community crafts center**.

The Fillmore East, which presented rock concerts around the corner on Second Avenue, is also long gone. But St Mark's Place is still one of the city's liveliest thoroughfares. Sidewalk cafés and restaurants are usually heaving with customers – and the bazaar-like atmosphere is enhanced by street vendors selling T-shirts, jewelry and bootleg CDs. Stop in at Trash and Vaudeville for retro-punk gear and **Dojo** (24–26 St Mark's Place) for a quick and nutritious vegetarian meal, then take a detour around the corner – down Third Avenue to East 7th Street – for a true

St Mark's-in-the-Bowery is the second-oldest church in Manhattan.

BELOW: the East Village is a place that stays up late.

drinking man's pub. **McSorley's Old Ale House** has been in business since the 1850s, although women weren't allowed inside until more than a century later. This was one of Irish writer Brendan Behan's favorite New York hangouts.

Continuing on St Mark's, the block between Second and Third is lined by a motley array of record shops, tattoo parlours and places to get various body parts pierced; it's also home to the **Pearl Theater Company** (80 St Mark's Place). In fact, the East Village has been a center for live performances since Second Avenue was lined by Yiddish theaters at the end of the 19th century. Today only a couple are still used as theaters (the Orpheum on Second Avenue is one). But there's also **La Mama** ETC just west of Second Avenue at 4th Street, a pioneer of avant-garde theater, and **P.S. 122** (First Avenue at 9th Street), where an annual benefit offers a microcosm of what's happening on the cutting edge of music, dance and poetry.

Little India

As befits a neighborhood that's a typical melting pot, you can find just about any cuisine here, from trendy to traditional. If cheap and exotic is your preference, you can't do much better than "**Little India**" ❼ on 6th Street between First and Second Avenues. All restaurants here are inexpensive, most stay open pretty late, and some even feature live Indian music on weekend evenings.

BELOW: McSorley's Old Ale House – in business since 1850 but only opened to women in 1970.

Walk north up Second Avenue to the corner of 7th Street, past the **Middle Collegiate Church** (a Reformed Protestant Dutch church built in 1891), and you'll find the Kiev. Eastern-European style meals can be enjoyed here, and it stays open late. Kosher meals are the staple at the Second Avenue Kosher Delicatessen and Restaurant on the corner of 10th Street. And, if you're hungry for

something sweet, there's Veniero's on 11th Street near First Avenue, where the Veniero family have been baking delicious Italian pastries since 1894.

The **Theater for the New City** on First Avenue was founded in 1971 as another venue for experimental Broadway productions. Not far away, the lovely **St Nicholas ❽** Carpatho-Russian Orthodox Greek Catholic Church is another reminder of this ethnic and religious melting pot. Originally built for a predominantly Anglican parish as St Mark's Chapel, its interior tiled walls and beamed ceiling date from 1894.

At 10th Street and Avenue A is the top of **Tompkins Square Park ❾**, a patch of reclaimed swamp used as a drill ground and recruiting camp during the Civil War. It was later the center of the *Kleine Deutschland* (Little Germany) community that thrived here more than a hundred years ago. A gathering place for hippies and runaways in the late 1960s, the park was a focal point for conflicts between homeless activists and police in the 1980s. Today, however, it's a generally peaceful place frequented by watchful young mothers with kids and neighborhood folk walking their dogs. Many of the homes in this area have been renovated by young professionals (the 19th-century rowhouses on 10th Street at the park's northern border are a good example), fueling a hike in rents that's led to further gentrification.

Along Avenues A and B, drug dealers and graffiti-covered walls have been usurped by bars and restaurants with a predominately young, hip clientele – although Odessa (119 Avenue A at 7th Street) is a surviving reflection of the neighborhood's Eastern European heritage, where specialties include home-cooked *pirogi*, *blintzes* and *borscht*. Other places reflect the neighborhood's cleaned-up image, like **Two Boots** (37 Avenue A), a family-friendly pizza joint with a Cajun twist, on the block between 2nd and 3rd streets. Nevertheless, strolling further into the heart of **Alphabet City** (Avenues C and D) is not recommended, especially late at night.

Nightlife in the area ranges from the **Pyramid Club**, which opened on Avenue A back when this was still frontier territory, to spots like **Brownies**, a showcase for local bands between 10th and 11th streets. And while CBGB-OMFUG on the Bowery is still going strong, the place where punk and new wave exploded in the 1970s has been eclipsed by newer venues on or below Houston Street.

The Lower East Side

This area technically starts east of Tompkins Square Park, where Avenue C becomes Losaida Avenue, but the traditional **Lower East Side**, with its immigrant roots firmly in place, is south of East Houston Street, bordered by the Bowery and the East River. This is where bargain hunters flock for wholesale deals in everything from bridal gowns to bathroom fixtures, and where the narrow streets are lined by tenements that date back 150 years.

Starting in the mid-19th century, successive waves of immigrants arrived here in pursuit of a new life: first free Africans, followed by Irish and Germans, and later by Eastern European Jews, mainly from Russia and Poland. These days you see stores with Jewish

Map on page 198

TIP

Relax with a steam bath and a *platza* (a rub-down with an oak leaf broom) at the funky Russian & Turkish Baths at 268 East 10th Street, going strong since 1892. Tel: 212-674 9250.

BELOW: Tompkins Square Park was used as a drill ground during the Civil War.

A sign of the times: the Lower East Side's Jewish heritage dates back to the mid-1800s.

BELOW: Orchard Street market is New York's favorite Sunday shopping bazaar.

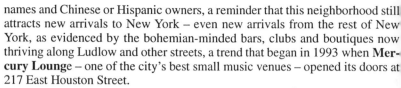

names and Chinese or Hispanic owners, a reminder that this neighborhood still attracts new arrivals to New York – even new arrivals from the rest of New York, as evidenced by the bohemian-minded bars, clubs and boutiques now thriving along Ludlow and other streets, a trend that began in 1993 when **Mercury Lounge** – one of the city's best small music venues – opened its doors at 217 East Houston Street.

Walk along East Houston to the top of **Orchard Street** and you've reached New York's favorite **Sunday shopping bazaar** (stores close Friday afternoons and all day Saturday for the Jewish sabbath). Once crowded with peddlers selling old clothes and cracked eggs, today you can find designer fashions, fabrics, linens and shoes at prices often half as much as Uptown. The scene is frenetic (bargaining encouraged), so you may want to stop in first at **Katz's Delicatessen** (205 East Houston, near Ludlow Street) for a little sustenance. The menu here has hardly changed since opening day in 1898 – and they make a pastrami sandwich that's considered a culinary landmark. For lighter fare, walk down Ludlow Street to the Pink Pony Cafe, which serves tea, coffee – and occasional poetry readings – next door to **Max Fish** (178 Ludlow Street), a lively bar with a pool table and jukebox.

Along with Katz's, traditional Lower East Side food and beverage options include the Schapiro Wine Company (126 Rivington Street, between Essex and Norfolk streets), a kosher winery with Sunday tastings. The city's best pickle experience is a few blocks south, at the corner of Hester and Essex Streets, where Hollander & Sons has barrels filled with the same homemade pickles featured in Joan Micklin Silver's 1988 movie *Crossing Delancey*.

For blintzes and onion rolls, stop in at **Ratner's** (138 Delancey, near Suffolk Street) or sit down at 175 Chrystie Street, just north of Delancey, to a memorable feast at **Sammy's Famous Roumanian Restaurant** where a traditional pitcher of chicken fat comes with every meal. Less-traditional is the nightlife exemplified by the **Bowery Ballroom**, a rock venue the owners of Mercury Lounge opened on Delancey between Chrystie and the Bowery.

History lives on

Grand Street's Seward Park High School counts Tony Curtis and Walter Matthau among its graduates; Sam Jaffe, another actor, was born in an 1863 tenement at 97 Orchard Street, between Delancey and Broome streets. Since 1988, the building and its cramped apartments have been part of the **Lower East Side Tenement Museum** (90 Orchard Street, tel: 431 0233, fee), which is dedicated to telling the story of what life was (and is) like for poor urban immigrants. In addition to changing exhibits, the museum offers tours of the building and the neighborhood.

In the 19th century, the area's substandard working and living conditions (ably chronicled by journalist-reformer Jacob Riis) were instrumental in spawning various anarchist and socialist movements. Emma Goldman preached her gentle anarchism here, radical newspapers, such as the *Jewish Daily Forward*, flourished, and settlement houses offering immigrants health and education assistance were formed.

In a sign of the times, the landmark building at 173 East Broadway where the old *Daily Forward* was published has been converted to condos (the faces of Karl Marx and Friedrich Engels peer from a frieze over the entrance). But some of the settlement houses are still in operation, including the **University Settlement House** on Eldridge Street, and the **Henry Street Settlement** (265 Henry Street), which was founded in 1893 as the country's first volunteer nursing and social service center. Today it continues to offer helpful programs for new arrivals, and has an active community arts center.

Religion played an important role in the lives of all immigrants, particularly those who had fled the pograms of their native lands. Although many of the old synagogues in the area are no longer used, the **Eldridge Street Synagogue**, a grand, 1887 Moorish-style landmark close to Division Street, has been restored as a cultural center (though it still has a small congregation.) For information about tours and exhibits, call 219 0888.

Map on page 198

The two-block stretch of the Bowery south of Delancy Street is lined with lighting stores, and is a good place to pick up a cheap chandelier.

Chinatown

One of the largest Chinese-American settlements in the US, as well as one of Manhattan's most vibrant and exciting neighborhoods, **Chinatown** got its start in the 1870s, when Chinese railroad workers drifted east from California in the wake of rising anti-Asian sentiment. Today, Chinatown – once squeezed into a three-block area bordered by Mott, Pell and the Bowery – encompasses almost 40 blocks, swinging around Little Italy to Houston Street, where a **Chinese vendor's market** recently opened at the northern end of **Sara Delano Roosevelt Park**, a narrow strip that stretches Uptown from Canal Street. Chinatown's heart lies south of Canal, not far from the city's civic center, where Worth Street,

BELOW: the menu at Katz's Deli has hardly changed since 1898.

Chinatown has spread from a three-block area to one that now sprawls for almost 40 blocks.

East Broadway and the Bowery meet at **Chatham Square ⑫**. Although the square is named after William Pitt, the Earl of Chatham, the **Kim Lau Memorial Arch** here was built in honor of a Chinese-American pilot who died a hero in World War II. Nearby, **Confucius Plaza ⑬** is a high-rise complex that includes apartments, shops, an elementary school and an interior tree-shaded park. A bronze statue of the philosopher Confucius stands in front, facing Chatham Square.

Tucked away among the Chinese banks lining the Bowery is a remnant of Old New York: **No. 18 Bowery ⑭**, a Federal-style house built in 1785 and now the oldest surviving rowhouse in Manhattan. Its original owner, Edward Mooney, was a wholesale meat merchant who dabbled in racehorses; ironically, in later years there was even an off-track betting parlor on the premises. Another interesting local landmark on the Bowery is the pagoda-style HSBC **Bank Building**.

Here we go 'round Mulberry Street

Walk west to **Columbus Park** and you're at the top of **Mulberry Street ⑮**, which, along with **Mott Street ⑯**, forms Chinatown's two main thoroughfares. In the early 19th century this area was part of the notorious Five Points slum region, where street gangs ran rampant and squatters' huts formed an equally notorious shanty town, later torn down to make way for the park.

The best place to learn about the neighborhood is at the old (1900s) school building on the corner of Mulberry and Bayard streets, which houses the **Museum of Chinese in the Americas ⑰** (70 Mulberry Street, tel: 619 4785, admission free for children under 12). Founded in 1970, when the area's population began to explode, the museum features a permanent exhibit on the

BELOW:
Chinatown's heart lies south of Canal Street near Chatham Square.

Map on page 198

Chinese-American experience, as well as regularly scheduled walking tours and lectures. Open Tuesday through Saturday from noon to 5pm, it also has a research library and a small gift shop. From here, walk past sidewalks thick with stands selling fruit, vegetables, fish and leaf-wrapped packets of sticky rice, and turn right on **Canal Street**. Crowded with vendors hawking Taiwanese tapes, old men and women reading fortunes, and shops stocked to the brim with imported goods, it's a scene that seems far from the rest of Manhattan. Turn right down Mott Street, and you'll notice shiny Singapore-style restaurants with marble facades and plastic signs, part of the "new" Chinatown built by recent, wealthier immigrants from Hong Kong and Shanghai.

Multi-armed goddess

Signs of the "old" Chinatown can still be found, however, especially at the **Chinese Community Center** run by the Chinese Consolidated Benevolent Association, which first opened on Mott Street in 1883. Next door, inside the **Eastern States Buddhist Temple** ⓲, there's a multi-armed statue of the Goddess Kuan-Yui. The air is thick with the scent of sickly sweet incense.

Nearby, **Quong Yuen Shing** opened as a general store in the 1890s. The oldest emporium in Chinatown, it's an interesting place to browse. Farther along, the **Church of the Transfiguration** was constructed for an English Lutheran congregation in 1801, became the Zion Protestant Episcopal Church in 1810, and was sold to the Roman Catholic Church in 1853. Today, it offers services in Cantonese and also runs a school for local children. Turn right down **Pell Street** and you'll see the **Sun Wui District Association** across from the **First Chinese Baptist Church**. This type of organization afforded Chinese

BELOW: the air is thick with incense at Chinatown's temples.

TIP

All the Manhattan telephone numbers in this book use the 212 code. The newer codes do not apply to existing numbers.

immigrants another means of coping with the new world they found themselves in. Unlike some of the other associations, this group constructed a more traditional-looking edifice, perhaps in an effort to combat homesickness. The pagoda roof is topped by two "good luck" ceramic fish. Nearby is the headquarters of the Hip Sing Association, one of Chinatown's many *tongs*, or fraternal organizations. From the 1870s until well into the 1930s, these groups were involved in often-violent disputes that were sensationalized as "*tong* wars," mainly by the non-Chinese press.

The narrow lane off to the right is the most crooked street in Manhattan; in the 1600s it was a cart path leading to Hendrik Doyer's brewery. Later, **Doyers Street** became an important communications center, where men gathered to get the latest news from China and to drop off letters and money for home with the small shopkeepers who served as combination banks and post offices. In keeping with this tradition, the current Chinatown post office was built on the site of the old brewery.

Dim Sum

Just before the post office is the **Nom Wah Tea House**, the oldest restaurant in the neighborhood. Unlike many places in the area, this one generally closes early (around 8pm), but it has some of the best *dim sum* in Chinatown. The interior is much the same as when it opened in 1921, with sagging red leather banquettes, linoleum floor and ceiling fans. The prices are just as old-fashioned.

Food is one of the main attractions of Chinatown and, with hundreds of restaurants to choose from, the hardest part is making a decision about where to eat. Choices range from the tiny five-table Malaysia Restaurant in the **China**

BELOW: food for the soul; a family eating by their altar.

Map
on page
198

town **Arcade** to the New Silver Palace which seats 800. There's also the Golden Unicorn on East Broadway, where house specialties are served in a rather luxurious atmosphere, and the Peking Duck House on Mott Street, a favorite of former New York mayor Ed Koch. For a taste of Chinese culture, drop in at one of the movie theaters that show films from Taiwan, Hong Kong and China, or visit the **Asian American Arts Center** (26 Bowery), across from the Confucius Plaza complex, which features ongoing exhibits. Upstairs, the **Asian-American Dance Theater** presents both traditional and contemporary dance productions.

Chinese New Year combines feasts, dance and musical presentations. Traditionally, it begins with parades and fireworks in a noisy, crowded celebration held between the end of January and the beginning of February. (Recently, however, the city banned the fireworks, a ruling contested by the community.)

Little Italy

Crowds – along with a bevy of tantalizing food stalls and raucous games of chance – are an integral part of the festivals that draw visitors to **Little Italy**: the Feast of St Anthony takes place on Mott Street between Grand and Canal streets in late May, and the 10-day Feast of San Gennaro, in September, when Mulberry Street from Canal to East Houston becomes a lively pedestrian mall.

Now squeezed between Chinatown and Soho, this area has been an Italian neighborhood since the late 1800s, when large numbers of immigrants arrived in New York from Southern Europe. The most pleasant bit is along **Mulberry Street**, north of Canal, where the atmosphere abruptly changes from boisterous to almost mellow, and the sidewalks are lined by cafés and social clubs rather than clamorous street vendors.

BELOW: death in Chinatown.

Most people come here to eat, and with good reason. **Luna's**, on Mulberry, is a long-time favorite, a reasonably priced restaurant that's been run by the same family since 1878. **Umberto's Clam House**, now on Broome near the corner of Mulberry Street, is another favorite (and was the place where gangster Joey Gallo met an abrupt and bloody end in 1972 while having dinner at its old Mulberry Street location). **Puglia** on Hester Street is another neighborhood standby that's been around since 1919. Keep walking north on Mulberry, past the headquarters of the Society of San Gennaro, and you come to one of the oldest houses in Little Italy. **Paolucci's Restaurant**, where strolling violinists entertain diners, is in a small white Federal-style house built for Stephen Van Renssellaer, a well-to-do New Yorker, in 1816. Originally located at 153 Mulberry Street, the entire house was moved to its present site at number 149 in 1841.

At the corner of Mulberry and Grand, you can browse through the gifts, novelties and religious relics sold at E. Rossi & Co., before sampling some of the famous products of **Ferrara**, a pastry shop and café since 1892.

NoLita

The **Police Building** ⓫ on Centre Street, an elaborate Beaux-Arts structure that dates from 1909, served as police headquarters until 1973 and was divided into expensive co-operative apartments in the 1980s – marking the start of this part of town's transition into an increasingly desirable locale for trendy shops, bars and restaurants.

Old St Patrick's Cathedral ⓴, on the corner of Mott and Prince Streets, was the seat of New York's Catholic archdiocese until 1879 (when the "new" St

BELOW: Little Italy's Feast of San Gennaro lasts for 10 days in September.

Patrick's Cathedral on Fifth Avenue was completed). Construction on the Cathedral began in 1809, was interrupted by the War of 1812, and was eventually finished in 1815. It was rebuilt in 1868 after being destroyed by fire, and remains a unique landmark on Little Italy's northern fringes. Across Mott Street from the cathedral's graveyard, a plaque on the wall of a red-brick Victorian building explains that this was the School of the Children's Aid Society, created for the care and education of neighborhood immigrant children. Designed in 1888 by Calvert Vaux, the architect who also helped to create Central Park, it's been residential apartments for a while – and probably a desirable place to live, now that Mott, Mulberry and Elizabeth streets from here to East Houston have been dubbed **NoLita**, for "**N**orth of **Lit**tle **Ita**ly".

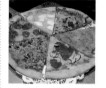
Map on page 198

Worth visiting

Edged by Soho to the west, this traditionally Southern Italian enclave (film director Martin Scorsese grew up on Elizabeth Street) has several interesting small boutiques, like **Gates of Morocco** (8 Prince Street), stocked with henna-painted sheepskin lamps and Moroccan rugs. Although an old luncheonette at the corner of Prince and Elizabeth has been transformed into Café Habana (serving relatively inexpensive Cuban specialities), there are still a couple of neighborhood standbys, like the butcher shop up toward Houston, where they cure their own bacon. On **Mott Street**, just below Prince, diehard cigarette smokers congregate at **Cafe Gitane**, a refuge for visiting Europeans since 1994. Slightly west toward Soho, **Le Jardin Bistro** is located on Cleveland Place. In warm weather, the back garden of this French-owned restaurant is the perfect spot to enjoy steak frites and a bottle of wine. ❑

ABOVE AND BELOW: most people come to Little Italy to eat; Puglia on Hester Street has been around since 1919.

NEW YORK'S LESSER-KNOWN MUSEUMS

Done the Met and MoMA? Feel like being a little unconventional in your culture-hopping? Then check out New York City's lesser-known museums

New York City has a museum of the American piano and a museum of skyscrapers; a museum for African art, one for folk art, one for illustration and another for photography. It seems there is a museum or cultural society to suit just about every minority, from the Kurds to the Chinese to the Swiss to the Puerto Ricans. Lovers of the traditional life should visit Historic Richmond Town *(see photograph above)*; followers of fashion should be in touch with Chelsea's Fashion Institute of Technology for exhibitions curated by specialists. Children can choose from three museums specially for them – who says the city's just for grown ups?

Cooper-Hewitt National Design Museum (2 East 91st St, tel: 212-849 8300); Wed–Sat 10am–5pm, Tues until 9pm, Sun noon–5pm. Fee.
Dyckman Farmhouse Museum (4881 Broadway at 204th St, tel: 212-304 9422); Tues–Sun 10am–4pm. Fee.
Historic Richmond Town (441 Clark Ave, Staten Island, tel: 718-351 1611); open Wed–Sun 1–5pm, extended hours July, Aug. Fee.
Jacques Marchais Museum of Tibetan Art (338 Lighthouse Ave, Staten Island, tel: 718-987 3500); Wed–Sun 1–5pm in summer; call for hours Dec–March. Fee.
National Museum of the American Indian (1 Bowling Green, tel: 212-668 6624); daily 10am–5pm, Thurs until 8pm. Donations welcome.
New York City Fire Museum (278 Spring St, tel: 212-691 1303); Tues–Sun 10am–4pm, Thurs to 9pm. Fee.
Teddy Roosevelt's Birthplace, 28 East 20th St, tel: 212-260 1616); Wed–Sun 9am–5pm. Fee.

▷ **JACQUES MARCHAIS**
This Staten Island museum has grounds arranged along the lines of a Tibetan monastery and houses one of the largest collections of Tibetan art in the West.

△ **FIRE! FIRE!**
Soho's NYC Fire Museum is housed in a renovated 1904 firehouse and has a huge collection of exhibits from the mid 18th century.

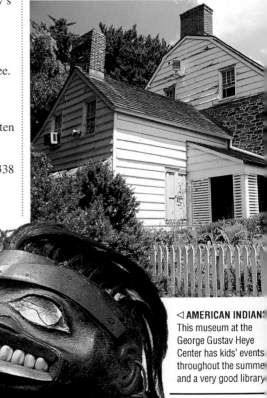

◁ **AMERICAN INDIAN**
This museum at the George Gustav Heye Center has kids' events throughout the summer and a very good library.

JOHN D. ROCKEFELLER

Born on a farm in upstate New York, John D. Rockefeller (1839–1937) established the Standard Oil Company in 1870 and became the country's first billionaire. Retiring in 1911, he spent the latter part of his life giving much of his fortune to various worthy causes and created a cultural legacy that was to span three generations. His namesake and son John D. Rockefeller, Jr (1874–1960) financed The Cloisters to house the Metropolitan Museum's medieval art collection, not only donating the tract of land it sits on but also providing land (and financing) for the Museum of Modern Art, which his wife co-founded. His grandson, Nelson Rockefeller (1908–79), who served as governor of New York and vice president of the US, continued the tradition of philanthropy by donating a superb collection of "primitive art" to the Met; another grandson, John D. Rockefeller III (1906–78) was a key financial supporter of the Lincoln Center and founded the Asia Society, to which he contributed nearly 300 works of art that form the basis of its collection.

△ TEDDY'S BIRTHPLACE
Roosevelt's personal mementos, plus house tours on the hour and occasional chamber music.

▽ COOPER-HEWITT
Museum Mile's National Design Museum's textiles and wallpapers are housed in an exquisite mansion.

FARMHOUSE MUSEUM
e Dyckman house on oadway is Manhattan's ly surviving 18th-century rmhouse and offers a mpse into a simpler age.

beau bru

SPRING CO
SPORT JA

SOHO AND TRIBECA

Decades after the first artists moved into its abandoned industrial lofts, Soho is still one of Manhattan's most stimulating neighborhoods

Map on page 198

When Abraham Lincoln made his first campaign speech at nearby Cooper Union, this was the center of the city's most fashionable shopping and hotel district. By the end of the 19th century, however, the narrow streets were filled by factories whose imaginative cast-iron facades masked sweatshop conditions so horrific that the city fire department dubbed the region "Hell's Hundred Acres." The entire area might have been razed in the 1960s if local artists hadn't started moving into the old lofts and the city hadn't changed zoning laws so they could do so legitimately. Around the same time, conservationists established the **Soho Cast Iron Historic District** to protect these elaborate "temples of industry."

Now too expensive for all but the most successful (or those who got in when prices were cheap), Soho, an acronym for **So**uth of **Ho**uston, is bordered by Canal Street to the south, Lafayette Street to the east, and the Avenue of the Americas (Sixth Avenue) to the west. If it's no longer strictly the artists' neighborhood of old, it maintains a uniquely New York combination of grit and blatant commercialism, where burly men unload trucks next to outrageous window displays and double-decker tour buses inch slowly along the cobblestone streets.

PRECEDING PAGES: reflections of fashions past. **LEFT:** Vesuvio; family-owned since the 1920s. **BELOW:** keys here.

West Broadway

Soho's main drag is **West Broadway ㉑**, lined by stores offering everything from jewelry to quirky household wares. On Saturdays, in particular, it's packed with crowds of tourists loaded down with shopping bags. From Houston to Canal, you'll find a clutch of boutiques hawking European fashions (René Lezard at 417) and footwear (Fortuna Valentino at 422), along with a bracing dose of imported Continental attitude. The selection of wares also includes the delicate lingerie at Joovay (436) and the neon cosmetics and clothing of Hotel Venus (366), all interspersed with tempting restaurants, bars and cafes.

Meanwhile, many of Soho's art galleries have relocated above street level to avoid exorbitant rents (and still others have absconded to Chelsea, Fifth Avenue or 57th Street). At last count, however, there were still close to 200 exhibition spaces in the immediate area (*see page 218*).

For instance, while **Prince Street ㉒** has also turned into prime shopping territory, a permanent art installation lingers on the Greene Street side of **114 Prince Street**, where the building's cast-iron facade was reproduced as a *trompe l'oeil* mural by artist Richard Haas. Next door, you can stop and shop for French ready-to-wear at Agnès b, or take a coffee break at any one of a number of watering holes or

espresso bars. Good places for meals around here include the diner-style Jerry's (101 Prince Street), a longtime local favorite; and **Fanelli's**, a landmark neighborhood bar and restaurant that's been standing on the corner of Prince and Mercer streets since the 1890s. The Romanesque Revival-style building on the opposite corner dates from the same period, but a century or so later has been transformed into **The Mercer**, a small luxury hotel with 75 rooms and an acclaimed basement-level restaurant called The Mercer Kitchen. High on the "being seen" scene is the queen bee of all Soho brasseries, **Balthazar** at 80 Spring Street between Broadway and Crosby Street.

The ghost of a young girl who was killed near the spring that still flows deep beneath the pavement on Spring Street has been said to haunt neighboring waterbeds.

Broadway and beyond

Once home to the city's most elegant shops and later to textile outlets, discount stores and delis, the stately cast-iron buildings on Broadway below Canal Street reacquired cachet in the 1980s first as museums, then as galleries, and then as stores like Pottery Barn and Eddie Bauer.

New Museum of Contemporary Art ㉓ (tel: 219 1222) paved the way when it relocated from lower Fifth Avenue to 583 Broadway in 1983. Founded in 1977 and now housed in an attractive stone building with carved columns, arches and floor-to-ceiling windows, its exhibits focus on everything from political issues to television's influence on society. The New Museum's bookstore is a hotbed of activity with readings, performances and book signings making it a good place to meet, or meet up with people; its one-off or limited-edition gifts provide great shopping opportunities. The museum is open Tuesday to Sunday with reduced admission Thursday evenings.

BELOW: window on the world of art and upscale shopping.

A 1904 cast-iron confection called the **Little Singer Building**, designed by

Ernest Flagg, stands across Broadway from the now-famous **Dean & Deluca** ㉔ store (560 Broadway), at the opposite corner of Prince Street. Dean & Deluca's, described by the *Washington Post* as "a combination of Paris's Fauchon, London's Harrod's Food Halls and Milan's Peck all rolled into one," is food-as-art: a cornucopia of fruits, vegetables and imported gourmet grocery specialities. This has proved to be so successful a formula that Dean & Deluca stores have now opened up in other cities, too. The stand-up coffee bar is stocked with delectable pastries, the perfect place for a quick snack.

Several galleries are located on the upper floors of buildings along this part of Broadway, with **Soho 20** at 545, PPOW at 532 and **Thread Waxing Space** at 476. If the Harry Potter novels made J.K. Rowling a millionaire, evidence that it did even more for publisher Scholastic Books is their huge new bookstore at 555 Broadway. Aisles of kids' books and reading events make this good family stop.

A walk east on Prince leads to Lafayette Street where bits of old New York, literally, can be purchased at Lost City Arts (275 Lafayette). In the opposite direction, the **Children's Museum of the Arts** ㉕ (182 Lafayette Street between Broome and Grand streets, tel: 941-9198, fee) has great interactive exhibits for kids; it's open every day but Monday and Tuesday. Back to Broadway, the Palazzo-style

Haughwout Building ㉖ at the corner of Broome Street is one of Soho's oldest – and most striking – cast-iron edifices. Designed by John Gaynor, it was constructed in 1857 as one of the country's first retail stores, complete with the country's first elevator. A left on Mercer leads to The Enchanted Forest, a whimsically decorated store between Spring and Broome that's a fantasy world of toys and children's games.

Flora and Miss Lizzie

Named after a Revolutionary War general, **Greene Street ㉗**, like Mercer and Wooster streets, runs parallel to West Broadway and Broadway. In the late 19th century it was the center of New York's most notorious red-light district, where brothels with names like Flora's and Miss Lizzie's flourished behind shuttered windows. As befits one of the Soho Cast Iron Historic District's prime thoroughfares, Greene Street also offers a rich concentration of this uniquely American architecture at its best, including (at the Canal Street end) the city's longest continuous row of cast-iron buildings.

At the corner of Broome Street, the **1872 Gunther Building** is particularly worthy of notice. Closer to Spring Street, 5 & 10 No Exaggeration is a quirky, cluttered restaurant where everything's for sale – and the only place in the city, says the owner, with both a liquor and an antique dealer's license. Before continuing onwards, stop and admire the cream-colored "king" (architecturally-speaking) of cast-iron splendor at **72–76 Greene Street** just opposite. It's an impressively ornate structure designed by Isaac Duckworth and built in 1873. Soho shopping continues at **Louis Vuitton** (116 Greene Street) and at **Back Pages Antiques** (125 Greene Street), where the speciality is classic jukeboxes.

Map on page 198

Greene Street has the city's, and maybe America's, longest continuous row of cast-iron buildings. These "temples of industry" are now protected and their distinctive exteriors cannot be altered.

BELOW: the Haughwout Building was constructed in 1857.

TIP

To buy a work of art without mortgaging your house, you might want to check out the galleries or artists' studios in Brooklyn's DUMBO or Williamsburg areas, where some of Soho's residents moved after rents became too high.

BELOW: a little something to go with the sofa, perhaps?

At the corner of Spring and Wooster, the white clapboard and brick house built in 1818 is home to Tennessee Mountain, a popular rib joint. The entrance is around the corner on Wooster Street and there's a nice view of Soho's weekend action from the second-floor windows.

Turn onto stone-cobbled **Wooster Street** ㉘ for the **Tony Shafrazi Gallery** (119 Wooster) and the **Howard Greenberg Gallery** (upstairs at 120 Wooster), which, like many galleries, seems to hop from street to street. A few have managed to anchor themselves at the same spot for years, however, including the **Dia Center for the Arts'** second-floor space at 141 Wooster Street, where *New York Earth Room* by Walter De Maria is on display (closed in summer). The Dia Center has another exhibition space on the second floor of a building on West Broadway (*see below*) and a major gallery in Chelsea. Another example of longevity can be found toward Broome Street, where Printed Matter (77 Wooster Street) specializes in books by artists, and another example near the corner of Grand Street, where the **Performing Garage** (33 Wooster) has presented experimental theater, dance and performance art since 1967. A great shopping stop on Wooster is number 136 where **Ad Hoc** stocks stacks of color-coordinated housewares, china, soaps and linens.

Cast-iron stomachs

John Broome was a successful merchant who imported tea and silk from China at the end of the Revolutionary War, so he might have appreciated the fresh produce and other goods sold at the Gourmet Garage (453 Broome, at Mercer Street) if not the pots, pans and garlic peelers stocked in abundance at Broadway Panhandler (477). In general, Broome Street is one of Soho's least jazzed-

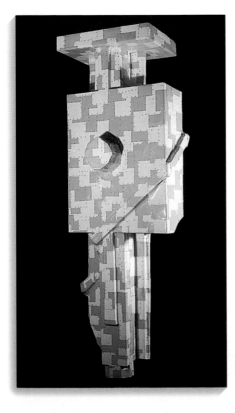

VISITING THE GALLERIES

Soho's days as the city's premier art center may be over but there are still enough exhibition spaces to make gallery-hopping in the area an endurance, as well as a cultural marathon. It all started in 1970 when the legendary Leo Castelli became the first major Uptown art dealer to migrate Downtown to Soho.

Although the late Castelli, who was also the first to represent artists Roy Lichtenstein, Willem de Kooning and Andy Warhol, followed the Uptown trend by moving to 59 East 79th (between Park and Madison), galleries worth visiting in Soho include O.K. Harris (383 West Broadway) and the always-interesting Dia Center for the Arts (393 West Broadway), home to Walter De Maria's *Broken Kilometer,* made of 500 shiny polished brass rods (this gallery is closed in summer.) Also look out for the Vorpai Gallery (459 West Broadway) another remaining pioneer.

For cutting-edge exhibits, head to the peripatetic Artists Space, currently at 38 Greene Street, founded more than a quarter of a century ago as a showcase for unknown and emerging artists. Among those who've shown at Artists Space are Robert Mapplethorpe, Cindy Sherman and Chuck Close.

up thoroughfares, unless you count the ornate Calvert Vaux-designed edifice at No. 448, built in 1872. If you're starved for lunch, keep going until you reach the corner of West Broadway and the **Broome Street Bar**. Located in an 18th-century house, this relaxed hangout is also open for brunch and dinner, and has been around a long time. Next door, the friendly Cupping Room Café specializes in breakfast, but offers lunch and dinner, too.

Crossing West Broadway, you're on the fringe of the South Village where, next to chic little shoe salons and boutiques, places like the **Vesuvio Bakery** on Prince between West Broadway and Thompson Street have been run by the same family since the 1920s. **Milady's**, a nearby neighborhood bar and restaurant has been around for close to half a century, while **Raoul's** (180 Prince) on the next block is a bistro long-favored by the hip, international crowd.

Map on page 198

Look, but don't touch.

Engine Company No. 30

If you've got the stamina, make a detour down Thompson to Spring Street – then walk west across Sixth Avenue to the **New York City Fire Museum ㉙** (tel: 691 1303, closed Mon, fee), at 278 Spring Street, between Varick and Hudson streets. It's worth the four-block hike to Engine Company No. 30's former headquarters to see the antique hand- and horse-pulled wagons *(also see page 210)*.

Back on West Broadway, Soho comes to a halt at **Canal Street ㉚**, where stores sell plastic odds and ends, rubber tubing, neon signs, household appliances and barrels of nondescript industrial leftovers. It's all mixed together in a bedlam of hot dog carts and street vendors displaying old books, new CDs and, on occasion, genuine treasures.

BELOW: The late Leo Castelli, the first dealer to represent Warhol and Lichtenstein.

The Taste of Tribeca Food Festival attracts foodies from all over New York, which itself has 5,000 annual street fairs.

To end a tour of Soho in grander fashion, stop in at the **Soho Grand Hotel** (310 West Broadway, between Grand and Canal streets). When it opened, this was the first hotel built in this part of the city since the mid-1800s, when the fashionable American House Hotel stood at the corner of Spring Street and the white-marble St Nicholas Hotel on Broadway and Broome held gala polka parties. Rising 15 stories above the rest of the neighborhood, the Soho Grand manages to fit in, thanks to its industrial-chic decor and cozy **lobby bar and lounge** that's become a popular meeting place for fashion and entertainment-industry types. It's also the only place in town where pets are not only welcome but as pampered as their owners; if you arrive without an animal companion, you can request a complimentary bowl of goldfish.

Tribeca

In the late 1970s, artists in search of cheaper rents migrated south from Soho to **Tribeca** – the **Tri**angle **Be**low **Ca**nal – which lies south of Canal Street to Chambers Street, and west from Broadway to the Hudson River. Called Washington Market in the days when the city's major produce businesses operated here (before they moved to Hunt's Point in the Bronx), this part of the Lower West Side is one of Manhattan's fastest-growing neighborhoods.

An eclectic blend of renovated commercial warehouses which sport Corinthian columns, condominium towers and celebrity restaurants, Tribeca was where artists like David Salle and Laurie Anderson showed their early works at the Alternative Museum and Franklin Furnace (both now closed). Today's Tribeca scene has more to do with the culinary arts than the fine arts, but its largely residential atmosphere is a pleasant change of pace from Soho's congested and tourist-packed streets.

A block south of Canal the **Tribeca Grand Hotel**, rising from the triangle bordered by Sixth Avenue, Walker and White streets, looms over one of the area's oldest survivors: an 1809 brick house at **2 White Street**, just off West Broadway, which dates back to an earlier era when this was the city's original residential enclave. The Tribeca Grand, a younger sister to the seriously cool Soho Grand, keeps the residential tradition alive with its trendy hospitality. Features for glamorous guests include an atrium lounge and 203 ergonomically designed rooms with extra-large windows and high-speed internet service.

From the block between Walker and White, where **Montrachet** produces some of New York's best French cuisine, West Broadway travels past El Teddy's, a trendy Mexican joint topped by a reproduction of the Statue of Liberty's crowned head, to Layla (at the corner of Franklin Street), a restaurant with Middle Eastern cuisine and belly-dancers. In between are down-home neighborhood bars like The Liquor Store, which actually used to be a liquor store as well as the more spiritual refreshments of Suf Books (225 West Broadway). Stop in to find out about lectures and meditation sessions.

Walk east on Leonard Street (the next street after Franklin) past some of Tribeca's finest cast-iron architecture, and you'll come to the **Knitting Factory** ㉛

(74 Leonard Street), one of the city's largest and worthiest new-music venues. The building, topped by an ornate clock tower that looms ahead, is the former New York Life Insurance Building, which was remodeled by Stanford White in 1898. It's belonged to the city since the late 1960s and now houses various offices as well as the top floor **Clocktower Gallery** (108 Leonard Street), occupied by artists' studios and affiliated with the PS 1 Museum in Queens. It's only occasionally open to the public for special exhibits or events, but go if you get a chance: the views of downtown New York from here are spectacular.

Map on page 198

Produce to pâté

On the corner of Thomas Street and West Broadway, two blocks below Leonard Street, a red neon sign spells out "Cafeteria" but don't be fooled. This 1930s mock-stone building has housed **Odeon**, one of Downtown's hippest restaurants since it opened in 1980. Unlike many trendy spots, it shows no signs of fading away and is still a favorite with the *cognoscenti*, especially late at night.

Across the street, you can browse through the city's largest collection of charts, maps and sailing accessories at the **New York Nautical Instruments Service Corp.** ㉜ (140 West Broadway), a store that's been serving the seagoing public since 1910, before turning right at **Duane Street**.

Named for New York's first post-Revolution mayor, this byway meets Hudson Street at tiny triangular **Duane Park** ㉝ — all that's left of a farm the city bought for $5 in 1795. **Staple Street**, a narrow strip of cobblestone where "staple" produce was once unloaded, connects the park with the ornate red-brick **Mercantile Exchange Building** ㉞, on the corner of Harrison and Hudson streets. Built in 1884 as the trading center for the egg and butter business (but

BELOW: although Soho and Tribeca now have as much to do with dining and shopping as with art, gallery openings are still an everyday occurrence.

Map on page 198

now offices), the ground floor is home to the decidedly upscale Chanterelle, another Tribeca temple of Gallic cuisine.

The neighboring **Western Union Building** ❸ at 60 Hudson Street soars 24 stories above the rest of the neighborhood like a layered missile and is made of 19 different shades of brick. Its interior lobby, where even the letterboxes are marvels of Art Deco artistry, is equally breathtaking – and makes for a diverting short cut if you're heading back to West Broadway.

Nearby, Puffy's Tavern (81 Hudson Street) is a former speakeasy that attracts a mix of office workers, artists and truck drivers until 4am. A short walk away, there's usually a line of locals waiting outside Bubby's (120 Hudson Street) on weekend mornings; it specializes in price-busting brunch specials but also serves lunch and dinner. Between these two spots, Nobu (105 Hudson) is the other end of the spectrum: a high-priced Japanese-inspired restaurant where the decor alone is worth the cost of admission.

Old and new

Greenwich Street is where much of Tribeca's new development is centered, although you can still find some authentic early remnants – like the 19th-century lantern factory between Laight and Vestry streets that's now million-dollar lofts and a wine and cigar club. At the corner of Greenwich and Franklin streets, where actor Robert de Niro transformed the old Martinson Coffee Factory into the **Tribeca Film Center** ❸, the ground-floor **Tribeca Grill** attracts bicoastal movie-makers and shakers. It's not cheap here, but the food is good and the bar scene generally hopping.

BELOW: escape from New York. *RIGHT:* Soho and Tribeca are both highly desirable residential areas.

The late 18th-and early 19th-century brick houses on **Harrison Street** look like a stage set plonked down in the shadow of adjacent **Independence Plaza**'s gargantuan 1970s apartment towers, but like the house on White Street they're survivors of Tribeca's residential beginnings. A block down, **Bazzini's** at 339 Greenwich Street, is a hardy remnant of the area's commercial incarnation; it has been a fruit and nut wholesaler since 1886, and it's still possible to buy 5-lb bags of pistachios and other yummy delicacies here.

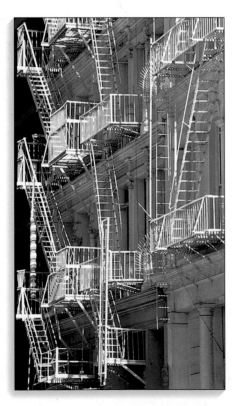

Grass and a gazebo

Opposite the stretch of condo dwellings between Duane and Chambers streets, **Washington Market Park** ❸ has a thick grassy meadow to stretch out on – even a fanciful gazebo to daydream in. Public School 234, its ironwrought fence embossed with Spanish galleons in full sail, is across from the park; a right turn here takes you to the Borough of Manhattan Community College, in a southern extension of Independence Plaza. This is where the **Tribeca Performing Arts Center** (199 Chambers Street) specializes in multi-cultural productions.

From Chambers and West Street, you can reach **Hudson River Park** via a **pedestrian bridge** that stretches across the West Side Highway. Landscaped walkways and leisurely bike paths extend north along the river beyond Pier 25, and south past Stuyvesant School to Rockefeller Park and Battery Park City. ◻

March, 2000

Oct. 12, 2001

LOWER MANHATTAN

Map on page 228

Lower Manhattan is where New York began. Now it's an area of high finance, poignant memories, South Street Seaport and the Staten Island ferry

Below Chambers Street to the west and the Brooklyn Bridge to the east is the original New York, where the Dutch and the English first settled, the country's first hotel was built, the first president was sworn in, and the city's first theatrical opening night took place. Clipper ships bound for the California Gold Rush sailed from Lower Manhattan's piers in the 1850s, and by 1895, the first skyscraper stood 20 stories above lower Broadway.

Over a century later, the city's traditionally staid financial and city government areas are bracketed by developments like the South Street Seaport and Battery Park City, and some of the landmark office buildings on or near Wall Street have been converted to high-tech business use and residential apartments. But Manhattan's oldest neighborhood is also one of its most moving, being the site of two memorials to modern tragedies. Just as events in the 20th century changed the area from a maritime economy to one based on financial commerce, so too, have events early in the 21st century changed the face of Lower Manhattan yet again. As has often been said about New York, just when you think you're beginning to understand it, the city metamorphoses into something else entirely.

PRECEDING PAGES: Lower Manhattan. **LEFT:** before and after the fall of the World Trade Center. **BELOW:** the interior of Trinity Church.

Moving memorials

The first memorial to the past lies on the southwestern tip of Manhattan. In a prime position overlooking the Hudson River is the **Museum of Jewish Heritage – A Living Memorial to the Holocaust ❶** (18 First Place, tel: 968 1800, closed Sat, fee). With more than 2,000 photographs, artifacts and 24 original documentaries, plus videotaped testimonies from victims of the Holocaust donated by Steven Spielberg after he directed *Schindler's List*, the museum has been so well received that a major expansion is in progress, due for completion in 2003. Among other things, a theater and a café will be added.

Beyond the museum, pathways wind through **Robert F. Wagner Jr Park**, which has beautifully landscaped gardens, a pair of deck-topped brick pavilions, and places to sit with fine views of New York Harbor. This provides an opportunity to meditate on the Jewish Museum's stated aim, which is to provide a thoughtful and moving chronicle of history, keeping the memory of the past alive and offering hope for the future.

If that thought make you particularly reflective, or you remember where you were on September 11, 2001 and would like to pay homage, walk several blocks north through **Battery Park City ❷**, the huge, 92-acre (37-hectare) development which stretches along the **Hudson River** between Chambers Street and Battery Park – and about which more is written later – to **Ground Zero ❸**, the site of the former

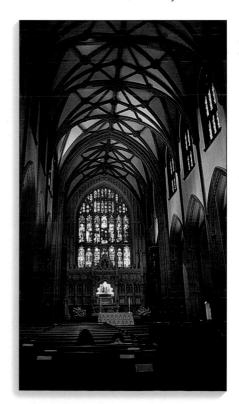

The World Financial Center: although damaged when the World Trade Center collapsed, its high-profile occupants were eager to return.

World Trade Center. Rising an impressive 110 stories into the sky and designed by Minoru Yamasaki, the World Trade Center was New York's biggest tourist attraction. An estimated 1.8 million visitors flocked to its twin towers every year, the best-known structures in a 16-acre (6.5-hectare), seven-building complex that took 17 years to complete. It was a classic piece of 1970s architecture, and the view from the South Tower's 107th-floor Observation Deck was, arguably, the best in the city (*see photographs on pages 96–97 and 244*). The World Trade Center's towers defined the skyline in countless memories and movies.

On September 11, 2001, a day no New Yorker will forget, nearly 3,000 people died as a result of two suicide terrorist attacks. Witnessed on TV screens around the globe, first one, than the other of the towers collapsed, killing not only many of their occupants, but burying policemen and, especially, firemen, who had raced to the scene to help. The outpouring of grief and bewilderment was unprecedented. New Yorkers engaged in uncommon acts of heroism both large and small, and President George W. Bush declared a war on terrorism. The

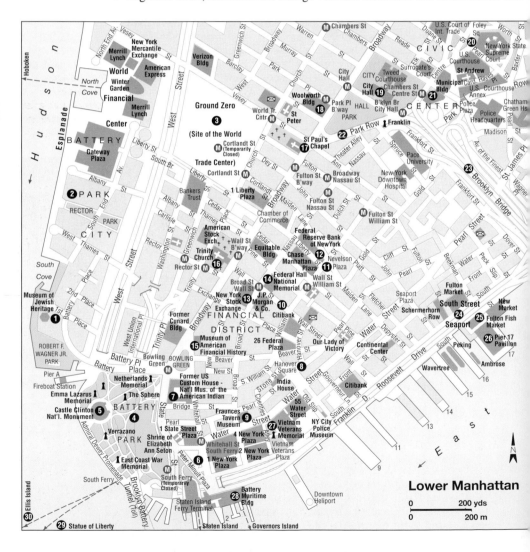

Lower Manhattan

site has since become a place of pilgrimage. Remarkably, a huge globe-shaped metal sculpture, *The Sphere* by Fritz Koenig, which stood for more than 30 years in the World Trade Center Plaza, survived the tons of metal and concrete that crashed down upon it. In March 2002, it was moved to Battery Park, where it is titled ***An Icon of Hope***, standing at the food of a bed of roses called Hope Garden. On the anniversary of the attack, an eternal flame was lit in memory of the victims.

The **World Financial Center**, with its towers and elegant **Winter Garden**, suffered structural damage during the attacks, but high-profile occupants such as Dow Jones and the *Wall Street Journal* were soon clamoring to move back in. Battery Park City, built on river-reclaimed land that included acres of earth from the construction of the World Trade Center, went through a shift in population. Many of its residents moved out to the suburbs. But in that regenerative way unique to world-class cities, other people moved in, bringing with them energy and a fresh new outlook. This welcome dynamism has played a much needed role in the aftermath of tragedy.

The attractions for newcomers can be readily seen. A third of Battery Park City is dedicated to public space, and is linked to Manhattan's riverfront expansion by scenic walkways that meander north to Tribeca and beyond. In the direction of the Jewish Museum is the **Esplanade**, stretching for more than a mile. In cold or rainy weather, a stroll here has a reflective mystique; on a sunny day this is a fine walk popular with strollers and dogs. Along the way are pocket parks decorated with environmental sculptures, like Ned Smyth's *Upper Room*, tucked between river-view apartment buildings. There are also benches where you can pause for a while and gaze out across the Hudson River.

Map on page 228

BELOW:
the smoking remains of the World Trade Center after the attack in September 2001.

Earliest New York

At the island's tip, **Battery Park** ❹ is where New York's history (and geography) began. Named for the battery of protective cannons that once stood here, the area includes **Castle Clinton** ❺, a reddish-stone former fort that was built as a defense against the British in the War of 1812 and originally stood about 200 feet (60 metres) offshore.

The old AT Stewart building, dubbed the "Marble Palace," and on Broadway between Chambers and Reade streets, was a shopping emporium in the 1840s.

In 1824, as Castle Garden, this was the city's premier place of amusement, where Samuel Morse gave his first public telegraph demonstration and Swedish singer Jenny Lind made her American debut in a tumultuously acclaimed concert in 1850 (for which some wealthy New Yorkers paid a then-unheard-of $30 a ticket). Not long after, it was joined to the mainland by landfill and served as the New York State Immigration Station, where more than 8 million immigrants were processed between 1855 and 1890.

For two years, potential settlers were processed on a barge moored in the Hudson River, but, when the new headquarters opened on Ellis Island in 1892, the tide of immigration shifted. Site of the New York Aquarium until 1941, Castle Clinton was declared a national monument in 1950 – and opened to the public in 1975. Today it's run by the National Park Service, and sometimes sells tickets for the Statue of Liberty/Ellis Island ferries.

At the water's edge, **Admiral Dewey Promenade** runs from the former Marine Company No. 1 building on Pier A (a fireboat station built in 1886 is now a **visitors' center**), in the direction of the Staten Island Ferry Terminal. Along the way are several monuments, including one to Giovanni da Verrazano, who sailed past New York in 1524 (85 years before the arrival of Henry Hudson and the Dutch West India Company), and the **East Coast War Memorial**, eight tombstone-shaped slabs of concrete engraved with the names of men who died in World War II Atlantic Ocean battles. A small plaque hidden on the patio of a nearby restaurant honors John Wolfe Ambrose, planner of the Ambrose sea channel "whose vision… and courage ended in making New York the greatest seaport of the world."

BELOW: Battery Park City and the Museum of Jewish Heritage.

New York unearthed

East of Battery Park, **Peter Minuit Plaza** ❻ is named for the first governor (director general) of New Amsterdam. In a tiny park nearby, a plaque commemorates some of the city's lesser-known arrivals: 23 Sephardic Jews, dropped off by a French ship in 1654, who founded New Amsterdam's, and the country's, first Jewish congregation, Shearith Israel. (The congregation's original graveyard is south of Chinatown, at the corner of Oliver Street and St James Place.)

Turn left on State Street, once lined by wealthy merchants' houses, and you come to the **Rectory of the Shrine of the Blessed Elizabeth Ann Seton** (7 State Street), in the only 18th-century mansion still standing here. The chapel next door contains a statue of this American-born saint, who founded the Sisters of Charity in 1809 and was canonized in 1975. New York novelist Herman Melville was born in a house near 17 State Street, where **New York Unearthed** (tel: 748 8628, closed Sun) offers a glimpse of what

Map on page 228

actually lies beneath the city streets. A particuarly interesting branch of the South Street Seaport Museum, it includes relics gleaned from ongoing digs in the historic Lower Manhattan area, as well an archaeological lab.

On the other side of State Street from Battery Park (and across from the Bowling Green subway station), the former **US Custom House** ❼ was designed by Cass Gilbert and built in 1907, more or less in the same location where Fort Amsterdam stood from 1626 to 1787. A magnificent example of Beaux-Arts architecture, with a facade embellished by ornate limestone sculpture that represents four of the world's continents and "eight races" of mankind, this grand edifice also has striking Reginald Marsh murals on the rotunda ceiling inside.

Smithsonian Indians

In a somewhat ironic development – considering that it stands opposite pretty **Bowling Green Park**, the spot where Peter Minuit is said to have purchased Manhattan from local Native Americans for $24 – the Custom House is the George Gustav Heye Center of the **National Museum of the American Indian** (One Bowling Green, tel: 668 6624). A division of the Smithsonian Institution, which is building a prestigious new venue for the collection in Washington, DC's Mall, these 800,000 objects were assembled by Heye, a New York banker. Exhibits range from Navajo blankets and a symbolic circle of beaded moccasins to interactive "discovery boxes" offering mini-histories about subjects like Mayan textiles. Admission is free, and the museum is open daily.

Bowling Green was actually New York's first public park ("created for the delight of the inhabitants" reads a plaque) and the fence that surrounds it dates back to 1771, when it was built to keep a statue of King George III safe from angry mobs. In a neat twist, and according to local lore, the statue ended up being melted down for bullets used by Revolutionary forces. From here you can wander up narrow Stone Street (the city's very first paved byway) to Broad Street, or take a quick detour back to State Street before following Pearl Street to **Hanover Square** ❽.

The city's smartest shopping center in the mid-to-late 18th century, Hanover Square burned to ashes in the Great Fire of 1835, one of many fires that virtually destroyed all remnants of Dutch New Amsterdam. According to one eyewitness who was watching from Brooklyn, "the sparks from that fire came over the river so thick that the neighbors… were obliged to keep their roofs wet all night."

The square recovered to become a thriving commercial center and includes **India House** (1 Hanover Square), an 1850s Italianate brownstone that's been home to a private club for maritime movers and shakers since 1914 (before that, it was a bank). You don't have to be a member, however, to drop in for a bit of refreshment at Harry's at Hanover Square, a popular bar and restaurant located beneath the club, or for dinner at Baynard's upstairs.

Further south at the corner of Pearl and Broad streets, **Fraunces Tavern** is a 1907 reconstruction of the old Queens Head Tavern run by Samuel Fraunces in the late 18th century, where the New York Chamber of

BELOW: the old Custom House is embellished by sculpture that represents four of the world's continents and eight races of mankind.

Commerce got its start over a few mugs of ale, and George Washington gave an emotional farewell address to his troops in 1783 in the Long Room. Still a restaurant, the premises also house the **Fraunces Tavern Museum** ❾ (54 Pearl Street, tel: 425 1778, closed Mon, fee), where exhibits include a lock of Washington's hair, the Long Room complete with period furniture; a fragment of one of Washington's teeth, and a shoe belonging to his wife, Martha. The Flag Gallery displays an exhibit of more than 200 Revolutionary War-era flags.

Wall Street

Captains of industry have dined at **Delmonico's**, at the corner of Beaver and William streets, since the mid 1800s, when two Swiss brothers established the city's first formal French restaurant. Stop and admire the impressive marble columns at the entrance, supposedly brought over from Pompeii, before walking north on William Street (its twists and turns a reminder of the days when it was known as Horse and Cart Street) to **Wall Street** ❿. Although some companies have moved their headquarters Uptown and some, in the wake of the 2001 terrorist attack, may well move out of Manhattan altogether, this is the traditional center of city commerce, where narrow stone canyons are lined by towering banks, brokerage houses and law offices.

Remembered for many traumatic scenes during the 1929 stock-market crash, the street took its name from a 17th-century wall – or, more accurately, a wooden stockade built by the Dutch as protection against the threat of Indian and British attacks. The privateer Captain William Kidd and his wife lived in a house at **56 Wall Street**, and the country's **first stock exchange** began just in front of **60 Wall Street** in 1792, when 24 brokers gathered beneath a buttonwood tree.

BELOW: Wall Street is named for the barrier erected by the Dutch in the 1600s against an attack by the British.

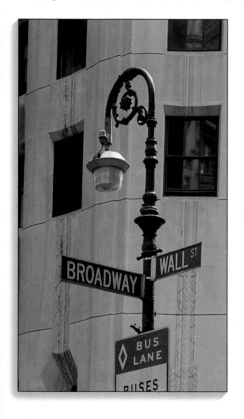

If they'd lived a few hundred years later, of course, they could have gathered at the Regent Wall Street Hotel (55 Wall Street), a massive columned landmark that dates to 1841 and served as the original Merchants' Exchange and later as headquarters for the influential First National City Bank.

Following William Street to Maiden Lane brings you to **Nevelson Plaza** ⓫, a narrow urban breathing space inhabited by a cluster of seven tall **abstract sculptures** by the late Louise Nevelson, a long-time New York resident. Nearby, **more sculpture** (including works by Isamu Nogachi and Jean Dubuffet) graces the Chase Manhattan Plaza between Pine and Liberty Streets.

Money may not be art, but there's alot of it at the **Federal Reserve Bank** ⓬ (33 Liberty Street), west of Nevelson Plaza. Constructed in 1924, this imposing edifice houses a quarter of the world's gold, as well as wheelbarrows-full of old and counterfeit cash. Tours are sometimes given, but call far in advance for information (tel: 720 6130; closed weekends).

Easy Street

For a close-up view of money in action, double back to Wall Street, where the **New York Stock Exchange** ⓭ building was constructed at the corner of Broad Street in 1903. Although fronted by an impressive facade of Corinthian columns, the building seems smaller than its status would imply, which explains why the Exchange might move out of Manhattan entirely, or might build new quarters nearby. In the meantime, the well-known **Visitors' Gallery** (20 Broad Street) remains closed to tourists following heightened security after the terrorist attack on the World Trade Center; check by phoning 656 5165 to see whether it's open before heading Downtown.

Map on page 228

The Greek temple-ish **Federal Hall National Memorial** ⑭ (26 Wall Street, tel: 825 6888) *is*, however, open to the public, but on weekdays only. Built on the site of the original Federal Hall, where George Washington was sworn in as the first President of the United States (there's an impressive statue of him on the steps); it later became a branch of the US Treasury Department. Today it's run by the National Park Service and includes exhibits of historical memorabilia, including the suit Washington wore to his inauguration. Occasional concerts are also presented here.

Financial history

A couple of blocks south, at the corner of Beaver Street, the intriguing **Museum of American Financial History** ⑮ (28 Broadway, tel: 908 4110, closed Sun, Mon) is appropriately located inside a landmark skyscraper built in 1922 by Standard Oil, the company that made John D. Rockefeller rich and famous. The interesting neo-Renaissance facade of the building curves in a fan shape to follow the contours of the road on which it was constructed, Broadway, while the museum is dedicated to the celebration of the trading and financial industries. It includes a collection of antique stocks and bonds, as well as memorabilia from the era of the robber barons, a group that included Messrs Carnegie and Frick, as well as canny John D. himself.

ABOVE AND BELOW:
The New York
Stock Exchange.

Badge of honor.

BELOW: for almost 20 years, the Woolworth Building was the tallest in the world.

At the very top of Wall Street, where it meets Broadway, the pretty, neo-Gothic **Trinity Church**  is a serene survivor of early New York. First established in 1698 (when its charter included the rights to all unclaimed shipwrecks and beached whales found in the vicinity), the present 1846 church is the third one built on the same site. The three bronze doors at the entrance were donated by William Waldorf Astor (John Jacob Astor's great-grandson). **Trinity Church graveyard** contains some of the oldest graves in the city – including that of Alexander Hamilton, the US's first Secretary of the Treasury, who owned a house at 33 Wall Street and was killed in a duel with Aaron Burr.

Public recitals and concerts are held in the church on a regular basis, and a small **museum** (tel: 602 0848) offers a look at the original charter, among other artifacts. Behind the church, the excellent **Trinity Bookstore** (74 Trinity Place) is the place to find books on theology and religion. Five blocks north on Broadway, between Fulton and Vesey streets, George Washington's personal church pew is preserved at **St Paul's Chapel**, part of the Trinity Church Parish and Manhattan's oldest public building in continuous use. Built in 1766, this Georgian-style landmark is the only church left from the colonial era, when luminaries like Prince William (later William IV) and Lord Cornwallis worshiped here. The interior, where 14 Waterford chandeliers hang from a pastel-green ceiling, is also a popular venue for recitals.

Though not exactly spiritual, the gargoyle-topped **Woolworth Building** (233 Broadway) was known in its heyday as the "cathedral of commerce." From 1913 until 1929, when the Chrysler Building was completed, its 60 stories and soaring height of almost 800 feet (245 meters) made it the tallest building in the world. Its architect, Cass Gilbert, described the building as terra cotta and masonry covering a steel frame. The Gothic-Revival tower cost five-and-dime baron Frank W. Woolworth $13 million, and was officially opened by President Woodrow Wilson, who pushed a button in Washington that successfully lit up all of the floors.

Be sure to take a peek inside the marble-encrusted lobby and admire the sculptural detail of Woolworth clutching a nickel, a telling image that has outlasted the company he founded. Nevertheless, at his death there were more than 1,000 stores in the mighty Woolworth chain.

Power complex

Since 1910, New York has honored everyone from Teddy Roosevelt to Nelson Mandela (and, of course, the New York Yankees) with ticker tape parades that conclude at **City Hall**. At the junction of Broadway and Park Row, this French Renaissance/Federal-style edifice has been the seat of city government since DeWitt Clinton was mayor in 1812, and was co-designed by French architect Joseph François Mangin, responsible for the Place de la Concorde in Paris.

City Hall Park, a triangular, tree-shaded former common in front of City Hall, has played an important role throughout the city's history: as the site of public executions, almshouses for the poor and a British prison for captured Revolutionary soldiers. It's also where Alexander Hamilton led a protest against the tea tax in 1774, and where, two years later, George Washington and his troops heard the Declaration of Independence for the first time. Behind City Hall stands the former New York County Courthouse, dubbed on its completion in 1878 the **Tweed Courthouse**. This was after the revelation that "Boss" Tweed and his Tammany Hall cronies had pocketed some $9 million of the final $14 million construction costs. The courthouse will also be the new home of the Museum of the City of New York.

Past the sumptuous **Surrogate's Court** (31 Chambers Street) with its eight Corinthian columns, **Foley Square ⑳** is named for another Tammany Hall politician. It's also the site of such worthy civic structures as the 1936 Cass Gilbert-designed **United States Courthouse** (1 Foley Square), and the **New York State Supreme Court** (60 Centre Street), built in 1913, where New Yorkers are summoned for jury duty selection.

As part of a massive reconstruction project, Foley Square is getting a central pool with a sculpture entitled "Triumph of the Human Spirit" – an appropriate motif considering that, when workers were excavating the foundations of a new Federal courthouse building, the skeletons of African slaves were discovered. Now a city, state and Federal landmark, the **African Burial Ground** is commemorated by a memorial at the corner of Duane and Elk streets.

Slightly to the south is the **Municipal Building ㉑** (1 Centre Street), an enormous, ornate 1914 McKim, Mead and White confection where, at the second-floor civil wedding chapel, you can tie the knot in about five minutes (after the proper preliminaries have been completed, of course). **City Books** in the lobby is the definitive book shop for the city and its memorabilia.

Newspaper row

A statue of journalist and newspaper editor Horace Greeley stands in City Hall Park, an appropriate location since **Park Row ㉒**, just opposite, was known as "Newspaper Row" between the mid-19th to the early-20th centuries, when most of the city's newspapers were published within scooping distance of municipal scandals. The **Pace University building** at 41 Park Row was the original headquarters of the *New York Times*. Other buildings here, including **15 Park Row**, the tallest building in the world from 1899 to 1908, are now occupied by J&R Music/Computer World stores. Not far away, the intimidating Metropolitan Correctional Center (a high-rise federal detention facility) is between Park Row and Pearl Street, beyond Police Headquarters at **One Police Plaza**, a sprawling orange-brick complex built in 1973. You can join cops and federal agents for lunch at the Metropolitan Improvement Company on the corner of Madison and Pearl streets.

For one of the best views of the **East River** and Lower Manhattan, walk down Frankfort Street or along Park Row. Both lead to the **pedestrian walkway** on the **Brooklyn Bridge ㉓**, one of the world's first suspension bridges. The bridge was the inspiration of engineer John Augustus Roebling, the inventor of wire cable, and the span between its two towers of almost 1,600 feet (488 meters) was for a time the

Map on page 228

BELOW: City Hall Park is a triangular, tree-shaded common where George Washington first heard the Declaration of Independence.

longest in the world. The bridge spans the East River from City Hall to Brooklyn's Cadman Plaza. The use of steel in a suspension bridge, until then unprecedented, was meant to provide unmatched stability and strength, as well as present a striking image to the public.

But the bridge's construction, which began in 1867 and took 16 years to complete, was marred by difficulty. Two years after approval was granted, Roebling was killed by a ferry boat. The project was handed to his son, Washington Roebling, who himself fell victim to the bends while working on the huge, wooden boxes (called caissons) from which the riverbed was excavated. An invalid for the rest of his life, Roebling, Jr, nevertheless carried on, monitoring proceedings through a telescope, and relaying messages to his managers via his wife. When the bridge was opened to the public in 1883, 12 people were trampled to death in a panic set off by a senseless warning that the construction was about to collapse. Despite its tortuous beginnings, however, the Brooklyn Bridge was seen as the "new eighth wonder of the world, " and has inspired artists and accolades ever since.

In the 1800s, the area around Fulton Street was the center of New York's ocean-going commerce, where spices came from China and rum from the West Indies.

South Street Seaport

Walk along **Fulton Street** toward the East River where, before the Brooklyn Bridge was built, ferries carried New Yorkers to Brooklyn from the Fulton Street pier. In the 1800s, this part of town was the center of New York's maritime commerce, where spices from China, rum from the West Indies and whale oil from the Atlantic were bought and sold; where ships were built; and where sailors thronged to enjoy a seedy red-light district.

All that ended after the American Civil War, when the old port fell into a

BELOW: al fresco refreshments at South Street Seaport.

decline that lasted until the mid-1970s. That's when the **South Street Museum** (founded in 1967) joined forces with the Rouse Corporation, which had previously revived historic areas in Boston and Baltimore, to create **South Street Seaport ㉔**, a 12-block "museum without walls."

Near the **Titanic Memorial Lighthouse**, at the corner of Fulton and Water streets, **Schermerhorn Row** is lined by the last surviving Federal-style commercial buildings in the city, and part of a block of early 19th-century warehouses. The **Museum Visitors' Center** (12 Fulton Street, tel: 748 8600) is halfway down the block and sells tickets for tours, cruises around the harbor and exhibitions at nearby galleries. Next door, the South Street Museum Shop sells books and gifts with nautical themes. **Cannon's Walk** is another block of restored buildings, between Fulton and Beekman streets. Stores on the Front Street side include a retail outlet of the J. Crew catalog clothing company. Around the corner on Water Street, the **Herman Melville Gallery** and the **Whitman Gallery** are on either side of **Bowne and Co.** (211 Water Street), a 19th-century printing shop.

Fulton Fish Market

Don't confuse the **Fulton Market** building across Front Street with the smelly but fascinating **Fulton Fish Market ㉕** just behind it on South Street. The former is a three-story atrium filled with take-out food outlets, boutiques and restaurants, while the latter – in the shadow of the FDR Drive – is the country's largest wholesale fish market. Started in 1831 (and at its present locale since about 1909), it's also one of the city's oldest continuously operating businesses. The action is heaviest between midnight and 8am, when burly men in rubber

Map on page 228

BELOW: the plaice to be; tours are available of the Fulton Fish Market, which has been on its present site for almost 100 years.

boots sell piles of fish to eager buyers (many of them chefs from the city's finest restaurants); more than 125 million pounds of seafood pass through here every year. Early morning tours are occasionally offered by the Seaport Museum; check with the Visitors' Center for details.

Red-light history

In 1985, when construction workers were excavating the foundations of a new office tower on Water Street, they discovered the remains of a merchant ship sunk as landfill between 1746 and 1755. **Water Street** ran along the river's edge back then, and was lined by bars and brothels that catered to a rough and rowdy sea-going clientele. A survivor of the bad old days is 273 Water Street, known to historians as the **Captain Rose House**. As Kit Burn's Sportsman's Hall in the mid 1800s, it attracted up to 500 spectators at a time to heavily wagered dog fights; even dog and rat fights. Dating to 1781, it's Manhattan's third-oldest house, but was never given landmark status and has been turned into apartments. The Seaport's red-light past may be history, but today the area is packed with establishments that cater to office workers from nearby buildings (on weekday nights) and hordes of out-of-towners on weekends. One of the most popular is the **North Star Pub** (93 South Street, at the corner of Fulton), which has a particularly lively bar scene.

Pier 17 ㉖ is a three-story pavilion that juts over the East River at the end of Fulton Street (behind the fish market). In addition to the third-floor food court's various ethnic delicacies, you can find the latest gadget at The Sharper Image or check out insect art at Mariposa, two of the more interesting shops here. In winter a nearby **skating rink** is crowded with kids; in summer free evening

BELOW: South Street Seaport is a 12-block "museum without walls."

concerts are presented on **Pier 16**. The adjacent booth sells tickets for one-hour **Seaport Liberty Cruises** and two-hour music cruises, operated by Circle Line (tel: 630 8888). The sloop *Pioneer*, along with the *Peking*, a four-masted sailing barque, and the *Ambrose*, last of the city's lightships, are part of the Seaport Museum's collection of **historic vessels**, graceful ships on which occasional cruises take place.

Map on page 228

Back to Battery Park

Several blocks south – past Pier 11, where the high-speed **Delta Shuttle ferry** departs for La Guardia Airport, and just beyond **Old Slip**, a landfilled 18th-century inlet where ships tied up to unload their cargo – is a park where stranded sailors used to congregate. Today the **Vietnam Veterans Memorial** ㉗, a 14-ft-high (4 metre) monument erected by the city in 1985, stands here, at the foot of a brick amphitheater near the corner of Coenties Slip and Water Street. Made of green glass etched with excerpts of letters written to and from soldiers serving in Vietnam ("I often wonder if what we're fighting for is worth a human life," reads one), it's eerily illuminated at night.

The crowning touch.

A few blocks away, the rusting steel **Battery Maritime Building** ㉘ (11 South Street), a landmark Beaux-Arts structure built at the end of Whitehall Street in 1909, has traditionally been the gateway for ferries to **Governor's Island**. It may or may not be renovated, depending on what happens with the island: a Coast Guard facility until 1998, future possibilities include everything from apartments to hotels to a casino. (Stay tuned.)

On the next pier down, the massive **Staten Island Ferry Terminal** at the end of South Street is embarking on an enormous reconstruction project that is

BELOW: the Staten Island Ferry.

Map on page 228

An estimated 40 percent of the American population has at least one ancestor who entered the country via Ellis Island between 1892 and 1924.

BELOW: "Give me your tired, your poor/your huddled masses yearning to breathe free…"

expected to be finished around 2004. In a separate shake-up, following the terrorist attacks on the World Trade Center, heightened security measures have been imposed, which sometimes affect ferries plying the waters to the Statue of Liberty, Staten Island and Ellis Island; call 269 5755 for the latest updates, times and prices.

The 25-minute cruise to Staten Island not only offers close-up views of the Statue of Liberty but is also free, making it the best bargain in town. There's a short wait at the other end before reboarding for the trip back to Manhattan. Ferries usually depart for the **Statue of Liberty** ㉙ *(see facing page)* and Ellis Island a few steps from the **East Coast War Memorial** in Battery Park.

Island of Tears

Ellis Island ㉚ was known as the "Island of Tears" during the 32-year period it served as a gateway to the United States. Today, it is a national monument and one of the city's most popular tourist destinations, although actual ownership has been oddly divided between New York and New Jersey. The original immigration station, transformed into a museum-of-the-melting pot in 1990, tells the often wrenching stories of the millions who passed through here on their way to new lives in the New World. Many new arrivals were turned away on grounds of poor health or for other reasons, but an estimated 40 percent of the American population has at least one ancestor who entered the country via Ellis Island between 1892 and 1924 (1,285,349 immigrants arrived in 1907 alone).

Outside the museum, a promenade offers wonderful views of the Statue of Liberty and the Lower Manhattan skyline – and includes the **American Immigrant Wall of Honor**, which is inscribed with more than 500,000 names. ❑

Statue of Liberty

L ike millions of other immigrants, Italian-born writer Edward Corsi's first glimpse of America was the heroic figure of the Statue of Liberty standing on tiny Liberty Island, her "beacon-hand" thrust skyward bearing a torch to light the way, the shackles of despotism broken at her feet. He wrote, "I looked at that statue with a sense of bewilderment, half doubting its reality. Looming shadowy through the mist, it brought silence to the decks of the *Florida*. This symbol of America – this enormous expression of what we had all been taught was the inner meaning of this new country we were coming to – inspired awe in the hopeful immigrants."

Of course, the Statue of Liberty is itself an immigrant. In 1865 Edouard-René Lefèvre de Laboulaye, a French intellectual, politician and admirer of America, made an off-hand suggestion to a young sculptor by the name of Auguste Bartholdi for a monument honoring French and American brotherhood.

Bartholdi seized the idea, seeing in it the perfect opportunity to indulge a longstanding interest in colossal statuary. It took more than eight years for the project to crystallize, but by 1874 enough money had been donated by the French people to begin construction. Gustave Eiffel, who later built the Eiffel Tower, designed the ingenious framework which supports the thin copper skin, hammered to less than an eighth of an inch thick but still weighing over 90 tons. In 1885, Bartholdi's *Liberty Enlightening the World* was shipped to the United States. It was formally dedicated in a ceremony on Bedloe's Island on October 28, 1886.

The statue, when not closed for security reasons, attracts well over a million tourists a year. In this age of high-tech wizardry, it's still a stirring and uncanny sight, made almost unreal by its enormous size. The big attraction, of course, is climbing to the top, which is a wonderful idea if you're in decent physical condition and don't mind waiting in line for at least an hour or two. This is one of the world's greatest tourist attractions, after all, and if you're going to schlep all the way out to Liberty Island it seems only right to get your money's worth. But discretion being the better part of valor, there are a few things you should keep in mind before making an assault on the summit.

For one thing, the only way up to the statue's crown is via a narrow spiral staircase that is many stories high (which may in fact be closed to the public, as it often is these days). There's no air conditioning either – which is no big deal on a cool day but is absolute hell on a hot one, especially when there are hundreds of people. Temperatures in excess of 100°F (38°C) are not that uncommon, and people with heart conditions should definitely consider just admiring the statue from the outside.

For those who stay behind, there are exhibits worth visiting at the base of the statue and views from the pedestal. Tickets for the Circle Line ferry to Liberty Island are sold at Castle Clinton in Battery Park. Depending on the time of year, the ferry departs every 45 minutes or every hour. ❏

RIGHT: the Statue of Liberty on Liberty Island was the "Mother of Exiles."

THE OUTER BOROUGHS

Is there intelligent life beyond Manhattan? Whatever Manhattanites may tell you, Brooklyn, Queens, Staten Island and the Bronx are all worth exploring

Map on page 246

A common nightmare for many Manhattanites is the thought of falling asleep on the subway as it dives beneath the East River (or worse, as it rumbles up to the Bronx), missing the last stop in Manhattan and ending up in the outer boroughs. Visitors, too, may panic at the idea of vacant lots. Airports. Discount furniture stores. Malls. Tract housing. They turn to the subway booth attendant and plead: "Help! Are we anywhere near the Bronx Zoo?"

If you suffer this Manhatto-centrism, you can be cured by a visit to Brooklyn, Queens, the Bronx, Staten Island – the four outer boroughs. All are rich in history, with an astonishing diversity of attractions. And by subway, bus, cab or ferry, no borough is hard to reach.

Neighborhoods

The key word in the boroughs is "neighborhood." Neighborhoods change. They overlap. They are also an ethnic delight. You can stroll through Middle Eastern shops that stock frankincense and myrrh. You can order your pasta in Italian; order your *kasha* in Yiddish.

The cultures clash, but that's nothing new. In 17th-century New York City, the Dutch fought their British neighbors. The Puritans frowned at the German Jews. The Chinese frightened the Europeans, then moved away from the Haitians. Hasidic Jews clashed with black Americans and immigrants from the Caribbean. Times change, problems with neighbors don't.

Some of these new neighbors are artists and young professionals in search of affordable rents. As the popularity and the price of Manhattan soars, the new generation is turning to former industrial zones, like **Long Island City** in Queens, **St George** in Staten Island, **Fulton Ferry Landing** and **Williamsburg** in Brooklyn. Co-ops flourish where warehouses once thrived. Burned-out buildings become galleries or restaurants. And real estate values skyrocket.

Amid the new is the older side of the boroughs: the boulevards, parks and palazzos built as grand civic projects at the end of the 19th century. Architects like Frederick Law Olmsted and Calvert Vaux found open space in the outer boroughs that was unavailable in Midtown. With sweeping gestures, they decked the boroughs with buildings that were inspired by Paris.

Until the population swelled after World War II, the boroughs had a rosy suburban image: agreeable housing, easy access to the "City" and a special civic pride. Moving out to the boroughs meant moving *up*, especially if your point of departure was a grimy tenement on the Lower East Side.

One thing the boroughs lack is Manhattan's easy grid system. Heading up the Moshulu Parkway or

PRECEDING PAGES: local character on Staten Island. **LEFT:** view of the outer boroughs from the late, great World Trade Center. **BELOW:** South Bronx; home of the Yankees.

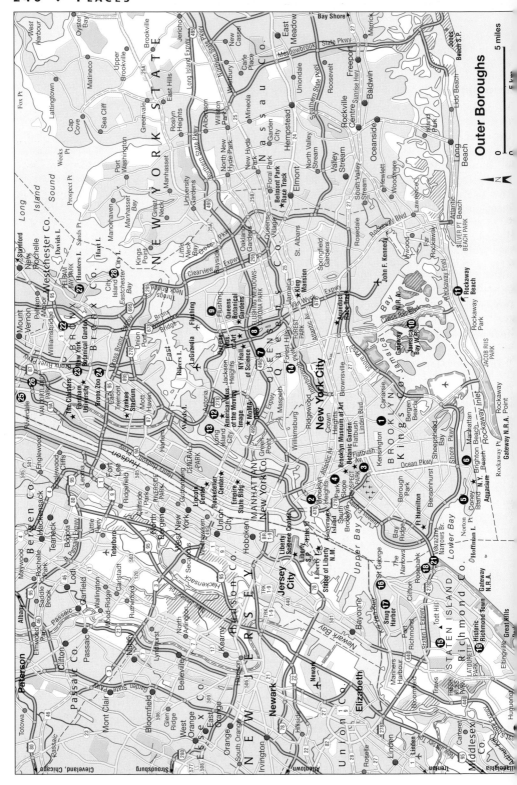

Outer Boroughs

Flatbush Avenue, you'll see that they're a maze of streets and expressways. With perseverance and a good map, however, you'll also find neighborhoods that can be explored easily on foot – places where the boroughs really breathe.

Map on page 246

Brooklyn

The 70 square miles (180 sq km) on the southeast tip of Long Island encompass the most populous borough of New York City, **Brooklyn ❶**. More than 2.3 million people live here, which would make it one of the largest metropolises in the United States if it weren't part of New York City. Its development commenced in the 1600s, when the Dutch bought Gowanus, then a Canarsie Indian village, and the land they called Breukelen was farmed and settled.

In the mid-18th century, Long Island farmers made frequent ferry trips across the river to sell off surplus fruits and vegetables. In the 1790s, Brooklyn Heights began to expand, due in part to a plague of yellow fever. The high, dry bluffs of Brooklyn were an escape from the unhealthy city. At the same time, Brooklyn was becoming a popular summer home for financiers who would then use the ferry to get to their offices on Wall Street.

Today, a scenic way to escape from Manhattan is via the **Brooklyn Bridge**. A stroll across the walkway will lead you to **Fulton Ferry Landing**, where cobblestone streets are coming back to life after lying dormant for decades. It was here that the borough set up up its first mass transit to Wall Street. In 1814, Robert Fulton's steam ferry, the *Nassau*, replaced the East River rowboats, flat sailboats and vessels powered by horses on treadmills. Brooklyn became an incorporated city in 1834, with a population close to 30,000.

A hub of homes and businesses grew up around the new docks. The area

According to the NYC & Company Visitor Information Center, more famous people – 1 in 7 – have been born in Brooklyn than in any other place in the US.

BELOW: the Brooklyn Bridge, looking towards Manhattan.

bustled with activity until 1883, when the Brooklyn Bridge was built, then slid into obsolescence not long after, when the city of Brooklyn was incorporated into New York City. Nowadays, artists have lofts in DUMBO ("Down Under the Manhattan Bridge Overpass") while there are occasional concerts and dance performances at **Empire-Fulton Ferry State Park**. You can even listen to chamber music at **Bargemusic** (tel: 718-624 4061), a converted coffee barge moored at the end of Old Fulton Street; it's on the other side of the Fulton Ferry Landing from the **River Cafe** (1 Water Street, at the Brooklyn Bridge), considered not only the city's most romantic restaurant but also one of its best.

Around the bend to the east is the old **Brooklyn Navy Yard**, where ships like the *USS Missouri* were built during World War II. Beyond it, the Williamsburg Bridge provides another connection to Manhattan; not far from its entrance is **Peter Luger's Steakhouse** (178 Broadway), considered one of New York City's best, as well as one of its oldest, restaurants; it opened here in 1887. Across Broadway, the Renaissance-style Williamsburgh Savings Bank building was constructed in 1875, while much further east, on Driggs Avenue, the "onion-domed" **Russian Orthodox Cathedral of the Transfiguration**, dating to 1921, indicates the area's traditional ties to Eastern Europe. Partly industrial, Williamsburg also includes one of New York's most vibrant new arts communities, with prices for lofts and apartments on the rise.

Brooklyn Heights

On the other side of the Fulton Ferry district, the housing market has always been hot. **Brooklyn Heights ❷**, where streets are lined with narrow rowhouses, brownstones change hands for more than a million dollars. Along the river edge of the Heights is the **Promenade**. This much-used and appreciated walkway overlooks the East River, the Brooklyn Bridge and offers a movie-star view of the Manhattan skyline.

A stroll along here and through the Heights is extremely pleasant. Each block is iced with wrought-iron flourishes, stained-glass windows and stone busts and trims. On the corner of **Willow Street** and **Middagh** is the oldest wooden house in the district, dating back to 1824. During the Civil War **Plymouth Church**, on **Orange Street** between Henry and Hicks, served as a stop on the Underground Railroad, while Henry Ward Beecher (Harriet Beecher Stowe's brother) preached abolitionism to the congregation.

"Young urban professionals" of the 19th century frequently settled into Brooklyn brownstones, which were popular homes for newlyweds. Today, the narrow buildings and quiet streets are still popular – the Heights are just minutes from Wall Street by subway. A few single-family mansions remain, but most brownstones have been divided into smaller apartments.

Many streets in the Heights, like Middagh and Hicks, take the names of the neighborhood's early gentry. Five, however, are named after the flora of the period – **Pineapple**, **Cranberry**, **Orange**, **Poplar** and **Willow streets**. It's rumored that the streets were christened by one of the Mistresses Middagh, who refused to consider using the names of the neighbors

BELOW: Manhattan Bridge with its elevated streets. Artists have named the area DUMBO, which stands for Down Under the Manhattan Bridge Overpass.

she detested. The **Brooklyn Historical Society** (tel: 718-624 0890) includes the **Brooklyn History Museum** (reopening late 2001) on the ground floor of its landmark Heights building, located at 128 Pierrepont Street. Browse around and enjoy its rich mix of Dodgers baseball memorabilia, scholarly exhibits, maritime artifacts and Coney Island exhibitionism. A block away is St Ann and the Holy Trinity Church, on the corner of Montague and Clinton streets. Dating to the 1840s, it includes the oldest stained-glass windows made in America as well an innovative cultural program called the **Arts at St Ann's** (tel: 718-834 8794), with everything from contemporary music to avant-garde dance performances offered on a regular basis.

At the foot of Brooklyn Heights is the **Civic Center**, with its Greek Revival **Borough Hall** (209 Joralemon Street, free tours every Tues). From here, a quick detour takes you to Gage and Tollner (372 Fulton Street, near Jay Street), a landmark restaurant that's been in business since 1892. This is the start of the **Fulton Mall**, a shopping district that includes 200 stores between Adams Street and Flatbush Avenue. From here it's a short walk down Boerum Place to the **New York Transit Museum** (Boerum Place and Schermerhorn Street, tel: 718-243 8601, closed Mon, fee). In a classic 1930s-era subway station, the museum includes changing exhibits on the city's transportation systems, along with vintage subway cars and buses.

Keep walking past State Street and turn right on **Atlantic Avenue**. Between Court and Henry Street, shops are bulging with imported spices, dried fruits, olives and *halvah*. Some bakeries cook their filo pastries in coal-burning ovens, and the Middle Eastern restaurants are worth visiting. Back towards Flatbush Avenue, this Middle Eastern bazaar shares the sidewalk with a growing number of antiques shops. The stores have plenty of interesting stock (Victorian, Art Deco, 1930s, 1940s), and are usually open on weekends if not every weekday.

BELOW: the Brooklyn History Museum is a mix of scholarly pursuits and pure Coney Island exhibitionism.

Another Brooklyn street which is a bazaar of ethnic enticements is **Court Street**. It begins at Cadman Plaza and travels, as the crow flies, through four Brooklyn neighborhoods – the Heights, Cobble Hill, Carroll Gardens and Red Hook. Many Italian establishments line Court Street, offering soft and hard imported cheeses, best-quality olive oils, freshly pressed pasta, baby artichokes, Italian broccoli and rich coffees. A hint of the earlier character of the street, when it bustled with immigrants from Galicia in the northwest of Spain, can be found in a few remaining stores that sell imported Spanish delicacies.

Flatbush

To the east, where Atlantic meets **Flatbush Avenue**, things get a lot grittier. But there is a high point at this junction, a great view of the monumental **Williamsburgh Savings Bank**, the tallest building in Brooklyn. Nearby on Lafayette Avenue at Ashland Place, is the innovative **Brooklyn Academy of Music** (BAM), where the performance spectrum has included multi-media maestro Laurie Anderson, Martha Clarke's performance art and the music of composer Philip Glass. Home to the innovative Next Wave Festival since 1982, it includes the beautifully restored

Map on page 246

Majestic Theatre, a few blocks from the main building, as well as a café and four screening rooms known as the BAM Rose Cinemas. (For information, call 718-636 4100.)

Beyond Flatbush Avenue, Atlantic stretches into the triangle known as **Bed-Stuy**. The old neighborhoods of Bedford and Stuyvesant are infamous for their urban problems, though the district is beginning to show new signs of prosperity. **Ebbets Field** is no longer the site of Dodger baseball miracles, but the acres of renovated homes here make this one of the largest minority home-owning communities in the whole of New York. There are also annual brownstone tours sponsored by a neighborhood association; further south, the **Weeksville Houses** on Bergen Street, between Rochester and Buffalo avenues, date from an early 19th-century settlement of freed slaves. They're open for tours by appointment (tel: 718-756 5250).

In neighboring **Crown Heights**, Hasidic Jews and immigrants from the West Indies are building communities worlds apart, but only doorsteps away. Even farther east is **Brownsville**. Before World War II, this was a mainly Jewish slum, where, say locals, a candy store on **Livonia Avenue** served as headquarters for Murder Inc., the notorious gangster ring of the 1930s. (For a Brownsville classic, check out *A Walker in the City* by Alfred Kazin.)

Brooklyn Museum of Art

The thoroughfare of eastern Brooklyn is **Eastern Parkway**. It runs through Bed-Stuy and Crown Heights to **Prospect Park ❸**, along the way passing the **Brooklyn Children's Museum** (145 Brooklyn Avenue, tel: 718-735 4403, closed Mon and Tues, fee). Founded in 1899, this is the oldest children's museum in America, and possibly the world. It's very much a hands-on learning experience, with thousands of interesting artifacts to wonder at – and almost as many buttons and knobs to play with.

The marvelous **Brooklyn Museum of Art** (200 Eastern Parkway, tel: 718-638 5000, admission fee) includes an Egyptian collection considered to be the best outside of Cairo and London. The museum also boasts a changing array of world-class exhibits, 28 period rooms and an unusual outdoor sculpture garden of New York building ornaments. Next door, at the pastoral 50-acre (20 ha) **Brooklyn Botanic Garden** (tel: 718-623 7200, closed Mon), the Japanese gardens alone are worth a visit, especially when the cherry trees bloom in the spring. The Steinhardt Conservatory here includes desert and tropical plants, and is a nice warm place for lingering in winter.

The huge roundabout at the western end of the Parkway is **Grand Army Plaza**, while the **Soldiers' and Sailors' Memorial Arch** provides a formal entrance to the 526 acres (213 ha) which make up Prospect Park. The park, plaza and boulevards were all designed by Frederick Law Olmsted and Calvert Vaux. The Plaza is their most literal tribute to Paris – an Arc de Triomphe at the focal point of the borough.

Prospect Park is considered to be Olmsted and Vaux's best work, even better, perhaps, than Central Park. Roam dreamily through the park's romantic

Map on page 246

regions: the Long Meadow, the Vale of Cashmere and the **Rose Garden**, or ride the antique carousel. The park also contains sports fields, tennis courts, a skating rink, and the Prospect Park Wildlife Conservation Center (tel: 718-399 7339, fee), which is geared toward children. Information from the renovated 1907 Beaux Arts boathouse, or by calling the park at 718-965 8999.

In an eastern corner of the park, off Flatbush Avenue at Empire Boulevard, the **Lefferts Homestead Children's Museum** (tel: 718-789 2822, open weekdays by appointment) is a two-story, eight-room Dutch farmhouse that was built between 1777 and 1783. For visitors, it offers valuable insights into 18th-century colonial life. There are interactive exhibits especially designed for children, along with several rooms which have been restored to their original early American appearance.

Park Slope

The neighborhood of **Park Slope ❹** runs along Prospect Park's western border and is filled with Victorian rowhouses, many of which have been divided up into apartments (not quite as expensive as Brooklyn Heights). From **Prospect Park West**, turn down Montgomery Place or Carroll Street. The shopping street, **Seventh Avenue**, is two blocks down from the park. Along the way, on **Montgomery Place**, there's a Roman arch, a Greek pediment and Chinese double arches – all in one building. Down the street, look for iridescent bricks framing peacock windows and be sure to check out the Venetian-style palazzo with an American Indian motif located at 25 Eighth Avenue. Unlike Park Slope's rowhouses, the homes in **Prospect Park South** are detached; huge gables nearly touch those of the houses next door. For an architectural treat, stroll down and around **Albemarle Road** to see copies of a Swiss chalet, a Japanese pagoda, and even a southern plantation.

Flatbush's best boulevard is **Ocean Parkway**, just to the west. It passes residential **Gravesend**, founded in the 1600s by the widowed Lady Deborah Moody and named for her home in Britain. Lady Moody was both the first woman settlement founder, and the first founder to guarantee religious freedom with a written law.

Coney Island

On the coast to the south lies **Coney Island ❺**, which is not actually an island, but a peninsula. At the western tip, the community of Seagate has a guarded entrance, but no apparent protection against encroaching shabbiness. The wealthier but basically uninspiring **Manhattan Beach** is at the other end of the boardwalk. The **Aquarium for Wildlife Conservation** (tel: 718-265 3474, open daily, fee), more familiarly known as the New York Aquarium, is located in-between, at West 8th Street and Surf Avenue. Overhauled not long ago, with an outdoor theater for sea lion performances, this metropolitan home for ocean life is one of the borough's most popular attractions.

The famous name of Coney Island really belongs to what was once Brooklyn's premier vacation center. New Yorkers have been escaping to Coney Island ever since the summers of the 1840s and in greater numbers after 1875, when the train connected the beach

Brownstone is iron oxide, and was used mostly in the 1840s in the construction of buildings. Skinny walk-ups built wall-to-wall with the houses next door, the design was meant to conserve heat and retard fire.

BELOW: walking the dog past Brooklyn's brownstones.

with the city. Garish hotels, little beach homes, the old Brighton Race Track and amusement parks were all erected; Dreamland (burned down in 1911), Luna Park (ditto in 1939) and Steeplechase (which was demolished by developer Donald Trump's father in 1964) were among them. But now, most of the holiday bungalows have been replaced by public housing. In summer, the remnants of the amusement parks seem to sag under the weight of the crowds. Off-season, the wintry beach can seem as desolate as a vacant lot. But all is not lost.

Question: how long does a ride on Coney Island's Cyclone roller coaster last? Answer: one minute and 50 seconds.

Sideshows by the Seashore

You can visit the small museum **Sideshows by the Seashore** (West 12th St and Surf Ave, tel: 718-372 5159, closed Mon and Tues in summer and weekdays in winter), which is operated by a local theatrical group. Inside are relics of Coney Island in its heyday, as well as an actual sideshow presented in the theater downstairs. You can still get **Nathan's famous hot dogs**, at the stand on Surf and Stillwell, where fans insist the mass-produced sausages were invented in 1916. The grills sizzle up to 1,500 dogs an hour on a hot summer's day. You can still tempt fate and hang on for dear life aboard the Cyclone, the grand-dad of roller coasters, with its 3,000 feet of wooden track and cars speeding down it at 68 mph. And you can still walk along the boardwalk and watch seagulls swoop over the ocean. More important, the future might well see the revitalization of Coney Island. There are ongoing plans to rebuild Steeplechase Park as an amusement center, and to create an elaborate new sports complex that might include a minor-league baseball field.

Private developers have long realized the potential of the island, only 25 miles from the heart of Manhattan. "A whole new generation is starting to come

BELOW:
New Yorkers have been escaping to Coney Island for over 150 years.

Map
on page
246

out here," said a spokesman for the Aquarium, speaking to the *New York Times*. "They don't know what Coney Island was, or anything about its decline."

Farther east on the boardwalk is **Brighton Beach** ❻, which for many years was an enclave of elderly Jews and made famous by playwright Neil Simon. As Coney Island slid into decay, Brighton's buildings stood like forts along the coast, waiting for crime to crack through the walls and for time to wash out their district. But in the mid-1970s, a wave of immigrants, mostly Russians and Ukrainians, began moving into Brighton Beach, which soon became known as "**Little Odessa**." Today, their children – teenagers with rosy cheeks and leather jackets – hang out under the subway "El," or elevated train tracks, while Russian restaurants, bookshops, markets and other businesses have infused the neighborhood with a sense of vitality. You can even dance the night away at a series of exuberant nightspots on **Brighton Beach Avenue**.

Just north of Brighton Beach is **Sheepshead Bay**, where the fishing boats are docked. You can buy fresh fish off the boats, or order it off the menu at restaurants like Lundy's (1901 Emmons Avenue). You can also charter a boat and captain, and bring home your own catch of the day. The boats leave early (and are expensive), so it is a good idea to stop by the day before and ask around for the best price.

Nathan's hot dogs: fans insist wieners were invented here in 1916.

Queens

Every visitor who lands at JFK International Airport and takes a taxi to Manhattan goes through **Queens** ❼. But this borough is more than just a point of arrival. Named for Queen Catherine of Braganza, wife of Charles II of England, this is one of the world's most diverse communities, with one of the largest

BELOW:
Coney Island
holidaymakers.

The Unisphere in Flushing Meadows-Corona Park, a relic from the World's Fair, is the largest globe in the world.

BELOW: drugs and crime are still a problem in some areas, but things are improving in others.

Greek neighborhoods outside of Athens and neighborhoods filled with immigrants from India, Pakistan, Thailand, South America and Europe.

The area between **Northern Boulevard** and **Grand Central Parkway**, which was once a swamp and later the "Corona Garbage Dump," ended up as the glamorous grounds of the 1939 and 1964 World's Fairs. The reconstruction work done for the fairs transformed the marshy land, and it was then renamed the more elegant **Flushing Meadows-Corona Park** ❽, an expanse of over 1200 acres (485 ha) that includes museums, sports facilities and botanical gardens.

World's Fair

Among the many relics of the two World's Fairs is the **Panorama of the City of New York**, a scaled replica of the city constructed in painstaking detail. It's on display in what was the 1964 Fair's New York City Building but is now the **Queens Museum of Art** (tel: 718-592 9700, closed Mon and Tues, fee). Close to the park's 111th Street entrance, the **New York Hall of Science** (tel: 718-699 0005, closed Mon, fee) is famous for its interactive high-tech exhibits. The nearby **Queens Wildlife Center** (tel: 718-271 7761, fee) has a geodesic dome that was designed by Buckminster Fuller and is now used as an aviary. Other reminders of the fairs, like the great steel **Unisphere** in the heart of the park, are close to such sporty attractions as the USTA **National Tennis Center**, the site of the annual US Open. Not to mention **Shea Stadium**, the Mets' home, just beyond the subway station (take the Flushing line No. 7 train), with its capacity to seat 55,000 cheering baseball fans. The park also has paths for biking and strolling; an indoor **skating rink** (in the same building as the Museum of Art), and an antique carousel. Close by, the 38-acre (15 ha) **Queens Botanical Garden** (43-50 Main Street, tel: 718-886 3800, closed Mon, fee) has the largest rose garden in the Northeast and is a popular spot for weddings.

Little Asia

Bordering the park, **Flushing** ❾ is packed with history, and perked up by its "**Little Asia**" section. Before the postwar building boom, the area was a quiet place with clapboard and shingle houses. The district's claim to history centers on a strong tradition of religious freedom. It is home to one of the biggest Hindu temples in North America, located on **Bowne Street**. The **Quaker Meeting House**, built in 1696, is the oldest house of worship in New York City. Nearby is the "Shrine to Religious Freedom," the historic **Bowne House**, on Bowne Street near 37th Avenue. In 1661, John Bowne, a Quaker leader, supposedly bought the land for eight strings of wampum. The best place to learn about local history is the Queens Historical Society at the **Kingsland Homestead** (tel: 718-939 0647), at 143-35 37th Avenue. Around the back is a weeping beech tree more than 150 years old – and one of only two "living landmarks" in the city (the other is a magnolia tree in Brooklyn).

Most people assume the most generous stretches of land in Queens belong to JFK and **LaGuardia airports**. These terminals with their long runways *are* huge, but more impressive acreage actually remains

undeveloped: nearly a quarter of the borough has been preserved as parkland.

Alley Pond Park, off Northern Boulevard near the borough's northeastern border with Long Island, includes the Alley Pond Environmental Center (tel: 718-229 4000), which offers trail walks through freshwater and saltwater marshes, and exhibits of natural history.

Just south of the JFK runways, however, the **Jamaica Bay Wildlife Refuge** ⑩ (tel: 718-318 4340) is home to more than 300 species of birds as well as small creatures like raccoons, chipmunks and turtles. Trail maps available at the visitor center, run by National Park Rangers, take you through groves of red cedar and Japanese pine trees; there are also year round birding workshops. (For the most part, the birds have so far avoided tangling with their jetpowered cousins, thanks to an innovative program that uses falcons to scare them off.)

The Rockaways

Along the southernmost strip of Queens, **the Rockaways** ⑪ form the biggest municipal beach in the country. To the east is **Far Rockaway**; to the west is **Neponsit**, where old mansions cling to the bygone splendor of Rockaway days when wealthy New Yorkers vacationed here. A similar neighborhood is **Belle Harbor**, the site of a tragic incident on November 13, 2001, when an American Airlines plane crashed into four buildings shortly after take-off from JFK, killing more than 250 people, including some residents. That the crash happened in Belle Harbor – a tight-knit, middle-class area – was particularly poignant, as the neighborhood had been mourning the many local people who were among the fire-fighters, policemen and Wall Street traders killed only two months earlier when the World Trade Center collapsed as a result of a terrorist attack.

Map on page 246

For nearly half his life, Louis Armstrong lived at 34-56 107th Street in Corona, Queens. The house is now a museum. Dedicated fans can traipse through the jazz musician's kitchen, bedroom and even his bathroom.

BELOW: serving up a salt-beef sandwich.

Astoria

Facing Manhattan from the other side of the East River, **Astoria** ⑫ is a modest section of small apartment buildings and semi-detached homes that has gained a new reputation as a center for New York's film industry. The motion picture business here dates back to the 1920s, when the Marx Brothers and Gloria Swanson were among those working at what was then the Famous Players-Lasky Studios. Now the **Kaufman Astoria Studios** occupy the old site, as well as many surrounding blocks *(see box on facing page)*. Films and commercials are rolling again, both here and at the Silvercup Studios not far away in neighboring Long Island City.

Traditionally a Greek enclave, Astoria has also attracted immigrants from other parts of the world. Along main drags like **Steinway Street** and **Broadway**, you'll find Greek delis, Italian bakeries, Asian markets and restaurants like Karyatis (35-03 Broadway, between 35th and 36th streets). Despite the movie stars working nearby, the side streets remain reasonably quiet. Kids play driveway basketball and pick-up soccer, while elderly men watch the action from lawnchairs.

Long Island City ⑬, an aging industrial section, was discovered in the early 1980s by artists. Status has been confirmed by siting **MoMA QNS** here, the temporary home of the Museum of Modern Art *(see page 132)*. Just three blocks from MoMa QNS at 43rd Avenue at 36th Street is the **Museum for African Art** (tel: 718-784-7700. closed Tue, Wed, fee), which moved here when Soho got too pricey. MoMA is also responsible for **PS 1**, a museum and contemporary art center at 22–25 Jackson Avenue at 46th Avenue (tel: 718-784 2084, closed Mon and Tues, fee). Dedicated to showing the work of emerging artists, it's one of the

BELOW: AMMI'S *Tut's Fever* movie palace by artist Red Grooms is a dazzling display of cinematic whimsy.

city's most exciting venues. Another is the **Isamu Noguchi Garden Museum** (32–37 Vernon Boulevard, tel: 718-721 1932, admission fee), where hundreds of works by the Japanese artist are displayed in a converted warehouse and harmonious outside sculpture garden. Just up Vernon Boulevard at Broadway, more art can be admired at the 4½-acre (1.8 ha) **Socrates Sculpture Park** (tel: 718-956 1819). Started by artists, this expanse of grass was proclaimed an official city park. The view of Manhattan from here, through giant sculptures (shows twice a year) is mesmerizing. It's open from 10am until sunset.

Another neighborhood worth exploring is **Forest Hills ⓮**, a section of Queens inspired by the English "Garden Cities" movement. Planning commenced in 1906 with an endowment for low-cost housing. But in 1923, when the project was only half completed, residents took over the management and began vetting newcomers. The district turned fashionable, and called itself the "lawn tennis capital of the western hemisphere." Although the courts of the **West Side Tennis Club** no longer host the US Open, Forest Hills remains a pleasant residential area; its mock-Tudor buildings and shops adding to the suburban appeal.

For a change of pace, a day at the racetrack should not be overlooked. Events at **Aqueduct** (Rockaway Blvd and 108th Street in Ozone Park) include the Wood Memorial and the Turf Classic, both significant races of their kind.

Staten Island

Once upon a time in New York, there was an island where roads were paved with oyster shells, where yachts stood guard by resort hotels, where proper European-style finishing schools were founded, and where Americans first played tennis.

ABOVE AND BELOW: queen of the screen: the American Museum of the Moving Image in Astoria shows films that are rarely seen.

AMMI

The American Museum of the Moving Image was the first institute in the US devoted to exploring the art, history, technique and technology of motion pictures, television and video. Although nowhere near as glamorous as LA's Hollywood History Museum, AMMI is still worth visiting if you're in Queens. Located at 35th Avenue at 36th Street, the landmark three-story building is part of the Astoria Studios complex – Paramount Pictures' East Coast facility in the 1920s. In this regard, the museum has a pleasing, archival feel about it, with many examples of early film and TV equipment. Renamed the Kaufman Astoria Studios, in recent years the complex has been used by both Woody Allen and Martin Scorsese.

Modern exhibits include interactive work stations where you can select the sound effects for famous movies or insert your own dialogue into classic scenes. Film retrospectives are held in the 200-seat Riklis Theatre; other viewing theaters include a 1960s-style living room, complete with shag rug and vinyl furniture, and the knock-out Tut's Fever by artist Red Grooms, an amusing homage to the lavish neo-Egyptian-style picture palaces of the 1920s. AMMI, tel: 718-784 0077, open Tues–Fri noon–4pm, Sat, Sun noon–6pm; fee.

TIP

The oldest restaurant in New York City is located on Staten Island. The Old Bermuda Inn opened in 1716 and is in a landmark colonial house at 2512 Arthur Kill Road, Rossville, Tel: 718-948 7600.

Could this place be **Staten Island ⑮**, the second-smallest and least known borough? To most New Yorkers, the island is only the place where the famous ferry goes: the excursion from South Ferry (next to Battery Park in Manhattan) includes a view of the Statue of Liberty and the Manhattan skyline, and runs well into the evening. As the poet Edna St Vincent Millay wrote: "We were very tired, we were very merry – we had gone back and forth all night on the ferry." Most people only come for the ride, but, in fact, it's worth disembarking on Staten Island itself.

Staten Island's oversimplified image is of a once-pastoral place gone suburban. Until the 1830s, it remained a quiet settlement of fishing and farming villages. About that time, the beach became trendy. A literary crowd arrived, along with a second crowd with enough money to build mansions. Island industry picked up steam and thrived well into the 20th century. But the area fell into dire straits during the Great Depression and many old landmarks slipped into a state of disrepair from which they've only recently awakened.

The ferry lands in the town of **St George ⑯**, where nearby attractions include the **Staten Island Institute of Arts & Sciences** (tel: 718-727 1135). Located in a dignified 1918 building, at 75 Stuyvesant Place, it contains a variety of local historical exhibits. Part the museum's extensive ferry collection is on display at the **St George Ferry Terminal**.

Snug Harbor Cultural Center ⑰ (1000 Richmond Terrace, tel: 718-448 2500) is a short S40 bus trip west of St George and opened in 1831 as Sailors' Snug Harbor, a home for retired seamen. Now its 83 acres (34 ha) of ponds, wetlands and woodlands are a haven for the arts and nature. The main buildings are Greek Revival landmarks. Neptune, tridents, parrots and ships still decorate the **Main Hall** interior, just as they did when the building served as quarters for the old sailors. Today, the **Newhouse Center for Contemporary Art** (closed Mon and Tues) features works by emerging and established artists in all media.

BELOW: Staten Island living.

Outside, close to the pretty and romantic **old gazebo**, Snug Harbor holds an impressive range of concerts and performances. Other parts of the renovation include the **Veterans Memorial Hall** and an 1892 **Music Hall**. Also on the grounds is the **Staten Island Botanical Garden** (tel: 718-237 8200), which is famous for its orchid collection and recently added a Chinese Scholar's Garden; and the **Staten Island Children's Museum** (tel: 718-273 2060, closed Mon, admission fee), another excellent interactive experience for kids.

East of the ferry landing – beyond **Stapleton** – the **Rosebank ⑱** section was home to Staten Island's first Italian-American community, although German and Irish immigrants lived here, too. It's also home to the **Garibaldi Meuci Museum** (480 Tompkins Ave, tel: 718-442 1608, closed Mon, admission fee). Antonio Meuci, who invented an early telephone years before Alexander Graham Bell, lived in this simple frame house until his death in 1889. Exhibits focus on this and other of his inventions, as well as his friendship with Italian hero Giuseppe Garibaldi, who stayed with Meuci when he came to New York in 1850.

A short bus or taxi ride away, the **Alice Austen House Museum** (2 Hylan Blvd, tel: 718-816 4506, closed Mon-Wed and Feb, admission fee) is a lovely, garden-surrounded cottage that was the home of a pioneering woman photographer from 1866 to 1945.

Because a glacier ridge runs right through the middle of the island, its six hills: **Fort**, **Ward**, **Grymes**, **Emerson**, **Todt** and **Lighthouse** are the highest points in New York City. Stately mansions with breathtaking views stand on the ridge of **Todt Hill**, the highest point south of Maine along the eastern seaboard.

Signal Hill

Take a taxi up **Signal Hill**, a narrow hairpin lane. Along the way, alpine homes peek out of the cliff, half hidden by rocks and trees. At the top, beyond the super views from the ridge, you will enter the core of the island. Called the **Greenbelt**, this verdant slice of trees and meadows – 2,500 scenic acres (1000 ha) of contiguous parkland – is the result of a civic plan that tightly controls or entirely prohibits development.

The heart of it all is **High Rock Park**, a 90-acre (36 ha) nature center that was once a Girl Scout camp, where a visitor center (tel. 718-667 2165) offers information about walking trails. Further west, the Greenbelt encompasses **Latourette Park and Golf Course**, one of the city's best public courses. Around the bend, on **Lighthouse Hill**, is an idyllic corner imported from the Himalayas. The **Jacques Marchais Museum of Tibetan Art** (338 Lighthouse Ave, tel: 718-987 3500, admission fee) includes two monastic-style stone buildings, a lotus pond and terraced garden. Inside, paintings, bronze Buddhas and Tibetan religious artifacts make up a small but fine collection that's open on Wednesday through Sunday afternoons in summer; call for opening hours during December to March *(see page 210)*.

BELOW: artist at home on Staten Island (that's her painting).

On the way down the hill, take a peek at the architecturally interesting **Crimson Beech**, a pre-fabricated house at 48 Manor Court and the only private residence in the city designed by Frank Lloyd Wright. The **Staten Island Lighthouse**, behind it on Edinboro Road, was built in 1912 and still guides ships into New York Harbor. (Like the house, however, it's not open to the public.)

Historic Richmond Town ⓭, less than a mile away on Richmond Road, is a restored 17th-and 18th-century village depicting 300 years of life on Staten Island. With its spacious grounds, costumed guides and demonstrations of old-style crafts, it's a worthwhile destination on its own *(see page 210)*.

From Richmond Town, **Amboy Road** leads down to **Tottenville** ⓴, the southernmost point in New York State. It's difficult to believe that this quiet community is part of New York City, since it more closely resembles a town in upstate New York. The major attraction for visitors is the **Conference House**, or Billopp House, (tel: 718-984 2086, closed Mon and Tues) at the end of **Hylan Boulevard**. This was the site of Benjamin Franklin's meeting in 1776 with the British commander, Admiral Lord Howe, in an attempt to prevent the American Revolution.

Hylan Boulevard travels back up the island, eventually reaching **Great Kills Park**. Follow the entrance road through fields of swamp grass to the beach. Behind a spit of land are marinas and a public boat ramp; the park also includes a swimming beach and miles of walking trails. Several of the island's best easterly views include the **Verrazano-Narrows Bridge** ㉑, built in 1964 as the longest suspension bridge in the world. The Verrazano connects Staten Island to Brooklyn and, often criticized, is known as the island's great change-maker. The traffic that poured across its span brought Staten Island's fastest and most uncontrolled boom in construction, especially inland.

While new building is still underway, better and more thoughtful planning – like that which resulted in the Greenbelt area – has become the rule rather than the exception. And though Staten Island may still be one of the city's smallest boroughs, its wealth of cultural and scenic attractions are helping ensure that it's no longer the least-known.

The Bronx

In 1641, a Scandinavian named Jonas Bronck bought 500 acres of the New World from Native Americans. After building his home on virgin land, he and his family found the area remote and lonely so they began to throw parties for their friends. The Indian land was called Keskekeck then, but the name was changed by Manhattanites who would say to their neighbors, "Where are you going on Saturday night?"

"Up to the Broncks. And you?"

The tale is debatable. Nevertheless, **the Bronx** ㉒ did begin with Jonas, and in the beginning it was virgin forest. In most sections of today's Bronx, idyllic woods seem inconceivable, but there is one place where part of the original hemlock forest remains untouched: the 250-acre (100 ha) **New York Botanical Garden** ㉓ (200th St and Southern Blvd, tel: 718-817 8700, closed Mon, fee).

The **Bronx River Gorge**, which cuts through 10 acres (4 ha) of woods, is best reached from its arched stone footbridge not far from the 19th-century **Lorillard Snuff Mill**, now a café and restaurant.

The grandest structure on the grounds is the **Enid A. Haupt Conservatory**, a veritable crystal palace built in 1901 which includes a central Palm Court and connecting greenhouses. But there are plenty of outdoor gardens to explore too, of course, including a spectacular **Rose Garden** and the new **Everett Children's Adventure Garden**, with tantalizing kid-size topiaries and mazes.

The 265-acre (107 ha) **Bronx Zoo/Wildlife Conservation Park** ㉔ (tel: 718-367 1010) is the country's largest urban zoo – and shares **Bronx Park** with the Botanical Gardens. The most decorative way to enter is by crossing Fordham Road to the **Paul Rainey Memorial Gate**, topped with Art Deco bronze casts of animals. Some of the most popular exhibits include the **World of Darkness** (nocturnal animals), the **Aquatic Bird House** and the **Butterfly Zone**.

There's a pleasant **Children's Zoo**, a two-mile monorail ride through **Wild Asia** and a 40-acre (16 ha) complex with moats to keep the big cats away from their prey (that means you). A new exhibit,

BELOW: ceiling of the Main Hall, Snug Harbor Cultural Center

Map on page 246

Congo Gorilla Forest, has nearly seven fun-filled acres of forest, bamboo thickets and baby lowland gorillas.

The zoo is at the geographic heart of the Bronx, but its nostalgic and architectural heart may well be the **Grand Concourse**. This Champs Elysées-inspired boulevard began as a "speedway" across rural hills. As the borough became more industrialized, the Concourse achieved a classy role as the Park Avenue of the Bronx, stretching as it does for more than 4 miles (6 km). Its Art Deco apartments remain, though few retain their luxury status.

Edgar Allan Poe

North of the Grand Concourse at **Kingsbridge Road**, poet **Edgar Allan Poe's cottage** sits humbly among high-rise housing. Poe moved here in 1846, hoping what was then country air would be good for his consumptive young wife and cousin, Virginia. But she died at an early age, leaving Poe frayed and destitute; the haunting poem *Annabel Lee* was a reflection of the poet's distress. The cottage has been a museum since 1917, and is now run by the **Bronx County Historical Society** (tel: 718-881 8900), which also runs the **Valentine-Varian House** (3266 Bainbridge Ave at 208th Street), a 1758 fieldstone farm dwelling where an early New York mayor grew up. Inside, there's a small but interesting **Museum of Bronx History**. Both are open weekends only, with a small fee.

The Little Italy of the Bronx is the **Belmont** section, just east of the Zoo. **Arthur Avenue**, near the fork of Crescent Avenue and East 187th Street, teems with people who flock here from all over the city to buy cured meats, pasta and freshly baked bread. It's also a great place for restaurants: try Dominick's, 2335 Arthur Avenue, across from the indoor market. (Tables are shared, the

"So neat, so poor, so unfurnished, and yet so charming a dwelling I never saw," remarked a guest after visiting Edgar Allan Poe at his little cottage in the Bronx.

BELOW: the Verrazano-Narrows Bridge connects Staten Island to Brooklyn.

atmosphere is boisterous, but it's not too expensive and the food is great.) Or stop in at the Belmont Library, around the corner at East 186th Street and Hughes Avenue, where the **Enrico Fermi Cultural Center** has books and research materials about the contributions made by Italians to American life. The staff, of course, speak Italian and will help with queries.

The Great Green Nipple of Knowledge

West of the Grand Concourse, **Bronx Community College**'s most famous landmark is the **Hall of Fame**, a tile-roofed colonnade lined by busts of famous Americans that wraps around Gould Memorial Library. Designed by Stanford White and no longer used as a library, the building's great copper dome was known by scholars as the Great Green Nipple of Knowledge.

There are seven other campuses located throughout the borough, including **Lehman College**, the **Albert Einstein College of Medicine** and **Fordham University**, at Fordham Road and Third Avenue. The most impressive landmark at Fordham is the chapel, which has fine stained-glass windows that were donated by Louis Philippe, the Citizen King of France.

ABOVE AND BELOW:
The Bronx Zoo is
the largest urban
zoo in America,
with gorillas, big
cats and bison like
the ones grazing in
the picture above.

Above University Heights is **Riverdale ㉕**, in the hilly northwest. It's hard to believe this is the Bronx. The curvy roads are lined with mansions – and a drive down Sycamore Avenue to Independence and West 249th Street brings you to **Wave Hill** (tel: 718-549 3200, varying hours, fee).

This formerly private estate, now a city-owned environmental center, has greenhouses and public gardens overlooking the Hudson and is one of the most beautiful spots anywhere. There are actually two houses here, the largest and most elegant of which is a 19th-century Greek Revival mansion that Mark Twain rented from 1901 to 1904. But it's the view and landscaped grounds that are extraordinary and, when combined with summer concerts and site-specific dance performances on rolling lawns, make a visit here memorable.

East of Riverdale, **Van Cortlandt Park ㉖** stretches from West 240th to West 263rd streets, and includes stables, tennis courts and acres of playing fields. On weekends, West Indians play rounds of cricket here and a league of waiters from the neighborhood's Irish pubs and restaurants has soccer games between meals. The **Van Cortlandt House Museum** (tel: 718-543 3344, closed Mon, fee), overlooks the park's lake from a perch at Broadway and 242nd Street. Built in 1748 by Frederick Van Cortlandt, son of a leading Dutch colonial-era merchant, its rooms are filled with some of the family's original furnishings and possessions.

On the park's other side, and edged by Webster Avenue, **Woodlawn Cemetery** is permanent home to about 300,000 New Yorkers. Herman Melville, Duke Ellington and five former mayors are just a few of the celebrities resting in elaborate mausoleums amidst over 300 acres (120 ha) of shady trees, hills and streams. It may be the perfect place to unwind after a morning of stressful sightseeing (and has been a weirdly popular tourist attraction since it opened in 1863). Occasional art shows are held here, too; for

Map
on page
246

information and a map, stop in at the cemetery's office at Webster Avenue at 233rd Street or call 718-920 0500. Marshland extends into Long Island Sound at the eastern corner of the Bronx, where the place to aim for is City Island. On the way, the highway passes Co-op City, a sprawling, brown-towered housing development that dates back to the 1960s and looms on the horizon like a huge urban beehive, with its own school, shops and about 50,000 tenants.

Pelham Bay Park ㉗, farther east, is one of the city's largest recreation areas and includes **Orchard Beach**, a popular summer destination created in 1936 by the Department of Parks, which imported tons of fine white sand from the Rockaways and Long Island. There are nature trails, riding stables and a public golf course here as well.

Past the turn-off for Orchard Beach, the road ends at **City Island** ㉘, the borough's slice of New England quaintness. Accessible by car, city bus, or by boat, this 230-acre (93 ha) island off the northeast Bronx coast has remained quietly detached from the rest of the city. The first industry on City Island, in the 1830s, was the Solar Salt Works, which marketed salt from evaporated sea water. Then oystering became big business, only to be replaced by shipbuilding; the boatyards along **City Island Avenue** eventually yielded masterworks like *Intrepid*, the 1968 winner of the America's Cup Race. Today, this main street sports attractions ranging from fishing gear emporiums and craft shops to galleries and seafood restaurants. At 620 look for romantic hideaway **Le Refuge Inn**, with both food and rooms to offer. Farther along the avenue is stately **Grace Church**, a fine example of Gothic Revival architecture. Behind the church you'll find peaceful side streets lined with weathered bungalows and cottages; even a few large, fading Victorian mansions that still have their original stained-glass windows in front, and overgrown gardens out back.

Yankees at home

The opposite end of the borough – in location and reputation – is the **South Bronx**. Its best-known landmark is baseball's **Yankee Stadium** (161st Street at River Avenue), known as The House That Ruth Built. Actually, the nickname is backwards. This is the house built for Ruth. Its shortened right field was designed for player Babe Ruth's special home-run record.

Other baseball stars associated with the stadium include Lou Gehrig, Micky Mantle, Joe DiMaggio and the 1998 team that won the World Series; in fact, more world championship flags and American League pennants have flown over Yankee Stadium than any other baseball field in the country. At one point, as the surrounding neighborhood suffered financial thirst, $100 million was pumped into rebuilding the stadium; at the start of a new century, however, its future is uncertain.

To some extent, the urban blight of the South Bronx has lessened. Not too far away from the stadium, at 165th Street, the **Bronx Museum of the Arts** (1040 Grand Concourse, tel: 718-681 6000, closed Mon and Tues, fee) features exhibitions of sculpture, graphics, paintings and photography. ❏

BELOW:
time to be tough.

☒ INSIGHT GUIDES
Travel Tips

✕® INSIGHT GUIDES Phonecard

One global card to keep travellers in touch. Easy. Convenient. Saves you time and money.

It's a global phonecard

Save up to 70%* on international calls from over 55 countries

Free 24 hour global customer service

Recharge your card at any time via customer service or online

It's a message service

Family and friends can send you voice messages for free.

Listen to these messages using the phone* or online

Free email service - you can even listen to your email over the phone*

It's a travel assistance service

24 hour emergency travel assistance – if and when you need it.

Store important travel documents online in your own secure vault

For more information, call rates, and all Access Numbers in over 55 countries, (check your destination is covered) go to www.insightguides.ekit.com or call Customer Service.

JOIN now and receive US$ 5 bonus when you join for US$ 20 or more.

Join today at

www.insightguides.ekit.con

When requested use ref code: **INSAD010**

OR SIMPLY FREE CALL
24 HOUR CUSTOMER SERVICE

UK	0800 376 1705
USA	1800 706 1333
Canada	1800 808 5773
Australia	1800 11 44 78
South Africa	0800 997 285

THEN PRESS 0

For all other countries please go to "Access Numbers" at www.insightguides.ekit.com

* Retrieval rates apply for listening to messages. Savings base on using a hotel or payphone and calling to a landline. Corre at time of printing 01.03

(INS001)

powered by ⊕ekit

"The easiest way to make calls and receive messages around the world"

CONTENTS

Getting Acquainted

The Place

Area: New York City lies in the southeast corner of New York State at the mouth of the Hudson River. It covers about 300 square miles (780 sq. km).

Geography: Greater New York is divided into five boroughs – Manhattan, the Bronx, Queens, Brooklyn and Staten Island. Manhattan is the smallest but most densely populated borough, with a population of 1.5 million people, all crammed onto an island that is 13 miles (21 km) long and slightly more than 2 miles (3.2 km) across at its widest point.

Population: 8,008,278 (Federal Census Bureau, 2000).

Nickname: The Big Apple.

Religion: Approximately 70 percent Christian, 11 percent Jewish, 1.5 percent Muslim, 7.4 percent agnostic, with Buddhists, Hindus and others also represented.

Time Zone: New York is in the Eastern Standard Time zone (EST). This is five hours behind London;

Dialing Codes

The most popular Manhattan code is 212. If no other area code is listed in this book, dial 212 before the seven-digit number. Area codes 646 and 917 are also used, but are newer and less common. The codes for Brooklyn, Staten Island, Queens, and the Bronx are the old 718, plus the newer 347 and 917. With the proliferation of cell phones, fax machines and other facilities requiring new numbers, telephone codes are changing rapidly, however, so be sure to check.

Fascinating Facts

Biggest: The biggest meteorite to hit the Earth weighed 34 tons, and is displayed at the American Museum of Natural History on Central Park West.

Longest: Originally an Indian trail, Broadway continues well beyond the city's boundaries; as the Albany Post Road, it goes all the way to the state capital – a distance of 175 miles (282 km).

Oldest: The oldest grave in New York is in Lower Manhattan's Trinity Churchyard, dated 1681.

Most clogged: According to the Bureau of Traffic, the city's most congested auto area is along 42nd Street, between Third and Madison avenues.

Waterlogged: It takes an average seven hours, 15 minutes to swim around the island of Manhattan.

one hour ahead of Chicago and three hours ahead of California.

Currency: US dollars and cents.

Weights and Measures: The United States uses the Imperial system of weights and measures. Metric weights and measures are rarely used.

Electricity: 110 volts.

Country Code: (1).

Climate

New York has four distinct seasons, and is generally at its best during the spring and fall months. Summer temperatures hover in the mid-70 to mid-80s°F (24–29°C), although heatwaves where the mercury rises to 100°F (37.8°C) may occur, and uncomfortable humidity is often the rule, especially in July and August. September and October sometimes usher in a balmy, dry "Indian summer" that fills parks and office plazas with sun-worshipers. Winter temperatures can drop below 10 or 15°F (-12 or -9°C), with the average temperature for January closer to 32° F (0°C). The average annual rainfall is 44 ins (112 cm) and the average annual snowfall is 29 ins

Making the switch: Radio City's Rockettes make an average of seven costume changes during the annual gala Easter Show.

Flipping the switch: Wall Street was one of the first publicly lit US streets. Thomas Edison personally flipped the switch in 1882.

City shore: New York City has 15 miles of beaches, the most popular being Coney Island.

City core: How New York got its well-known nickname "The Big Apple" is open to dispute. Some say it came from a 1920s newspaper column about horse racing called "Around the Big Apple." Others say it was first used by jazz musicians who, when getting a gig in New York, saw it as the top of their profession, or reaching "the Big Apple."

(74 cm). Raincoats are advised year-round and – except for casual wandering – dress can be fairly formal compared to other cities.

Economy

The city has some of the best of everything in the USA. New York City is the country's foremost **financial center** (the New York Stock Exchange, the Federal Reserve Bank, and the commodities exchanges are all located here). It holds a leading position in the **retail and wholesale trades,**as well as in **manufacturing**, **fashion**, **art** and the **service industries**. New York is also a major center for **media** (advertising, television, movies book publishing, magazines and newspapers), with **new-media** companies that develop interactive software and on-line computer services an important segment of the industry.

Government

New York City was first incorporated as a city in 1653 and expanded as "Greater New York" in 1898 (when it grew to include the outer boroughs). The city is governed by a mayor and a strong city council – which was made even stronger a decade ago, when the US Supreme Court ruled that the city's old Board of Estimate system (in which the presidents of each borough had a single vote) was unconstitutional. The result is an expanded 35-member city council.

Culture and Customs

New York is a fast-paced town, whose residents are possessed of a restless energy that legend says is necessary for survival. Few people seem to have time for anything not on their mental schedule, and even asking for directions in the street is best done with an awareness of this, ideally while moving at the same pace and in the same direction as the informant.

New Yorkers have persuaded themselves that living at breakneck speed, always under pressure, is stimulating and is what gives them their edge and makes Manhattan the center of the universe (which all New Yorkers believe implicitly). It may also explain why few people choose to live out their latter years in the city, if, indeed, they survive long enough to make that choice.

The city is undeniably stimulating and exciting not only for the wealth of its social and cultural pleasures but also because of its fascinating and truly varied, almost 24-hour street life. Its multifarious neighborhoods, segueing from one to another, offer boundless diversions to the eye and ear.

A casual stroll in almost any direction rewards the explorer with guaranteed serendipity. Rockefeller Plaza at lunchtime, Soho's West Broadway on Saturday, Central Park on Sunday, or Washington Square on any summer weekend will provide a visitor with as much entertainment as the best Broadway show.

Planning the Trip

Entry Regulations

VISAS AND PASSPORTS

A passport, a passport-size photograph, a visitor's visa, proof of intent to leave the US after your visit and, depending upon your country of origin, an international vaccination certificate, are required of most foreign nationals for entry. Visitors from certain countries staying less than 90 days no longer need a visa. Vaccination certificate requirements vary, but proof of immunization against smallpox or cholera may be necessary.

Canadian and Mexican citizens, and British residents of Canada and Bermuda, are normally exempt from these requirements but it is wise to check for specific regulations on international travel in your country.

Extension of Stay

Non-US citizens should contact the **US Immigration and Naturalization Service** at 425 I. St, NW, Washington, DC 20536. Tel: 202-514 4316.

CUSTOMS

For a breakdown of customs allowances write to: **United States Customs Service**, P.O. Box 7407, Washington, DC 20044. Tel: 202-927 6724.

Meat or meat products, illegal drugs, firearms, seeds, plants and fruits are among the prohibited goods. Also do not bring in any duty-free goods which are worth more than $400 (returning Americans) or $100 (foreign travelers). Visitors

over 21 may bring in 200 cigarettes, 3 lbs (1.3 kg) of tobacco or 50 cigars and 34 fl. oz (1 liter) of alcohol.

GIFT EXEMPTION

A non-resident may claim, as free of duty and internal revenue tax, articles up to $100 in value for use as gifts for other persons, if you remain in the US for at least 72 hours and the gifts accompany you. This $100 gift exemption or any part of it can be claimed only once every six months. You may include 100 cigars within this gift exemption. However, alcoholic beverages may not be included in the gift exemption. *Do not have your articles gift wrapped, as they must be available for customs inspection.*

If you are not entitled to the $100 gift exemption, you may bring in articles up to $25 in value free of duty for your personal or household use. You may include any of the following: 50 cigarettes, 10 cigars, 150 ml. of alcoholic beverages, or 5 fl. oz. (150 ml.) of alcoholic perfume or proportionate amounts. If any of these limits are exceeded or if the total amount of all dutiable articles exceeds $25, no exemption can be applied. Articles bought in "duty-free" shops in foreign countries are subject to US Customs duty and restrictions but may be included in your exemption.

Health

Medical services are extremely expensive. Always travel with comprehensive travel insurance to cover any emergencies.

Money

The dollar comes in denominations from $1 through $5, $10, $20, $50, $100, and up. It is always green, although bearing the head of different presidents. There is a $2 bill, although it is considered unlucky and is rarely seen. Coins begin with the penny (1¢) and ascend through the nickel (5¢), dime (10¢), quarter (25¢), half-dollar (50¢) and the infrequent $1 coin, which is unpopular as it closely resembles a quarter.

US VISITORS

Credit cards are accepted almost everywhere, although not all cards at all places. Along with out-of-state or overseas bank cards, they can also be used to withdraw money at ATMS (automatic teller machines), which are marked with the corresponding stickers (i.e. Cirrus, Plus, Visa, MasterCard, American Express, etc.)

OVERSEAS VISITORS

There are numerous outlets for exchanging currency in New York (although a check not written in dollars can take weeks to clear), and a few banks still charge a fee to cash traveler's checks. Traveler's checks (as long as they are in dollar amounts) are accepted in most hotels and good restaurants, so long as they are accompanied by proper identification. Keep your passport handy.

It is advisable to acquire enough dollars at one of the airport banks or currency exchanges to last for a day or two at least. Once in Manhattan, money can be exchanged seven days a week at three branches of **Thomas Cook Currency Services**, tel: 1-800 287 7362; 1590 Broadway at 48th St, tel: 265 6063; 1271 Broadway at 32nd St, tel: 679 4365; and 511 Madison Ave at 53rd St, tel: 753 0117.

Thomas Cook's offices also sell and cash traveler's checks, as do the numerous **American Express** offices around town, including 374 Park Ave, tel: 421 8240.

Among the city's foreign exchange centers offering full services is **Ruesch International** at 608 Fifth Avenue, tel: 581 8821. There is also an automated self-change kiosk at the **Times Square Visitors Center** at 1560

Public Holidays

As with other countries in the world, the US has gradually shifted most of its public holidays to the Monday closest to the actual dates, thus creating a number of three-day weekends throughout the year. Holidays that are celebrated no matter what day on which they fall are:
New Year's Day (January 1).
Independence Day (July 4).
Veterans' Day (November 11).
Christmas Day (December 25).

Other holidays are:
Martin Luther King Jr Day (third Mon in Jan).
President's Day commemorating Lincoln and Washington (third Mon in Feb).
Memorial Day (last Mon in May).
Labor Day (first Mon in Sept).
Columbus Day (second Mon in Oct).
Election Day (first Tues in Nov, every four years).
Thanksgiving (last Thurs in Nov).

Broadway (between 46th and 47th streets).
Citibank offers exchange facilities at most of its 200 or so branches around the five boroughs. Tel: 1-800-285 3000.

Getting There
BY AIR

East of Manhattan on Long Island, New York's two major airports, **John F. Kennedy International** and **LaGuardia**, are respectively 15 and 8 miles (24 km and 13 km) from the city, with driving time from Kennedy estimated at just under one hour. In practice, heavy traffic can sometimes double this. Most charters and domestic flights and some international flights use LaGuardia.

New York's third airport, **Newark**, is actually in New Jersey and, although further away from Manhattan than JFK and LaGuardia, can be easier to reach.

BY SEA

Stretching along the Hudson River from 48th to 52nd streets in Manhattan, the **Passenger Ship Terminal**, tel: 246 5450, at Piers 88, 90 and 92, has customs facilities, baggage handling, rooftop parking and bus connections to Midtown.

BY RAIL

Trains arrive and depart from Manhattan's two railroad terminals: **Grand Central Terminal** at Park Ave and 42nd St, and **Pennsylvania Station** at Seventh Ave and 33rd St. City buses stop outside each terminal and each sits atop a subway station. **Amtrak information**, tel: 582 6875, or (toll-free) 1-800-872 7245.

BY ROAD

From the south, the **New Jersey Turnpike** leads into lower Manhattan via the Holland Tunnel or Lincoln Tunnel (Midtown) and offers access farther north via the George Washington Bridge, across which traffic from the west also enters the city off the Bergen-Passaic Expressway. From the northwest, the **New York State Thruway** connects with the Henry Hudson Parkway leading into northern Manhattan. Driving in from the Long Island airports, access is via the Midtown Tunnel or across the Triborough Bridge and down Manhattan's East River Drive. The city's main bus terminal, the **Port Authority** (Eighth Ave between 40th and 42nd St), sits atop two subway lines and is serviced by long-distance bus companies (including **Greyhound**, tel: 1-800-231 2222) as well as local commuter lines. City buses stop outside. A modern, air-conditioned terminal with several shops and facilities, it tends to attract its share of riff-raff; although well-policed, it's not the sort of place to trust strangers or to leave bags unguarded.

Special Facilities

CHILDREN

Most of the sightseeing activities that adults might take part in are likely to appeal to children as well, especially the **Circle Line boat trip** around Manhattan, **Macy's Thanksgiving Day parade**, the **July 4th fireworks** display over the East River, and visits to the **Statue of Liberty** or **Empire State Building**. Some supposedly adult activities, such as visiting the **Fulton Fish Market** at six o'clock in the morning, might even appeal more to children than to their parents.

Central Park has an entire children's district, including a children's zoo, an antique carousel and a marionette theater, tel: 988 9093. Saturday morning story-telling sessions take place in summer at the statue of Hans Christian Andersen near the Conservatory Water (East 74th St), which is also a popular spot for model boat racing. For **park information**, tel: 794 6564.

There's a wonderful children's zoo in Brooklyn's **Prospect Park**, tel: 718-399 7339; hundreds of exotic fish for kids to wonder at in the **New York Aquarium**, West 8th St and Surf Ave, Coney Island, tel: 718-265 3474 (FISH); while the **Bronx Zoo**, tel: 718-367 1010, is worth an entire day's adventure.

At the **American Museum of Natural History**, Central Park West and 79th St, tel: 759 5100, the dinosaur collection is always popular. Not far away, the **Children's Museum of Manhattan**, 212 West 83rd St, tel: 721 1234, encourages hands-on participation. There's a similar hands-on museum at **Snug Harbor** in Staten Island, tel: 718-273 2060, while the **Brooklyn Children's Museum** at 145 Brooklyn Ave, tel: 718-735 4400, is the country's oldest.

You may also want to consider the **New York City Fire Museum**, 278 Spring St, tel: 691 1303; the dazzling **Liberty Science Center** (just across the Hudson River, in New Jersey), tel: 201-200 1000;

and the **South Street Seaport's Children's Center**, tel: 748 8600.

There are **playgrounds** throughout the city, including Central Park; Washington Square Park; at West 82nd St and Riverside Drive; at Second Ave and 93rd St; and in Queens, where the **New York Hall of Science**, tel: 718-699 0005, in Flushing Meadows-Corona Park, not only has the largest outdoor science playground in the US but also features more than 100 indoor "experiments" for kids to work on.

For organized sightseeing, contact **Small Journeys** (tel: 874 7300) a company that specializes in educational tours and sites of special interest to the young.

It's also a good idea to check weekly listings in local papers and magazines for children's events, including theatrical productions. Among the more established troupes and venues are: **The Paper Bag Players**, 50 Riverside

Student Visitors

Columbia University, tel: 854 1754, operates an International Students Office to give advice on visas and other documents; the university also has an **Information and Visitors Service**, tel: 854 4902, which publishes a weekly calendar of events at the university. Similar information services are offered by **Hunter College**, 695 Park Ave, tel: 772 4000, and **New York University's Office of Student Affairs**, Loeb Student Center, 566 La Guardia Place, tel: 998 4900, where there's a lounge and basement dining room, plus free literature about student activities.

For a reasonable fee (slightly more if applying by mail) and proof of student status, the **Council on International Educational Exchange (CIEE)** at 633 Third Avenue, New York NY 10017, tel: 822 2600, issues a student identity card good for discounts on services, plus also on museums and hotels.

Dr, tel: 362 0431; **New Victory Theater**, 209 West 42nd St, tel: 239 6200.

PEOPLE WITH DISABILITIES

Disabled travelers can obtain information about rights, facilities, etc., from the **Mayor's Office for People with Disabilities**, 52 Chambers St, Room 206, New York, NY 10007. Tel: 788 2830.

GAYS

The Gay and Lesbian Hotline, tel: 989 0999 (closed mornings), provides information to gay men and women about all aspects of gay life in New York including recommendations of bars, restaurants, accommodations, legal counseling, etc. **The Lesbian and Gay Community Services Center**, 208 West 13th St, tel: 620 7310, is another helpful organization. Bookshops, such as **A Different Light**, 151 West 19th St, tel: 989 4850, and the **Oscar Wilde Memorial Bookshop** at 15 Christopher St, tel: 255 8097, stock various useful publications, and can often offer advice.

Useful Addresses

NYC & Company Visitors Information Center, 810 Seventh Ave, New York, NY 10019, tel: 212-397 8222, 1-800-NYCVISIT; www.nycvisit.com, has brochures, maps and information about special hotel packages and discount admission programs to various attractions.

They also publish the *Official NYC Guide*, a mini but comprehensive listing of activities, hotels, tours, restaurants, etc. Visitors are welcome in person at NYC & Co.'s **Visitor Information Center,** tel: 484 1222 (which is the same address as above), located between 52nd and 53rd streets. The office is open Mon–Fri 8:30 am–6pm, weekends 9am–5pm.

City Websites

Several boroughs have their own websites, listed here under "Useful Addresses." Other websites that provide helpful information include: www.newyork.citysearch.com for listings and reviews of current arts and entertainment events, as well as restaurants and shopping. Excellent for links to every conceivable aspect of New York. www.newyorktoday.com offered by *The New York Times* and filled with details about everything from poetry readings in the Bronx to traffic in Midtown.

www.nypl.org for everything you ever wanted to know about (and from) the New York Public Library. www.queens.nyc.ny.us for Queens' cultural attractions, including places like the American Museum of the Moving Image. www.si-web.com for general chat about the city's second-smallest borough – Staten Island – with links to museums and attractions. www.bronxmall.com for events in the Bronx, links to various cultural institutions and lots of Bronx trivia. www.centralparknyc.org for tours and special events in Central Park.

● **The Times Square Visitors Center** at the Embassy Theater, 1560 Broadway between 46th and 47th streets. Another good source of citywide information, with a ticket center for Broadway shows, as well as e-mail and currency exchange facilities. Open daily 8am–8pm, with free walking tours of Times Square every Friday at noon.
● **The Harlem Visitors & Convention Association**, 219 West 135th St, New York, NY 10030. Tel: 212-862 8497; fax: 862 8745. An essential source of information about tours, events and landmarks in Harlem. Visit also: www.harlem.cc
● **The Bronx Council on the Arts**, 1738 Hone Ave, Bronx NY 10461. Tel: 718-931 9500. Offers information about art, music and other events.
● **The Brooklyn Tourism Council**, 30 Flatbush Ave, Brooklyn, NY 11217. Tel: 718-855 7882; www.brooklynX.org. Provides useful information on culture, shopping, history, local parks, events and historic sites.
● **Queens Council on the Arts**, 79-01 Park Lane South, Woodhaven, NY 11421. Tel: 718-291 ARTS (2787).
● **Staten Island Tourism Council**, 1 Edgewater Plaza, Staten Island, NY 10305. Tel: 718-442 4356, 1-800 573 7469. Cultural events and places of interest. It also

maintains an information kiosk in the Ferry Terminal at Battery Park. **The NYC & Company Visitors Information Center** has recently opened an overseas office in **London, England**. Brochures about the city, maps, airlines and other practical information about visiting New York can be sent to you by calling 44-20-7202-6368 from Monday to Friday, 9am to 5pm.

Tour Information

Among the dozens of tour operators offering sightseeing trips around the city, the most popular include: **Gray Line New York**, tel: 397 2600, which features double-decker buses with hop-on, hop-off itineraries; **Circle Line**, tel: 563 3200, which operates boat trips around Manhattan, as well as harbor cruises from South Sreet Seaport; and **NY Waterway**, tel: 1-800-533 3779, featuring harbor cruises, entertainment cruises and boat trips to Yankee Stadium during baseball season.

Other interesting options include:
● **Art Horizons International**, tel: 969 9410. Visits to galleries, museums, and artists in their studio lofts.
● **Central Park Bicycle Tours**, tel: 541 8759. Guided bike tours, including bike rentals, through the wilds of Central Park.

● **Municipal Art Society**, tel: 935 3960. Architectural highlights.
● **92nd St Y**, tel: 415 5599. In-depth look at neighborhood attractions.
● **Shopping Tours of New York**, tel: 873 6791. Buying sprees, by limo.
● **Radio City Music Hall**, tel: 247 4777 or 246 4600. Go behind the big gold curtain and find out who plays the gigantic Wurlitzers.
● **Tombstone Tours**, tel: 718-760 8662. Famous crime scenes explored by hearse.

The **Lower East Side Tenement Museum** at 90 Orchard St, tel: 431 0233, offers walking tours through a neighborhood rich with 19th-century immigrant history, led by local historians. Call for a current schedule.

Another view of the immigrant experience is provided by the **Museum of Chinese in the Americas**, 70 Mulberry St, tel: 619 4785, which sponsors walks around one of the city's most fascinating ethnic enclaves.

Buildings around which tours are

Specialized Tours

There are numerous specialized tours, such as:
Harlem Spirituals/NY Visions, tel: 757 0425, with its Sunday Morning Gospel Tour.
Big Onion Walking Tours, tel: 439 1090, for strolls through interesting neighborhoods.
CityQuest CD Tours, tel: 1-888-HEAR-NYC, self-guided walking tours, narrated on CD by famous New Yorkers.
Spirit Cruises, tel: 727 7735, for moonlit cruises with dining and dancing.
Liberty Helicopter Tours, tel: 967 6464, offering spectacular aerial views of the city.
● A look at local wildlife is provided by the **Urban Park Rangers,** at the New York City Department of Parks and Recreation (tel: 1-888-NY PARKS) who lead hikes through parks in all five boroughs; they also conduct ecology workshops and other events.

Consulates and UN Missions

Note that additional listings can be found in the telephone book.

● **Australia**, 150 East 42nd St. Tel: 351 6600.
● **Austria**, 31 East 69th St. Tel: 737 6400.
● **Belgium**, 823 United Nations Plaza. Tel: 599 5252.
● **Canada**, 1251 Avenue of the Americas. Tel: 596 1700.
● **Denmark**, 1 Dag Hammerskjold Plaza. Tel: 223 4545.
● **Finland**, 866 UN Plaza. Tel: 750 4400.
● **France**, 934 Fifth Ave. Tel: 606 3600.
● **Germany**, 871 United Nations Plaza. Tel: 610 9800.
● **Ireland**, 345 Park Ave. Tel: 319 2555.
● **Israel**, 800 Second Ave. Tel: 499 5000.

● **Italy**, 690 Park Ave. Tel: 737 9100.
● **Japan**, 299 Park Ave. Tel: 371 8222.
● **Mexico**, 2 United Nations Plaza. Tel: 752 0220.
● **The Netherlands**, 1 Rockefeller Plaza. Tel: 246 1429.
● **New Zealand**, 1 UN Plaza. Tel: 826 1960.
● **Norway**, 825 Third Ave. Tel: 421 7333.
● **People's Republic of China**, 520 12th Ave. Tel: 736 9301.
● **South Africa**, 333 East 38th St. Tel: 213 4880.
● **Spain**, 150 East 58th St. Tel: 366 4080.
● **Sweden**, 1 Dag Hammerskjold Plaza. Tel: 583 2550.
● **Switzerland**, 633 Third Ave. Tel: 286 1540.
● **UK**, 845 Third Ave. Tel: 745 0200.

conducted include **Carnegie Hall**, tel: 247 7800; **Gracie Mansion**, tel: 570 4751; **Lincoln Center**, tel: 875 5350, including the **Metropolitan Opera House**; **Radio City Music Hall**, tel: 632 4041; the NBC **Studio**, tel: 664 7174, and **Rockefeller Center**, tel: 632 4000; **Madison Square Garden**, tel: 465 5800; the **United Nations**, tel: 963 7713; and **Grand Central Terminal**, tel: 935 3960. The **South St Seaport Museum** (tel: 748 8600) runs 6am tours of the Fulton Fish Market from April–October, and harbor cruises on board the historic schooner *Pioneer* from May–September.

Touring Out of Town

In summer, New Yorkers love to get out of town, preferably to the **Hamptons** or **Fire Island** but sometimes just to **Jones Beach** (tel: 516-785 1600), a great stretch of sand and surf relatively close to the city. All these places are on **Long Island** to the east, serviced by the Long Island Railroad (tel: 718-217 LIRR) from Pennsylvania Station with crowded trains that nevertheless usually arrive faster than driving on

the congested highways. (There are also limousines, helicopter and jitney bus services to the Hamptons. Call the **Long Island Convention & Visitors Bureau** at 1-800-441 4601 for more information or go to: www.licvb.com.)

East Hampton and **Southampton** are very pretty, with interesting shops, trendy clubs and restaurants and loads of celebrity sightings, but nearby **Sag Harbor** and **Shelter Island** are just as scenic and much quieter. Day-trippers in search of an even less exclusive beach ambiance can visit Fire Island, to which ferries run from Bay Shore (tel: 516-665 3600) across to **Ocean Beach**, the most popular community, and from Sayville (tel: 516-589 8980) to the national park at **Sunken Forest/ Sailors Haven.**

In winter the Scandinavian Ski & Sports Shop (tel: 757 8524) offers day trips to **Hunter Mountain**; ski rentals and lift tickets are included in the package price. Amtrak (tel: 1-800-872-7245 or 1-888-AMTRAK-1) offers excursions to Saratoga Springs during the summer horse-racing season and to the Hudson River Valley for a look at fall

foliage and historic houses. **New York Waterway** (tel: 1-800-533 3779) operates day cruises up the Hudson River from Pier 78 in midtown Manhattan to such scenic spots as the US Military Academy at West Point.

New York's **Catskill Mountains** region is another popular destination, with skiing, health spas and year-round luxury resorts. For more information about upstate attractions, contact the **New York State Division of Tourism**, 1 Commerce Plaza, Albany, NY 12245, tel: 1-800-CALL NYS (225 5697); www.iloveny.state.ny.us.

Popular out-of-town places to visit also include the old whaling town of **Mystic**, Connecticut, where Mystic Seaport (tel: 860-572 0711) is the country's largest maritime museum; for general information about lodgings and sightseeing call 1-800 863 6569. The town of **New Hope**, Pennsylvania (tel: 215-862 5880) is an artists' and writers' colony with small-town ambiance, barge rides on the Delaware Canal and numerous quaint B&B inns, less than two hours from Manhattan by bus from Port Authority.

Gray Line (tel: 397 2600) operates round-trip gambling excursions to **Atlantic City** in New Jersey. The Indian-owned **Foxwoods** and **Mohegan Sun** casinos in Connecticut are equally popular. For bus information, call Foxwoods at 1-888-BUS-2-FOX and Mohegan Sun at 1-888-226 7711. Metro-North Railroad offers year-round excursions to Foxwoods from Grand Central Terminal; call 532 4900 or 1-800-METRO INFO.

Practical Tips

Business Hours

New Yorkers work long and hard in a city where this is generally seen to be an advantage. Normal business hours are 9am–5/6pm but shops, particularly, tend to stay open much later. Needless to say, there is no close-down at lunchtime, which for many stores is the busiest time of day. Some shops are open on Sundays. Banking hours are nominally 9am–3pm but increasingly, banks are opening as early as 8am and staying open until late afternoon or early evening. ATM machines are everywhere.

Tipping

Most New Yorkers in the service industries (restaurants, hotels, transportation) regard tips as a God-given right, not just a pleasant gratuity. The fact is, many people rely on tips to make up for what are often poor hourly salaries. Therefore, unless service is truly horrendous, you can figure on tipping everyone from bellmen and porters (usually 50¢ a bag; or $1 if only one bag); to hotel doormen ($1 if they hail you a cab); hotel maids ($1 a day, left in your room when you check out), rest room attendants (at least 25¢) and room-service waiters (approximately 15 percent of the bill unless already added on). In restaurants, the best way to figure out the tip is to double the tax (which adds up to a little more than 16 percent; add or subtract a dollar or two depending on how the service was). In taxis, tip as much as 15 percent of the total fare, with a 50¢ minimum.

Religious Services

Some 6,000 churches, temples and mosques are scattered throughout the city's five boroughs, including the following:

MIDTOWN

Central Synagogue, 123 East 55th St, at Lexington Ave. The city's oldest synagogue in continuous use.
St Patrick's Cathedral, Fifth Ave, between 50th and 51st streets. The city's most famous Catholic church.
St Peter's Lutheran Church, 619 Lexington Ave, at East 54th St. Jazz eucharists on Sunday afternoons.
Fifth Avenue Presbyterian Church, 705 Fifth Ave, at West 55th St. Frequent Sunday concerts.
Marble Collegiate Church, Fifth Ave and West 29th St. Former pastor Dr Norman Vincent Peale put this 1854 Dutch Reform church on the map.

UPPER EAST SIDE

St Nicholas Russian Orthodox Cathedral, 15 East 97th St. Built in 1902; traditional Russian Orthodox.
Temple Emanu-el, 840 Fifth Ave at East 65th St. Built in 1929, the world's largest Reform temple.
The Mosque of New York, Third Ave and East 96th St. New York's newest mosque, catering to all Muslims.

UPPER WEST SIDE

Riverside Church, 490 Riverside Drive at West 122nd St. Interdenominational; features the world's largest carillon and bell.
Islamic Center of New York, 1 Riverside Drive at West 72nd St. Muslim center.
Buddhist Church of New York, 332 Riverside Drive at West 105th St. Zen meditations are held here.
Cathedral of St John the Divine, Amsterdam Ave and West 112th St. The world's second-largest Gothic cathedral offers weekly concerts and special events, as well as religious services.

HARLEM

Canaan Baptist Church, 132 West 116th St. One of the best places to hear soul-stirring music.
Abyssinian Baptist Church, 132 West 138th St. Former church of Adam Clayton Powell, Jr and an integral part of Harlem's religious and political history.
Mother A.M.E. Zion Church, 140–146 West 137th St. The city's first African-American church, established in 1796.
St Philip's Episcopal Church, 208 West 134th St. Since 1818 has played a key role in the religious, political and economic life of the city's African-American community.

THE VILLAGES/LOWER MANHATTAN

Grace Church, 802 Broadway at East 10th St. Designed by James Renwick, this Gothic Revival Episcopal church was also the site of Tom Thumb's wedding in 1864.
John Street Methodist Church, 44 John St. The "mother church" of American Methodism, built in 1841.
Trinity Church, Broadway and Wall St. The city's oldest Episcopal parish (Alexander Hamilton is buried in the graveyard); frequent concerts and special events.

THE OUTER BOROUGHS

Friends Meeting House, 137–16 Northern Blvd, Flushing, Queens. The oldest house of worship in New York City, built in 1694.

Media

PRINT

The internationally known New York Times is the paper of choice for most well-informed readers, with its bulky Sunday edition listing virtually everything of consequence. On a daily basis, two tabloids compete for the rest of the audience: the New York Post, famed for its garish headlines and downmarket appeal;

and the *Daily News*, which until outsold (by the *Los Angeles Times* and *The New York Times*), boasted of having the largest daily circulation of any newspaper in America. The free weekly *Village Voice* has comprehensive listings and classified advertisements, as does the free *New York Press*. Respected local magazines include *New York*, the *New Yorker* and *Time Out* New York.

TELEVISION

The three major networks – all with New York headquarters – are **ABC**, 77 West 66th St, tel: 456 7777; **CBS**, 51 West 52nd St, tel: 975 4321; and **NBC**, 30 Rockefeller Plaza, tel: 664 4444. The **Public Broadcasting System** (PBS) can be found on channels 13 and 21 on the VHF band (for those without cable). The other three local stations are affiliated with the **Fox** (5), **UPN** (9) and the **WB** (11) networks and broadcast nationally aired shows as well as local programming. In addition, there are half a dozen UHF stations which broadcast in Spanish and other languages.

Various **cable companies** – at least four under the umbrella of Time Warner – offer 50 or more basic cable and movie channels, although the exact number differs from borough to borough. Most hotels offer cable in guest rooms as well as – for a fee – up-to-the-minute Hollywood movies. Some of the Manhattan public access TV programs (particularly late at night) are pretty sexually explicit, so you may want to put the kids to bed first before tuning in.

How to See a Television Show

With advance planning, you can join the audience of a New York-based TV show, many of them shown overseas. For full details, write to the NYC & Company Information Center or visit their website at www.nycvisit.com. Here's just a selection:

● *Late Show with David Letterman*
Tapings of this popular, wacky talk show are Mon–Fri at 5:30pm. Audience members must be 16 or older; proper ID required. Tickets must be requested six to eight months in advance by postcard, with standby tickets available on the day (not Friday) at 2.30pm from the box office.
Late Show Tickets, Ed Sullivan Theatre, 1697 Broadway, New York, NY 10019. Tel: 212-975 1003 or 975 2476.
www.cbs.com/navbar/home.html

● *NBC Today Show Through the Window*
Tapings of this early-morning show are Mon–Fri from 7–9am. An audience is welcome, but you will have to be there by 6am. Go to the kiosks at 30 Rockefeller Plaza.

NBC Today Show Tickets, 30 Rockefeller Plaza, New York, NY 10112. Tel: 212-664 4249.

● *Saturday Night Live*
Tapings of this venerable comedy show are on Saturday from 11.30pm–1am. Audience members must be 16 or older. A ticket lottery is held at the end of each August. Only one postcard per person sent in August will be accepted. Standby tickets available at 9:15am on the 49th St entrance, but do not guarantee admission.
NBC Tickets (as above). Tel: 212-664 4000; www.nbc.com.

NBC Studio Tour
To guarantee that you will at least see the studios of *Saturday Night Live*, the *Today Show* and other top TV programs (as long as they're not taping at the time) you could go on the NBC Studio Tour. Attractions include blue-screens to let you "join" presenters on the sets. The tours start at the NBC Experience Store at 30 Rockefeller Plaza, leaving every 15 minutes, 7 days a week (www.nbcsuper-store.com, tel: 664 7174, fee).

Telecommunications

Most Manhattan attractions have the established 212 telephone code, which has been in existence for decades; newer places might use the 646 or 917 prefix. Brooklyn, Queens, Staten Island and Bronx numbers are prefixed by 718 (or the newer 347 or 917).

Toll-free calls are prefixed by 1-800, 888 and 877; remember to dial 1 first when calling these numbers and when calling from one

area code to another. **Telephones** accepting credit cards can be found in various major centers, including Grand Central and Pennsylvania stations. For all calls, be sure you're using a phone owned by **Verizon**, not a private company, or you can be charged triple the normal cost. Most hotels also add on a hefty charge.

Most major hotels offer **fax services**; faxes can also be sent from many of the copy and printing shops around the city, as well as from the numerous branches of Kinko's (see phone book for locations), which offer computer access and **e-mail** for a fee.

E-mail can also be sent from most branches of Kinko's copy shops or from computers at the **Science, Industry and Business Library**, 188 Madison Ave at 34th St, tel: 592 7000; one-hour limit per day, by appointment.

Useful Numbers

● **International calls**, dial: 011 (the international access code), then the country code, city code and local number.
● **Directory help**, including toll-free numbers, dial: 411
● **Complaints**, dial: 811

● **Wrong number refunds**, dial: 211
● **Current time**, dial: 976 1616
● **Emergencies**, *see page 274*
● **AT&T**, 1-800-CALL ATT
● **Sprint**, 1-800 877 8000
● **MCI**, 1-888 757 6655

Postal Services

Manhattan's main post office (tel: 967 8585) on Eighth Ave between 31st and 33rd St is open 24 hours a day for stamps, express mail and certified mail.

Security and Crime

Despite its recent reputation as a "caring, sharing New York", parts of the city are still reasonably dangerous and visitors should not be lulled into any false sense of security. Miscreants whose lives are devoted to exploiting the unwary will be quick to seize advantage of your bewilderment, so adopt the typical New Yorker's guise of looking street-smart and aware at all times.

Ostentatious displays of jewelry or wealth invite muggers; foolhardy excursions into deserted regions at night (such as Central Park or Battery Park) are equally unwise. Lock your hotel door even when you are inside, and travel to places like Harlem in a group. And even though Times Square itself has thrown off its seedy mantle, the streets around it still attract loiterers and pickpockets.

Although the subways are much safer than they were, women traveling alone late at night should be on full alert. Once having passed through the turnstile, stay within sight – or at least within shouting

Emergencies

● **Police, fire** or **ambulance**, dial: 911.
● **Deaf Emergency Line**, tel: 1-800-421 1220 or TTY 1-800-662 1220 (police, fire, ambulance).
● **Physicians Home Care**, tel: 718-238 2100.
● **Dental emergency**, tel: 573 9502.
● **24-hour pharmacy**, CVS, 72nd St and Second Ave, tel: 249 5699.
● **Sex Crimes Report Line**, tel: 267 7273.
● **Alcoholics Hotline**, tel: 1-800 56 SOBER.
● **Suicide Prevention HelpLine**, tel: 532 2400.

range – of a token booth. When boarding, try to get on a carriage where there are other women. In emergencies, **dial 911 for police, fire or ambulance**.

POLICE PRECINCTS

Call for non-emergencies only.

Downtown
1st, 16 Ericsson Place (West Canal St). Tel: 334 0611.
5th, 19 Elizabeth St (Chinatown). Tel: 334 0711.
6th, 233 W. 10th St (Greenwich Village). Tel: 741 4811.

Hospitals with Emergency Rooms

Call **911** for an ambulance. (US medical services are expensive. Make sure you are insured.)

Midtown/Downtown
Bellevue Hospital, First Ave and East 27th St. Tel: 562 4141.
Beth Israel Medical Center, First Ave at East 16th St. Tel: 420 2840.
NYU Medical Center, 550 First Ave at 33rd St. Tel: 263 7300.
St Luke's-Roosevelt Hospital, 59th St. between Ninth and Tenth avenues. Tel: 523 6800.

St Vincent's Hospital, Seventh Avenue at 11th Street. Tel: 604 7000.

Uptown
Columbia Presbyterian Medical Center, 622 West 168th St. Tel: 305 2500.
Lenox Hill Hospital, 77th St and Park Ave. Tel: 434 2000.
Mount Sinai Hospital, Fifth Ave and East 100th St. Tel: 241 6500.
New York Hospital, 525 East 68th St. Tel: 746 5454.

7th, 19 Pitt St (Lower East Side). Tel: 477 7311.
9th, 321 E. 5th St. Tel: 477 7811.
10th, 230 W. 20th St. Tel: 741 8211.
13th, 230 E. 21st St. Tel: 477 7411.
17th, 167 E. 51st St. Tel: 826 3211.
Midtown South, 375 W. 35th St. Tel: 239 9811.
Midtown North, 524 W. 42nd St. Tel: 767 8400.

Uptown
19th, 153 E. 67th St. Tel: 452 0600.
20th, 120 W. 82nd St. Tel: 580 6411.
Central Park, Transverse Road at 86th St. Tel: 570 4820.
23rd, 162 E. 102nd St. Tel: 860 6411.
24th, 151 W. 100th St. Tel: 678 1811.
25th, 120 East 119th St. Tel: 860 6511.
26th, 520 West 126th St. Tel: 678 1311.
28th, 2271 Eighth Ave (near 123rd St). Tel: 678 1611.
30th, 451 W. 151st St. Tel: 690 8811.
32nd, 250 W. 135th St. Tel: 690 6311.
33rd, 2120 Amsterdam Ave. Tel: 927 3200.
34th, 4295 Broadway. Tel: 927 9711.

LOSS OF BELONGINGS

Your chances of retrieving lost property are not high, but the occasional public-spirited individual may turn items in to the nearest police precinct.

To inquire about items left on public transportation (**subway and bus**), tel: 712 4500, open Mon, Wed, Fri 8am–12pm, Thur 11am–6.45pm. For items left in **taxis**, tel: 302 TAXI (8294).

Lost or stolen credit cards
● **American Express**, tel: 1-800-528 4800.
● **Visa**, tel: 1-800-847 2911.
● **Carte Blanche/Diners Club**, tel: 1-800-234 6377.
● **MasterCard**, tel: 1-800-826 2181. All 1-800 calls are free of charge.

Getting Around

On Arrival

ORIENTATION

Most of the city's best known hotels, as well as offices, the Broadway theater district and major shops, are concentrated in the Midtown area, which runs from about 30th St north to Central Park at 60th St. Generally, avenues in Manhattan run north to south; streets run east to west. Even-numbered streets tend to have one-way eastbound traffic; odd-numbered streets, westbound traffic. There are very few exceptions. Most avenues are one-way, either north or south, the major exception being Park Avenue which is wide enough for two-way traffic north of 44th St.

Buses do not run on Park Avenue but do run on most other avenues, as well as on major cross-streets (also two-way): Houston, 14th, 23rd, 34th, 42nd, 57th, 66th, 86th, 116th, 125th and a few others. Subway trains cross town at 14th and 42nd St but there is no north–south line east of Lexington Ave or west of Eighth Ave and Broadway above 59th St.

RECOMMENDED MAPS

The NYC & Company's Visitor Information Center, 810 Seventh Ave at 53rd St, has a useful pull-out map in its *Official NYC Guide*, as well as a separate *Official NYC Map*. These can also be ordered (for a small fee) by calling 212-397 8222 or (US and Canada) 1-800-NYCVISIT.

Subway and bus maps are available at subway station booths, or from the New York City Transit Authority booth in Grand Central Terminal and the Long Island Rail Road information booth in Penn Station, as well as the MTA booth at the Times Square Visitors Center at 1560 Broadway. You can also request bus and subway maps by mail from New York Transit Authority Customer Assistance, 370 Jay St, Room 702, Brooklyn NY 11201 (with a self-addressed stamped envelope.)

Airport to City

AirTrain is an airport rail system that the Port Authority of New York and New Jersey has recently built connecting **JFK** and **Newark** airports with the region's existing rail transportation network. At all AirTrain rail link terminals, travelers are able to check their flight times and board AirTrain for a short ride to their airline terminals. AirTrain arrives every few minutes and is approximately 10 minutes from each airline terminal.

AirTrain JFK information:
tel: 1 718 244 4444 or go to www.airtrainjfk.com

AirTrain Newark information:
tel: 1-888 EWR INFO or www.airtrainnewark.com

The New York Airport Service operates **buses** from both **JFK** and **LaGuardia** airports to Manhattan drop-off points, including Grand Central Terminal. New Jersey Transit and Olympia Trails Coach Service operate regular express buses between **Newark** airport and Manhattan, the former to the Port Authority Bus Terminal at Eighth Ave and 41st St, the latter to Penn Station and Grand Central Terminal.

A **minibus** service from all three airports to many major Manhattan hotels is provided by **Gray Line Air Shuttle** (tel: 1-800-451 0455) at fares averaging $20. **Super Shuttle Blue Vans** (tel: 1-800-258 3826) offer a door-to-door transportation service at competitive prices. All of these can be booked at airport ground transportation centers or

Airport Taxis

Taxis are metered with a flat rate, plus tip, from JFK. The fare from LaGuardia is slightly lower, while the fare from Newark is slightly higher. Bridge and tunnel tolls are extra. Unsuspecting visitors straight off an airplane are often besieged by private taxi drivers offering rides into the city; the more naïve you look, the higher the price quoted. Most drivers are, in their own fashion, reputable enough – out to make a buck, not interfere with your life. But it can be unnerving traveling a little-known route with an unfamiliar, unregistered driver, even if you've negotiated a reasonable price. Unless you have great savvy and a keen sense of direction, stick to the official taxi stands.

from well-marked courtesy phones.

The **cheapest route** from JFK to the city is via Green Bus Lines to the Lefferts Boulevard subway station (from which A trains run to Brooklyn, lower Manhattan and the West Side) or to the Kew Gardens-Union Turnpike station (E and F trains to Queens and mid-Manhattan). From LaGuardia, the Triboro Coach Corporation operates the Q-33 bus to the 74th St subway station in Jackson Heights, Queens, from which various trains run to Manhattan. For information about this and other routes to and from airports, call 1-800 AIR RIDE.

Note that 12 airlines maintain a joint ticket office at the Satellite Airlines Terminal (125 Park Ave, tel: 986 0888) opposite Grand Central, which is also a drop-off and pick-up spot for airport buses

Public Transportation

SUBWAYS AND BUSES

Subways and buses run 24 hours, less frequently after midnight, with the fare payable by token or (buses only) exact change, as well as by MetroCard pass (available at subway ticket booths), which allows free transfers within two hours of use. Unlimited-ride passes good for seven or 30 days are also available, as is a day pass sold at newsstands, hotels and electronic kiosks in some subway stations. For **general bus and subway information** call: 718-330 1234; for details about the **MetroCard pass**, call 212-METROCARD (1-800-METROCARD from outside the city).

PATH (Port Authority Trans Hudson) trains run under the Hudson River from six stations in Manhattan to New Jersey, including Hoboken and Newark. The flat fare is very reasonable; for more information call 1-800-234 PATH.

TAXIS

Taxis, all metered, cruise the streets randomly and must be hailed, although there are official taxi stands at places like Grand Central Terminal. Be sure to flag down an official yellow cab, not an unlicensed gypsy cab.

One fare covers all passengers up to four (five in a few of the larger cabs). After 8pm there is a small surcharge on all taxi rides. Call 302 TAXI (8294) for lost property or to make a complaint.

Private Transportation

BY CAR

Driving around Manhattan is not much fun although, should the need arise, there is a generous range of firms available at all airports from which cars can be rented. In order to rent a car, you must be at least 21, have a valid driver's license and at least one major credit card.

Be sure that you are properly insured for both collision and liability. Insurance is not usually included in the base rental fee. Or, you may already be insured by your own insurance or credit card company. It is also a good idea to inquire about an unlimited mileage

Car Rental Companies

Alamo: US	1-800-327 9633	
International	+1-305-522 0000	
Avis: US	1-800-331 1212	
International	+1-918-664 4600	
Budget: US	1-800-527 0700	
International	+1-214-404 7600	
Dollar: US	1-800-800 4000	
International	+1-813-877 5507	
Enterprise: US	1-800-325 8007	
International	1-314-781 8232	
Hertz: US	1-800-654 3131	
International	+1-405-749 4424	
National: US	1-800-227 7368	
International	+1-612-830 2345	
Thrifty: US	1-800-331 4200	
International	+1-918-669 2499	

package. If you don't have one of these packages, you may well be charged extra per mile over a given number of miles.

Rental fees vary depending on the time of year, how far in advance you book, and if you travel on weekdays or weekends. Inquire about any discounts or benefits, including corporate, credit card or frequent-flyer programs.

BY LIMOUSINE

For the ultimate luxury in road transportation, contact one of the following private car companies for a limousine at your beck and call. These include:
● **Absolute Class**, tel: 227 6588; 1-800-546 6644.
● **Carey Limousine**, tel: 599 1122; 1-800-336 4646.
● **Smith Limousine**, tel: 247 0711.
● **Dav-El Limousines Inc.**, tel: 645 4242.
● **Gotham Limousines**, tel: 1-888-227 7997.

Where to Stay

The old adage that New York has more of everything than virtually anywhere on earth is only a slight exaggeration when it comes to hotel accommodations. The following list is hardly exhaustive, but rather represents a sampling of the best hotels in Manhattan in the moderate to luxury price range, plus a few inexpensive "characters."

When making reservations, ask specifically about special weekend or corporate rates and "package deals." Telephone reservations staff in America are notorious for quoting only the most expensive rates, but many hotels offer an ever-changing variety of discounts and promotions. You are well advised to book your room by credit card and secure a guaranteed late arrival, in the foreseeable circumstance that your flight is interminably stacked up over the airport or your 40-minute limo ride from the airport turns into a two-hour nightmare of traffic jams. New York City is the last place on earth

Discount Bookings

Because the average night's stay now hovers close to the $200 mark (and rooms at a few luxury hotels, such as the Peninsula and Four Seasons, cost at least $500 a night), it may also be helpful to use a **discount reservation service**, which sometimes provides rates cut by as much as half. Contact the NYC & Company Visitors Information Center for a list of reliable firms, or call Quikbook, tel: 1-800-789 9887; fax: 212-779 6120; www.quikbook.com; e-mail: info@quikbook.com.

you want to find yourself stranded without a hotel room.

In addition to standard hotels, we have included a short list of "suite hotels" and bed and breakfast accommodation services.

The former are basically apartments, available from a few nights, up to rates by the month. The latter are modeled on those in the UK and Europe. As with B&Bs everywhere, reservations should be made as far in advance as possible.

Be sure to specify if you want a room where smoking is allowed.

Hotels

MIDTOWN

The Algonquin, 59 West 44th St. Tel: 840 6800, 1-800-548 0345; fax: 944 1618. Once a haven for the Round Table (New York's version of the Bloomsbury literary set), still a favorite of the theater set, the Algonquin retains an atmosphere of sedate, oak-paneled charm. Clubby and Victorian in demeanor, civilized in its treatment of guests, and right in the heart of the Broadway theater district. **$$$$**

Comfort Inn Midtown, 129 West 46th St. Tel: 736 1600 or 790 2710, 1-800-567 7720; fax: 790 2760; www.applecorehotels.com. A reasonably priced hotel in the Apple Core Hotels range, this has a fine location not far from Times Square. Fairly small (80 rooms) and a recent, successful $2 million renovation means there are more than a couple of personal touches, like on-demand movies. All rooms are non-smoking. **$**

Drake SwissHotel, 440 Park Ave at 56th St. Tel: 421 0900, 1-800-372 5369; fax: 371 4190. A Swiss-owned model of decorum and efficiency, much favored by corporate executives for its clean, hushed, boardroom atmosphere. Very large and very comfortable rooms. **$$$$**

Hotel Inter-Continental, 111 East 48th St. Tel: 755 5900; fax: 644 0079. Opened in the 1920s as

The Barclay, this hotel blends executive-class efficiency with majestic spaces and a full range of pampering services. Public rooms include two fine restaurants, a clothier, and a luxury gift shop. **$$$$**

Hotel Iroquois, 49 West 44th St. Tel: 840 3080, 1-800-332 7220; fax: 827 0464. Built in the early 1900s, this once-shabby hotel has received a $10 million facelift and now offers upscale single, double and suite accommodations on the same block as the more expensive Algonquin and Royalton hotels. James Dean lived in room 83 (now renumbered as room 803) from

Price Categories

Price categories are based on the average cost of a double room for one night.

$$$$	=	$250 and up
$$$	=	$180 to $250
$$	=	$135 to $180
$	=	$135 and under

1951 to 1953. **$$$**

Hotel Pennsylvania, 401 Seventh Ave at 33rd St. Tel: 736 5000, 1-800-223 8585; fax: 502 8712. With 1,700 rooms, this large hotel is centrally located across from Madison Square Garden and Penn Station. Its range of packages makes it good value for the area, and few can compete with its history. Built in 1919 by the Pennsylvania Railroad, the building was designed by the renowned firm of McKim, Mead and White. The hotel's Cafe Rouge Ballroom played host to many of the Big Band era's greats, including Count Basie, Duke Ellington, and the Glenn Miller Orchestra – who immortalized the hotel and its phone number in the 1938 hit *Pennsylvania 6-5000*. It has had the same phone number ever since. **$–$$$**

Intercontinental Central Park South, 112 Central Park South. Tel: 757 1900, 1-800-WESTIN-1; fax: 757 9620. Formerly the Ritz-Carlton, and still tweedy, refined and plush

without being overdone, it's favored by the international corporate elite and Old Money. **$$$$**

La Quinta Manhattan, 17 West 32nd St. Tel: 736 1600 or 790 2705, 1-800-567 7720; fax: 563 4007 or 790 2760; www.applecorehotels.com. Like others in the Apple Core Hotels group, rates at this 176-room hotel, a short walk from Macy's and Madison Square Garden, are extremely reasonable, especially considering that the comfortable rooms come with such conveniences as data ports and voice mail. There's also a lobby café with entertainment, a restaurant with room service, and an open-air rooftop bar where music and snacks can be enjoyed in summer, along with views of the Empire State Building. **$**

New York Palace, 455 Madison Ave at 50th St. Tel: 888 7000, 1-800-NY-PALACE; fax: 303 6000. A grandiose monument to lavish, American-style pomp and excess. Appointed in a style that can only be called post-modern rococo – all gilt and marble and floral splashes – the Palace has a regime of flawlessly detailed service that can make the average guest feel like an imperial Pasha. In its brashly high-style way, it's a *very* New York experience. **$$$$**

New York Hilton and Towers, 1335 Avenue of the Americas. Tel: 586 7000, 1-800-HILTONS; fax: 315 1374. A typical Hilton: huge, modern, impersonal but consistent. **$$$**

Omni Berkshire Place, 21 East 52nd St. Tel: 753 5800, 1-800-THE-OMNI; fax: 754 5020. Although it's been acquired by the Omni chain, the Berkshire retains its old-fashioned grace and attention to personal services. Known by some frequent guests as "a junior Plaza," it's comfortable and comforting, a tastefully appointed oasis of calm right in the heart of the Midtown shopping and business bustle. **$$$$**

The Paramount, 235 West 46th St (between Broadway and Eighth Ave). Tel: 764 5500, 1-800-225 7474; fax: 354 5237. A New York fashion statement in the heart of Times Square (and one of former Studio 54 king – now hotel king – Ian Schrager's ever-growing roster of hotels). The Paramount's rooms and public spaces, designed by Philippe Starck, dazzle and amaze: amenities include beds with headboards made of reproductions of famous paintings, a fitness club, a supervised playroom for children, and The Whiskey, a trendsetting small bar. Rooms are also small, but well-equipped. **$$–$$$**

Le Parker Meridien, 118 West 57th St. Tel: 245 5000, 1-800-543 4300; fax: 708 7477. Part of the internationally known French chain: modern, airy, with an excellent restaurant, and health facilities that include a swimming pool. **$$$$**

Peninsula New York, 700 Fifth Ave at 55th St. Tel: 247 2200, 1-800-262 9467; fax: 903 3943. One of the city's most expensive hotels, where richly appointed rooms go for about $500 (slightly less with corporate rates). The hotel's health club and spa is truly luxurious. In a prime location on Fifth Ave. **$$$$**

Pickwick Arms Hotel, 230 East 51st St. Tel: 355 0300, 1-800-742 5945; fax: 1-800-PICKWICK. Rooms are about the size of a postage stamp at this popular budget hotel, which is on a pleasant tree-lined street across from a "pocket park". The least expensive rooms have shared baths. A short walk from the UN and other Midtown attractions; close to Second Avenue's strip of restaurants and Irish bars. **$**

The Plaza, Fifth Ave at 59th St. Tel: 759 3000, 1-800-759 3000; fax: 759 3167. Once of New York's grand hotels, the venerable Plaza underwent a loving renovation that restored its Edwardian-style decor to dazzling splendor. Rooms are furnished with fine antiques; the high ceilings decorated with charming murals; and the service as close to Old World elegance as you'll find in America. The Plaza also features the Oak Bar and the Edwardian Room, two of Old Money's favorite before-and-after theater spots. **$$$**

Regal UN Plaza, One United Nations Plaza (44th St. and First Ave). Tel: 758 1234, 1-800-222 8888; fax: 702 5051. The clientele for this modern establishment is obvious, although its location is inconvenient for some visitors. Others appreciate the busy atmosphere as United Nations representatives and staff bustle through the heroically proportioned lobby. Benefits to non-ambassadorial guests include rooms with views of the East River, and good fitness facilities that include a tennis court and a swimming pool. **$$$**

Renaissance New York, 714 Seventh Avenue. Tel: 765 7676, 1-800-682 5222; fax: 765 1962. A star of the recently improved and cleaned up Times Square, with 300-plus rooms, most of them featuring large-screen televisions, oversized bathtubs and other ample comforts. Very convenient for theaters, restaurants and Midtown businesses. **$$$$**

The Royalton, 44 West 44th St. Tel: 869 4400, 1-800-635 9013; fax: 869 8965. Another chic, ultra-exclusive and ultra-modern creation from Ian Schrager of Studio 54 fame. Every line and appointment from the lobby to the lavatories is as boldly, coldly futuristic as the set of a sci-fi film, complete with state-of-the-art video and stereo gadgetry. Yet the Royalton bends over backwards to provide the scurrying, "can-do" pampering expected by its clientele. Convenient to the theater district. **$$$$**

St Regis, 2 East 55th St. Tel: 753 4500, 1-800-759 7550; fax: 350 6900. A grand Edwardian wedding cake of a building, filigreed and charmingly muraled (by the likes of Maxfield Parrish). The St Regis is a magnet for somewhat older, moneyed guests who appreciate the ambiance of a more regal age than ours. The convenient location doesn't hurt, either. **$$$$**

The Sherry-Netherland, 781 Fifth Ave at 59th St. Tel: 355 2800; fax: 319 4306. An old-fashioned luxury hotel also redolent of a bygone era, with such a faithful club

of visitors that reservations must be made well in advance. Grandly expansive spaces, both public and in the 40 rooms and suites (the rest of the building is private apartments), with royal treatment to match. **$$$$**

Super-8 Hotel Times Square, 59 West 46th St. Tel: 719 2300, 1-800-567 7720; fax: 790 2760; www.applecorehotels.com. More reasonably priced lodging from the Apple Core Hotel group, especially considering this is geared for the business traveler. Located between 5th and 6th avenues, there's the usual on-demand movies and free local phone calls, plus a business center with computers and a fax, a conference room that seats 30 people and an 80-seat meeting room. **$–$$**

W New York, 541 Lexington Ave. Tel: 755 1200; fax: 319 8344. The flagship of a chain of upscale sybaritic hotels-as-spas, W's interior was designed by entertainment architect David Rockwell and features Zen-like rooms where grass actually grows on the windowsills and pastel quilts are inscribed with New Age-y aphorisms. There's a juice bar, an extensive spa with good fitness facilities, and a trend-setting restaurant called Heartbeat. **$$$–$$$$**

The Waldorf-Astoria, 50th St and Park Ave. Tel: 355 3000, 1-800-925 3673; fax: 872 7272. The most famous hotel in New York City during its gilded heyday in the 1930s and 1940s, with a sweeping pre-war panache that's been restored to something like its early glory. The grand look of the lobby and public spaces combines H.G.

Wells' heroic view of the future with Hollywood's Cecil B. DeMille's view of Cleopatra's Egypt, and the combination never fails to lift the visitor's spirits. Most of the rooms have a gracious, welcoming, old-world charm, and the central location is very convenient, not only to Midtown shopping, but to the theater and business districts as well. **$$$**

The Wyndham Hotel, 42 West 58th St. Tel: 753 3500, 1-800-257 1111; fax: 754 5638. A charming 1920s hotel (favored by some of the musicians performing at nearby Carnegie Hall) and known for its spacious rooms and extremely reasonable rates. Near Fifth Avenue shopping and Midtown restaurants, and only a short walk from leafy Central Park. **$$**

UPPER EAST SIDE

The Carlyle, 35 East 76th St. Tel: 744 1600, 1-800-227 5737; fax: 717 4682. Posh, reserved and serene in its elegance, The Carlyle remains one of the city's most highly acclaimed luxury hotels. The appointments are exquisite, the furnishings antique and the service tends to be on the formal side. Home of Café Carlyle and Bemelmans Bar, two of the city's most enduring and upscale evening spots. The Carlyle is a favorite with visiting royalty. **$$$$**

The Franklin, 164 East 87th St. Tel: 369 1000, 877-847 4444; fax: 369 8000. A bargain for the Upper East Side, this charming boutique hotel offers free parking, free breakfast, free coffee and dessert, and in-room movies guests can select from a library of classic films. Rooms tend to be small but beautifully equipped, and convenient for museums, shopping and Central Park. **$$–$$$**

The Pierre, 2 East 61st St. Tel: 838 8000, 1-800-743 7734; fax: 758 1615. Justly renowned as one of New York's finest hotels, with a fabulous pedigree of guests that goes back to its opening in the early 1930s. (It's now run by the Four

Seasons luxury chain.) The location on Fifth Avenue is perfect for those intent on business or Midtown shopping and there is also a lovely view of Central Park. Rooms are large and elegant; service is top flight; and dining in the Café Pierre or having afternoon tea in the beautiful Rotunda are among the city's most civilized experiences. **$$$$**

Hotel Wales, 1295 Madison Ave (at 92nd St). Tel: 876 6000, 1-800-428 5252; fax: 860 7000. The Wales was once known for its low rates and splendid views of Central Park. Today it costs more, but still offers a great location in the upmarket Carnegie Hill neighborhood, close to Museum Mile, chic restaurants and Central Park. You can feast on the best breakfast in New York next door at Sarabeth's Kitchen, or enjoy the complimentary light breakfast offered in the hotel's tea salon, also the setting for afternoon teas and chamber music concerts. **$$$**

UPPER WEST SIDE

Beacon Hotel, 2130 Broadway at 75th St. Tel: 787 1100, 1-800-572 4969; fax: 724 0839.

Suite Hotels

Manhattan East Suite Hotels. Tel: 465 3600, 1-800-ME-SUITE; fax: 465 3697; www.mesuite.com. The concept is akin to renting an apartment on a nightly, weekly, or monthly basis. Accommodations range from one-room without kitchen (but with refrigerator) to two-person studios and one- or two-bedroom suites with kitchens. More "homey" than a hotel, they may be ideal for experienced travelers or for families. Manhattan East operates more than 2,000 such suites at 10 locations from 31st St up to 76th St. **$$$**

The Marmara-Manhattan. 301 East 94th St. Tel: 427 3100, 1-800-621 9029; fax: 427 3042;

A well-located Upper West Side hotel within an apartment building, where rooms include kitchenettes with coffee-maker, full refrigerator, stove and sink. Suites, with a separate bedroom, can accommodate four. **$–$$**

Hotel Excelsior, 45 West 81st St. Tel: 362 9200, 1-800-368 4575; fax: 721 2994. An old-fashioned hotel dating from the 1920s, recently renovated, and located on a pleasant block between Central Park West and Columbus Ave shopping. **$$**

Malibu Hotel, 2688 Broadway. Tel: 663 0275, 1-800-647 2227; fax: 678 6842; www.malibuhotelnyc.com. At 103rd St, this budget hotel's compact and newly renovated rooms have cable TV, CD players, etc. The cheapest share bathrooms. As an added bonus, guests (mostly students and younger travelers) receive passes to popular nightclubs. **$**

The Milburn, 242 West 76th St. Tel: 362 1010; 1-800-833 9622; fax: 721 5476. A bargain 16-floor hotel with refurbished rooms that have TVs and kitchenettes; it also has a fitness facility. The Milburn is situated on a quiet side street within walking distance of Lincoln Center. **$**

www.marmara-manhattan.com. This luxury property targets business travelers on lengthy assignments (at least a month) and others in need of long-term, elegant studio or suite accommodations. Rates include breakfast buffets, and maid and laundry service. There's also a rooftop terrace with East Side views. **$–$$$**

Off Soho Suites, 11 Rivington St. Tel: 353 0860, 1-800-OFF SOHO; fax: 979 9800. Though geographically more Lower East Side than Soho, the suites here are clean and comfortable, and include TV and fully-equipped kitchens. Attracts a casual, mostly overseas clientele. **$**

Bed and Breakfasts

B&B Network of New York, 134 West 32nd St, Suite 602, New York, NY 10001. Tel: 645 8134.
City Lights Bed & Breakfast Ltd, Box 20355 Cherokee Station, New York NY 10021. Tel: 737 7049; fax: 535 2755. An agency that lists B&Bs as well as studios, suites, and short-term apartments in locations around the city.
Urban Ventures, 38 West 32nd St, Suite 412, New York NY 10001. Tel: 594 5650; fax: 947 9320.

MURRAY HILL/ GRAMERCY PARK/ CHELSEA

The Chelsea Hotel, 222 West 23rd St. Tel: 243 3700; fax: 675 5531. A red-brick, Victorian landmark of bohemian decadence, home to beatnik poets, then Warhol drag queens, then Sid Vicious, and now… some of all of the above. For some, a stay at the Chelsea can be part of a ritual pilgrimage to all that is hip Downtown, as redolent with arty history as West Village streets and Lower East Side clubs. Accommodations vary from a few inexpensive "student rooms" to suites. **$$–$$$**
Doral Park Avenue, 70 Park Ave at 38th St. Tel: 687 7050, 1-800-223 6725; fax: 973 2440. Cozy boutique-style hotel, in a convenient location near Midtown business, shopping and transportation. **$$$**
Gramercy Park Hotel, 2 Lexington Ave at 21st St. Tel: 475-4320, 1-800-221-4083, fax: 505 0535. Antique and genteel as a dowager princess, a little shabby but comfortable and agreeably moderate in price. The dimly lit, old-fashioned lobby bar is a favorite with visitors seeking a quiet place to relax after a hard day. Guests also have access to Gramercy Park itself, a private pocket of *fin de siècle* calm and greenery, where squirrels cavort in enormous old trees. **$$**

Inn at Irving Place, 56 Irving Place. Tel: 533 4600, 1-800-685 1447; fax: 533 4611. A pair of graceful townhouses transformed into a facsimile of a country inn, with a cozy fireplace-lit tea salon, and 12 elegant rooms and suites featuring four-poster beds. A two-block walk from Gramercy Park and a short distance from Union Square. There's a nice little restaurant on the Inn's lower level that provides guests with room service. **$$$$**
Morgans, 237 Madison Ave at 37th St. Tel: 686 0300, 1-800-334 3408; fax: 779 8352. The original brainchild of Ian Schrager and the late Steve Rubell, and, surprising for ultra trend-conscious New York, still one of the most fashionable temporary addresses in Manhattan; an ultra-exclusive, ultra-modern enclave for hip young movie stars and other millionaires. The decor's original stark grays have been replaced by warmer tones, but there's still a minimalist ambiance at work. Service is extraordinarily pampering; it is said there is *nothing* the staff won't do for guests. **$$$**
Quality Hotel East Side, 161

Price Categories

Price categories are based on the average cost of a double room for one night.

$$$$	=	$250 and up
$$$	=	$180 to $250
$$	=	$135 to $180
$	=	$135 and under

Lexington Ave at 30th St. Tel: 545 1800, 1-800-567 7720; fax: 481 7270 or 790 2760; www.applecorehotels.com. A cozily refurbished early-1900s hotel, with a friendly staff and 100 reasonably priced rooms, some with views of the Empire State Building. The location, within walking distance of Gramercy Park, Union Square and Midtown, is very convenient. **$**
The Roger Williams Hotel, 131 Madison Ave at 31st St. Tel: 448 7000, 888-448 7788; fax: 448

7007. Affordable style is the keynote of this sleek, stark "boutique hotel." A grand piano (and pianist) in the lobby greet new, afternoon arrivals; free cappuccino on tap; CD players and VCRs in each room all ensure a very Manhattan experience. Guests have been known to "network" after having met over breakfast, and the breakfast is included in the price. Penthouses have nice little balconies with great views of the Empire State Building. **$$$**
W The Court, 130 East 39th St. Tel: 685 1100, 1-800-223 6725; fax: 889 0287. Now part of the W chain *(see page 278)*, this small hotel in the Murray Hill area offers a prime location near Midtown business, shopping and transportation (including Grand Central Terminal). **$$$**

GREENWICH VILLAGE/ SOHO/ LITTLE ITALY

Holiday Inn Downtown, 138 Lafayette St. Tel: 966 8898, 1-800-HOLIDAY; fax: 966 3933. In a renovated historic building, this downtown hotel is much nicer than you might expect from an international chain hotel. **$$**
The Mercer Hotel, 147 Mercer St. Tel: 966 6060, 888-918 6060; fax: 965 3838. In the heart of Soho, a converted 1890s landmark building with 75 rooms that feature high loft ceilings, arched windows and (for New York) spacious bath facilities. Andre Balazs, the owner, also owns Chateau Marmont in LA, and the clientele here is similarly stylish. Facilities include a second-floor roof garden, a library bar with 24-hour food and drink service, and the acclaimed Mercer Kitchen restaurant. **$$$$**
The Soho Grand, 310 West Broadway. Tel: 965 3000, 1-800-965 3000; fax: 965 3200. A sophisticated yet totally comfortable 15-story addition to downtown Manhattan, with industrial-chic decor throughout,

and stunning upper-floor views. Service is excellent, and the lobby and bar is the rendezvous of choice for cool media types, music stars and others in town to see and be seen. As befits a place owned by the heir to the Hartz Mountain pet empire, pets are welcome (in rooms far from other guests who might be allergic). Exercise, grooming and feeding services are available – and if you arrive without an animal companion, the management will provide a complimentary bowl of friendly goldfish. **$$$$**
Washington Square Hotel, 103 Waverly Pl. Tel: 777 9515, 1-800-222 0418; fax: 979 8373. An almost century-old hotel that offers the perfect Village locale. The rooms are small but nicely appointed. In a former incarnation, this was the seedy Hotel Earle, where Papa John wrote the 1960s rock classic *California Dreaming*. **$**

LOWER MANHATTAN

Best Western Seaport Inn, 33 Peck Slip. Tel: 766 6600, 1-800-HOTEL-NY; fax: 766 6615. A block from South Street Seaport, this converted 19th-century warehouse has 72 rooms featuring Federalist-era antiques and modern amenities like VCRs and mini-fridges. Some rooms on the sixth floor have Jacuzzis and/or terraces with views of the Brooklyn Bridge. **$$**

Youth Hostels

New York International Youth Hostel, 891 Amsterdam Ave, at West 103rd St. Tel: 932 2300; fax: 932 2574. Accommodations in dormitory-style rooms range from $25–30 per person per night; $3 less for IYH members.

YMCAs also offer inexpensive accommodations, including:
YMCA-Vanderbilt, 224 East 47th St. Tel: 756 9600; fax: 752 0210. The best of four Ys in Manhattan, with recently modernized rooms that have cable TV and air conditioning, but only a few with private baths. Doubles from around $80.

Where to Eat

There are literally thousands of restaurants in New York, of all sizes, types, specialties and qualities. The following does not even begin to hint at an "exhaustive" list. We cite here some of the best, those we recommend with few or even no qualms at all – enough to keep any visitor happily dining for weeks. (A couple of places are mentioned mainly for their status as pilgrimage sites for tourists, and because to omit them would be an oversight.)

To the dismay of travel guide editors, restaurants bloom and fade, appear and disappear with startling abruptness. Changes in management, chefs or decor can, seemingly overnight, make or break a restaurant. We have tried to list consistent, long-running successes, but no one can issue guarantees.

In order to calculate the tip, most New Yorkers simply double the sales tax shown on the bill, leaving a tip of about 16 percent at the current rate *(see page 272)*. In restaurants with a "greeter," it is customary to leave an additional 5 percent. In most instances, we indicate which restaurants accept major credit cards, and others that accept only American Express or none at all. Your best bet is to ask when you call to make reservations.

Reservations are often necessary and almost always recommended; at the top of the line establishments, such as the Four Seasons and the River Café, they may be required as much as two weeks in advance. Of course, not all holders of reservations appear at their appointed hour, so you can take the chance of showing up without one. You may be forced to wait in line (or at the bar), which

can be a tedious experience, and doesn't necessarily add anything to the enjoyment of dining. Since some restaurants close on Sunday or Monday, and a few close altogether in August, it's even more important to call ahead of time.

Restaurants

Eating establishments of all types are mentioned throughout the main body of this book, but listed below is a selection of restaurants particularly worth seeking out. As a basic guideline, they've been divided into categories based on the *average* cost of dinner and a glass of wine, before tip. (Prices may be lower or higher, depending on what's ordered; some of the city's most expensive restaurants, for instance, offer *prix fixe* lunches that are relative bargains.)

Price Categories

Price categories based on the average cost of dinner and a glass of wine, before tip.

$$$$ = Top of the line $50 or more
$$$ = Upscale $35 to $50
$$ = Reasonable $25 to $35
$ = Inexpensive $25 or less

MIDTOWN

Top of the line $$$$
The Four Seasons, 99 East 52nd St. Tel: 754 9494. A Manhattan favorite, although the cuisine does not always live up to its reputation as one of *the* restaurants in New York. But the restaurant is remarkable, partly for its modern decor, all marble and copper and New York-style swagger. Partly it's the clientele in the famous Grill Room, cutting deals over their scotches and bourbons, and their New Orleans-style shrimp and meaty crab cakes. And partly it's the fantasy setting of the Pool Room, with its grand marble pool and palm trees. The menu changes with the seasons of the

year (hence the name) and is wildly eclectic, with the roast duck and grilled fish often cited as favorites. Popular, so make your reservations two weeks in advance. All major credit cards. **Le Bernardin**, 155 West 51st St. Tel: 489 1515. One of the city's most elite establishments, offering excellent dining for a clientele of powerful corporate and financial leaders. Known for the delicacy of its seafood, ranging from its pearly oyster and sea urchin appetizers, to its variety of fresh ocean catch which is then prepared in light wine sauces. The atmosphere and service are quite formal and a little aloof, which is somehow fitting; the hotel is more conducive to settling business than to romantic trysts. All major credit cards. Reservations are necessary.

Price Categories

Price categories based on the average cost of dinner and a glass of wine, before tip.

$$$$ = Top of the line $50 or more
$$$ = Upscale $35 to $50
$$ = Reasonable $25 to $35
$ = Inexpensive $25 or less

La Cote Basque, 60 West 55th St. Tel: 688 6525. More outstanding French cuisine in a lovely setting. The prices are high, but worth it. Well-located for theaters. Most major credit cards.
Le Cirque 2000, 455 Madison Ave, in the New York Palace Hotel. Tel: 303 7788. Extremely elegant French restaurant, with excellent cuisine, where New York social types hobnob. Make reservations as far in advance as possible. Major credit cards.
Le Perigord, 405 East 52nd St (between First Ave and the East River). Tel: 755 6244. A formal, old-world French restaurant with taste, staying power – and first-class, classic Gallic cuisine. All major credit cards. Reservations are required.

Lutece, 249 East 50th (between Second and Third avenues). Tel: 752 2225. Once considered New York's finest French restaurant, Lutece was sold by chef/owner Andre Soltner and is under new management. You'll still need to book in advance to dine in this pretty townhouse, however, but the atmosphere is intimate and friendly. Accepts major credit cards. *Prix-fixe* menus are available for lunch and dinner.

Upscale $$$

China Grill, 60 West 53rd St. Tel: 333 7788. Nouvelle-Oriental, in a spacious, dimly lit interior that stretches to the 54th St side of the CBS building. An extremely popular lunch and dinner hangout for media types. Major credit cards accepted.
Jezebel, 630 Ninth Ave at 45th St. Tel: 582 1045. Convenient to the theater district, this is one of the city's most atmospheric restaurants, with soul food served beneath fringed lamps and hanging antique lace dresses. Most major credit cards. Open late for dinner every night except Sunday. Reservations necessary.
The Palm, 837 Second Ave (between 44th and 45th streets). Tel: 687 2953. Sawdust on the floor, waiters who've been here at least a century, and steaks and more steaks are the hallmark of this former speakeasy. A bit pricey. Most major credit cards.
Smith & Wollensky, 201 East 49th St. Tel: 753 1530. Another bustling, efficient steakhouse where portions are gigantic. A good wine list here, too. Accepts all major credit cards. No lunch served on weekends.
Sparks Steakhouse, 210 East 46th St. Tel: 687 4855. The granddaddy of New York steakhouses, Sparks is burly, boisterous, and unabashedly American. Not for the painfully shy, but a great spot to see successful New Yorkers having fun the old-fashioned way: loud and fast, whether they're drinking whiskey and telling jokes at the smoky bar or consuming huge steaks cooked

to precision and placed between their elbows by the tirelessly brisk staff. Do not be misled by the high spirits, however: dinner is not particularly cheap, and reservations are needed. All major credit cards. Dinner till 11.30 on Friday and Saturday; closed Sunday.
San Domenico, 240 Central Park South. Tel: 265 5959. One of the most highly rated Italian restaurants in the city, this Central Park South establishment offers unusual Bolognese fare, with a wide variety of Northern Italian pastas and an extremely large wine list. A fine place to take a big party, but not necessarily for an intimate romantic meal. Reservations required. All major credit cards.
Sardi's, 234 West 44th St. Tel: 221 8440. Recommended more for sightseeing than its cuisine, this once-glamorous, now touristy Theater District bar and grill is again under its original ownership. Go for drinks, and to admire the celebrity caricatures hanging on the walls. Closed Sunday.
"21", 21 West 52nd St. Tel: 582 7200. A clubby playpen for the business and social elite that's been more or less restored to its former glory, with a new menu of classic American specialties. Reservations essential. All major credit cards.

Reasonable $$

Billy's, 948 First Ave at 52nd St. Tel: 753 1870. Checked tablecloths and old-timey waiters give this East Side neighborhood hangout, which opened in 1870, a "real New York" feeling. The menu includes specials like corned beef and cabbage; open seven days for lunch and dinner. All major credit cards.
Bryant Park Grill & Café, 25 West 40th St. Tel: 840 6500. Just around the corner from the entrance to the main Public Library at 42nd Street and Fifth Avenue, both indoor and (in warm weather) outdoor dining. American-style cuisine, with Continental flavor. Popular and usually crowded.
Café Centro, 200 Park Ave at 45th St. Tel: 818 1222. In the lobby of the MetLife Building, above Grand

Central Terminal, this is a popular and noisy place for lunch during the week; the dinner crowd is slightly quieter. The food is French/Continental – except in the adjacent Beer Bar, which has dozens of beers on tap and serves some of the best burgers in town. All major credit cards. No lunch on Saturday; closed Sunday.

Café Un Deux Trois, 123 West 44th St. Tel: 354 4148. A bustling before-and-after theater favorite, which features friendly service and French bistro-type fare in a former hotel lobby. A fun place. Open late, every day. Major credit cards.

Joe Allen, 326 West 46th St. Tel: 581 6464. A friendly, long-time Theater District favorite (with branches in London and Paris), where you might spot your favorite celebrity having meatloaf and mashed potatoes. The burgers are excellent. Open for lunch and dinner during the week; brunch and dinner on weekends.

Oyster Bar, lower level, Grand Central Terminal. Tel: 490 6650. A New York institution and a must for seafood lovers. The best fresh oysters and clam chowder in town, and you can sit at the counter or sit down in the dining room or salon. Accepts all major credit cards. Open during weekdays and evenings; closed weekends.

Rosa Mexicano, 1063 First Ave at 58th St. Tel: 753 7407. Also at 51 Columbus Ave at 62nd St. Tel: 77 7700. Perhaps the most authentic Mexican fare in New York, scarcely resembling the greasy, gloppy messes passed off on the unsuspecting by gringo cooks in so many South o' the Border theme restaurants. Start at the lively bar, with an excellent margarita. The traditional Mexican main courses are delivered with admirable restraint – this is *not* fire-breathing "Tex-Mex," though you can pepper it to taste. The professional and friendly staff are accustomed to explaining the finer points of the menu. Reservations are recommended. All major credit cards.

Inexpensive $

Carnegie Deli, 854 Seventh Ave at 55th St. Tel: 757 2245. A pilgrimage site in the heart of Midtown, this is one of New York's most famous Jewish delicatessens, where the corned beef sandwich is a must. Very crowded at lunchtime, but open from 6–4am every day. No credit cards.

Johnnie's, 135 West 45th St. Tel: 869 5565. Italian standards in an intimate setting. The *prix-fixe* dinners are a bargain. All major credit cards.

Siam Inn, 854 Eighth Ave, near 53rd St. Tel: 757 4006. Excellent Thai food, close to theaters and a short walk from Carnegie Hall and Midtown museums. Most credit cards accepted.

Stage Delicatessen, 834 Seventh Ave at 54th St. Tel: 245 7850. Another New York landmark deli, open since 1937, where the sandwiches are huge. As with the Carnegie Deli, service is legendary for its brusqueness (and part of the appeal). Major credit cards accepted. Open for breakfast, lunch, dinner and late-night noshing. No lunch served on Saturday.

UPPER EAST SIDE/UPPER WEST SIDE

Upscale $$$

Café des Artistes, 1 West 67th St, off Central Park West. Tel: 877 3500. Romance is in the air at this elegant French restaurant, decorated by murals of naked nymphs. All major credit cards. Open: Mon–Sat noon–midnight, Sun to 11pm. Reservations advised.

Café Luxembourg, 200 West 70th St. Tel: 873 7411. Well-established, once impossibly trendy Upper West Side eatery where the French-American menu has a definitive *nouvelle* slant – and the occasional local celebrity sighting makes for a satisfying night out. All major credit cards. Reservations required. Dinner, plus Sunday brunch.

Elaine's, 1703 Second Ave between 88th and 89th Streets. Tel: 534 8103. Mentioned mainly for its

celebrity-watching appeal – never mind the food, just check the stars.

Primavera, 1578 First Ave at 82nd St. Tel: 861 8608. Primavera attracts a tweedy, well-heeled crowd of Upper East Side regulars with its refined atmosphere similar to a private men's club. It is therefore a rather formal experience, which some visitors find soothing and others off-putting. The kitchen is best known for standard pasta entrées handled with a minimum of frills or fanciful gestures. It's rarely spectacular, but then spectacle would be frowned upon here. One pays to sup among the city's power brokers. Reservations essential. All major credit cards.

Tavern On The Green, Central Park West at 67th St. Tel: 873 3200. The Tavern is perhaps better known for its festive atmosphere and landmark tourist status than for its menu, though the mostly American specialties have greatly improved over the past few years. An enormous faux-palace sprawled among the greenery of Central Park, it has the lovably daffy scale and good-natured brio of an airport terminal designed by Lewis Carroll. (It is said to serve more dinners than any other restaurant in the US. Watch the dizzying bustle of waiters serving a few hundred tables and you'll believe it.) All major credit cards. Reservations recommended.

York Grill, 1690 York Ave between 88rd and 89th Streets. Tel: 772 0261. A congenial Upper East Side favorite, with a great fish and meat menu. Major credit cards accepted.

Smoking Zones

On March 30th, 2003, Mayor Bloomberg's smoking bill went into effect, banning smoking in bars, restaurants and nightclubs. There are a few exemptions, including existing cigar bars and some parts of sidewalk terraces. Cigarettes and the "city that never sleeps" have been immortalized in countless black-and-white movies; sadly, the Big Apple's jazz clubs will never be the same again.

Reasonable $$

Fujiyama Mama, 467 Columbus Ave, between West 82nd and 83rd streets. Tel: 769 1144. Upper West Side hangout with an eclectic Japanese menu, cool decor and loud music that attracts a lively young crowd. Reservations suggested. Most major credit cards.

Mme Romaine de Lyon, 132 East 61st St. Tel: 758 2422. Since 1932 (at various Upper East Side locations), serving more kinds of delicious omelettes than you ever imagined, most recently from this extremely pleasant bistro setting just around the corner from Bloomingdale's. Major credit cards accepted. Open for lunch and dinner daily.

Pamir, 1437 Second Ave between East 74th and 75th streets. Tel: 734 3791. This places serves some of the best Afghan cuisine in New York. (Also in Midtown, on First Avenue at 58th St.)

Parkview at the Boathouse, Central Park near 72nd St. Tel: 517 2233. Another tourist landmark, in a fabulous setting overlooking the Lake in Central Park, and recently renovated. In its previous incarnation the Parkview was open only in the summer; now you can dine year-round. The menu includes Asian-style seafood specialties. All major credit cards. Reservations suggested.

Sarabeth's, 1295 Madison Ave at East 92nd St. Tel: 410 7335. Bright, cheery and incredibly popular, best for its home-style breakfasts and brunch. Also at 945 Madison at 75th St, in the architecturally extravagant Whitney Museum, and at 423 Amsterdam Ave between 80 and 81st St on the Upper West Side. Tel: 496 6280.Major credit cards accepted.

HARLEM

Upscale $$$

The Terrace, 400 West 119th St. Tel: 666 9490. Located in Columbia University at Morningside Drive and better known for 1960s controversy than fine dining, this is a wonderful eagle's nest situated 14 stories above street level, with a magnificent view of the Hudson River and Manhattan's famous skyscrapers. At night one can almost forget to eat for ogling the beautiful lights. The atmosphere here is quite formal, so expect to dress up. The predominately French-Mediterranean cuisine is equally elegant. Major credit cards accepted. Reservations necessary. Closed Sunday and Monday.

Inexpensive $

Amy Ruth's, 113 West 116th St between Lenox and 7th Ave. Tel: 280 8779. Big portions of the classics: fried chicken, BBQ ribs, plus killer desserts. Or there's chicken and waffles for breakfast.

Copeland's, 547 West 145th St. Tel: 234 2356. A well-known favorite for Southern-style food, with a jazz brunch on Sundays.

Sylvia's, 328 Malcolm X Blvd (Lenox Ave). Tel: 996 0660. Hearty, home-cooked meals make this Harlem standby a popular pilgrimage site for Sunday brunch with a soulfood flavor.

Price Categories

Price categories based on the average cost of dinner and a glass of wine, before tip.

$$$$ = Top of the line $50 or more
$$$ = Upscale $35 to $50
$$ = Reasonable $25 to $35
$ = Inexpensive $25 or less

CHELSEA/GRAMERCY PARK/UNION SQUARE

Upscale $$$

Gramercy Tavern, 42 East 20th St. Tel: 477 0777. Creative American food in a comfortably rustic setting, with top-notch service. Reservations are necessary, but not in the less-expensive front room (where you can eat at the bar). All major credit cards.

Periyali, 35 West 20th St. Tel: 463 7890. A fine Greek restaurant in Chelsea. The long wooden bar and dining areas are appointed with an eye to spare lines and bare walls. The meals are similarly straightforward: the expected variations on lamb, moussaka, calamari, and baklava, all treated with a respect for natural tastes and subtleties. Service is friendly, the atmosphere casual but refined. Most major credit cards. Reservations required. Closed Sunday.

Union Square Café, 21 East 16th St. Tel: 243 4020. Possibly the friendliest service in New York and some of the best new-American cuisine anywhere. It can be hard to get a reservation at this very popular restaurant, where the innovative menu attracts a hip, appreciative crowd. Definitely call ahead – or take a chance that you'll be able to grab a spot at the bar. Most major credit cards. Open for lunch every day but Sunday; dinner served every night.

Reasonable $$

Chelsea Commons, 463 W 24th St (at 10th Ave). Tel: 929 9424. In front it's a downhome pub; in the middle room, a jazz piano bar; and out back, in season, one of the most delightful little courtyard bistros in Manhattan, with small trees dappling aged brick walls that shut out virtually all the noise, bustle and smells of the city. The mood is extraordinarily relaxed, to the point where you may have to wave vigorously to get your waiter's notice but in Manhattan, such pleasurable lethargy is a rare commodity. Kitchen open daily till 1am, bar till 4am.

Tello's, West 19th St. Tel: 691 8696. Popular both with locals and with Chelsea-spotting tourists, this cozy Italian features food like seafood-packed fettucini and fennel sausage. There's also brunch on Saturday and Sunday.

Inexpensive $

America, 9 East 18th St between Fifth Ave and Broadway. Tel: 505 2110. Huge. Noisy. Fun. With one of the largest selections of casual American food in the world, some of

which may remind you of the meals you once had in school cafeterias. A good place to bring the kids. Major credit cards. Open until midnight.
Lady Mendl's, Inn at Irving Place, 56 Irving Place. Tel: 533-4466. The perfect place for that perfect late-lunch alternative: afternoon tea – complete with scones, cakes and finger sandwiches.

THE VILLAGES

Upscale $$$
Da Silvano
260 Sixth Avenue, New York, NY 10012. Tel: 982 2343. Everyone's favorite restaurant – The A-list celebs are gluttons for the earthy Tuscan fare served in unpretentious surroundings by conservative waiters. Good for people-watching. Reservations recommended. All major credit cards.
Il Mulino, 86 West 3rd St between Thompson and Sullivan streets. Tel: 673 3783. The large portions, variety of pastas and almost smothering service make this Greenwich Village institution a favorite of New Yorkers, so reservations well in advance are essential. Come prepared to eat well; from the instant you sit down and are confronted with plates of cold meats and freshly baked breads, to the piping hot fusilli with truffles, to the stunningly thick veal chops.
Indochine, 430 Lafayette St. Tel: 505 5111. An excellent Vietnamese restaurant in Noho, not far from St Marks Place, with reliable food and a hip ambiance. Open late (dinner only) every day. Reservations necessary. Most major credit cards accepted.
Provence, 38 MacDougal St. Tel: 475 7500. A warm, romantic restaurant with southern French food. Very popular. Open for lunch and dinner daily.

Reasonable $$
The Grange Hall, 50 Commerce St. Tel: 924 5246. On a charming corner of the West Village, this is a good place to unwind after a long day of sightseeing. Casual, folksy ambiance and good regional American cuisine. Plus, a cool bar. Major credit cards.
Home, 20 Cornelia St, between Bleecker and West 4th streets. Tel: 243 9579. Very small, very simple, on the narrow ground floor of a Civil War-era townhouse, where the menu might include grilled New York State brook trout and garlic potato cakes with sautéed greens or corn meal fried rabbit with a side order of farm-grown vegetables. Ask to sit in the pretty garden in the back. Reservations recommended. Major credit cards.
Japonica, 100 University Place at 12th St. Tel: 243 7752. A fine, not-too-fancy downtown Japanese restaurant. Lunch and dinner daily.
Knickerbocker Bar and Grill, 33 University Place. Tel: 228 8490. A bar and restaurant that epitomizes New York; dark wood paneling, and – after 9.30pm – cool, traditional jazz. A great place for steak or just a burger. All major credit cards. Lunch and dinner daily.
Taka, 61 Grove St. Tel: 242 3699. A tiny, often busy, and very authentic Japanese sushi and sashimi restaurant in the West Village. Dinner only; closed Monday. Major credit cards accepted.

Inexpensive $
Cedar Tavern, 82 University Pl., between 11th and 12th streets. Tel: 929 9089. Once famous as a hangout for poets and Abstract Expressionist painters, this dark yet chummy restaurant-pub is still a favorite with downtown New Yorkers. Regulars are a diverse lot: business people, office workers, students and professors from nearby NYU. The carved bar from which it derives its name features pints of Guinness and fine bartenders. A large back room and smaller rooftop terrace serve hearty American grub such as hamburgers and roast beef sandwiches. A great spot to withdraw from the city's hurly-burly and relax. Most major credit cards. Kitchen generally open until 2-3.30am; bar until 4am.

Florent, 69 Gansevoort St, near Greenwich St. Tel: 989 5779. Situated deep in the heart of the meat-packing district, this stainless-steel café serves everything from *escargot* to onion soup. Attracts an extremely eclectic clientele, especially in the early morning hours. Open 24 hours on weekends, until 5am Mon–Thur. No credit cards.
Two Boots, 37 Ave A, between 2nd and 3rd streets. Tel: 505 2276. An East Village favorite for Cajun-style pizza, with several branches around the Village; all stay open late. Offers good value and a fun, casual atmosphere. Open for dinner every night, and brunch on weekends only.

SOHO/LITTLE ITALY/ CHINATOWN/ LOWER EAST SIDE

Upscale $$$
Raoul's, 180 Prince St. Tel: 966 3518. A sleek, dark French bistro in Soho, elegant and eternally trendy, with a satisfying menu and famous fellow diners to ogle at. Most major credit cards. Reservations suggested.

Reasonable $$
Canton, 45 Division St, near the Bowery. Tel: 226 4441. A pleasant, midsize space patrolled by a polite staff. Best known for seafood, it's expensive by Chinatown standards; be sure to ask the price of any seasonal dishes before ordering. No credit cards.
Le Jardin Bistro, 25 Cleveland Place, near Spring St. Tel: 343 9599. A fine French restaurant, located just east of Soho, with a pristine back garden that is open during the summer months and has a romantic, leafy arbor of grapevines. The cassoulet, bouillabaisse and steak frites are especially good, as is the wine list. Major credit cards accepted.
Il Palazzo, 151 Mulberry St. Tel: 343 7000. Civilized and untouristy. The food is delicious and so is the tranquil back garden in Little Italy.

Inexpensive $

Broome Street Bar, 363 West Broadway at Broome St. Tel: 925 2086. When you've had enough of the stylish snobberies and outrageous prices of Soho, nip over to this old-timey pub-restaurant and relax. It's not exactly a hideaway, and when hordes of shoppers descend on weekends, it can catch the overflow. But mid-afternoon through early evening on weekdays, it's a relatively quiet treat, with a well-stocked bar and a large number of tables where you can loll over American-style pub grub (burgers, quiche, thick Reuben sandwiches of corned beef and sauerkraut). Open daily until 11pm or so.

Price Categories

Price categories based on the average cost of dinner and a glass of wine, before tip.

$$$$ = Top of the line $50 or more
$$$ = Upscale $35 to $50
$$ = Reasonable $25 to $35
$ = Inexpensive $25 or less

Ear Inn, 326 Spring St, between Greenwich and Washington streets. Tel: 226 9060. Tucked in the far-west corner of Soho, this small, dark bar and restaurant in a landmark 1817 house is a casual, funky spot for good pub meals and, sometimes, live music.
Excellent Dumpling House, 111 Lafayette (just below Canal St). Tel: 219 0212. Unpretentious, unadorned and on the outskirts of Chinatown proper; always packed with locals and devoted visitors who love its no-nonsense atmosphere, reasonable prices, and stellar dumplings (especially the vegetable dumplings, steamed or fried). No reservations, but there's sometimes a short wait; best for mid-afternoon lunch. No credit cards.
Katz's Deli, 205 East Houston St at Ludlow St. Tel: 254 2246. An authentic Lower East Side delicatessen, which means no fancy decor, grumpy waiters, and

enormous corned beef sandwiches. Try it for lunch, between 11am and 4pm. No credit cards.
Thailand, 106 Bayard St. Tel: 349 3132. One of the early pioneers of Thai food in New York, and still good, if somewhat lacking in atmosphere. They'll spice your meal extra-hot if you ask; a specialty is the frog sautéed with garlic sauce. The shrimp and chili salads and the coconut curries are also winners. Order a premium Singha Beer to cool you down. Major credit cards accepted. Lunch and dinner daily.

TRIBECA/ FINANCIAL DISTRICT

Top of the Line $$$$

Chanterelle, 2 Harrison St, at Hudson St. Tel: 966 6960. A highly regarded restaurant in Tribeca, noted for its exquisite nouvelle American creations. Reservations essential. *Prix-fixe* menu only; dinner Tues–Sat.
Nobu, 105 Hudson St at Franklin St. Tel: 219 0500. With its decor of birch trees and stone walls, and innovative Japanese-style cuisine, this Tribeca restaurant is a favorite special-occasion splurge. Major credit cards accepted; reservations are essential.

Upscale $$$

Montrachet, 239 West Broadway (below Canal). Tel: 219 2777. Another very elegant, expensive restaurant. Light and inventive nouvelle French cuisine and professional service warm up the somewhat frigid attitudes of the "Beautiful People" who frequent this spot. Make reservations. American Express only. Dinner Mon–Sat; open for lunch Fri.
Tribeca Grill, 375 Greenwich St at Franklin St. Tel: 941 3900. Robert DeNiro's trendy place-to-be-seen, serving upscale drinks and bistro fare. Reservations recommended.

Reasonable $$

El Teddy's, 219 West Broadway, between Franklin and White streets. Tel: 941 7070. The exterior of this

Tribeca landmark features the Statue of Liberty sinking behind its facade; the interior looks like a Salvador Dali peyote dream. But it's the inventive nouvelle Mexican cuisine: softshell crab tacos, steak and salsa burritos, and gigantic, salty margaritas that consistently lures a downtown mix of Wall Streeters, art dealers and well-heeled tourists. Most credit cards (but not Diner's Club) accepted.
Odeon, 145 West Broadway, between Duane and Thomas streets. Tel: 233 0507. French-American bistro fare in a converted luncheonette that's been packing in late-night (and earlier) crowds since the early 1980s. Still hip after all these years. Most major credit cards.

Inexpensive $

Bubby's Restaurant, 120 Hudson St, at North Moore St. Tel: 219 0666. Since its beginning as a pie company in the 1980s, Bubby's has grown to become downtown Manhattan's favorite weekend brunch spot. Expect to wait in line, or come for lunch or dinner, when you can wait at the friendly little bar. The food is basic Americana and comes in ample portions. Most major credit cards accepted.
Walker's, 16 N Moore St (Varick St). Tel: 941 0142. Old New York feel in trendy Tribeca. Great for burgers and very unpretentious.

THE OUTER BOROUGHS

Top of the Line $$$$

The River Café, 1 Water St. Tel: 718-522 5200. Make your reservations at least two weeks ahead, because this barge, situated on the East River at the Brooklyn end of the Brooklyn Bridge, is justly famous for its spectacular view of lower Manhattan's skyscrapers. The superior American cuisine (steak and seafood, with fanciful desserts) lives up to its setting. New York rarely feels so romantic and beautiful as during a sunset dinner here. All major credit cards. Open for lunch on weekdays, brunch on Sunday and dinner every night.

Upscale $$$

Peter Luger, 178 Broadway. Tel: 718-387 7400. A Brooklyn landmark, near the Williamsburg Bridge. Preserving a gaslight-era charm, this family-run establishment has been in operation since 1887 – ancient history by US standards. Steak, steak and more steak is the heart of the simple menu. Exposed wood beams, a smoky bar, and a clientele in which downhome Brooklynites rub elbows with business types from "The City" make for a loose, sometimes loud, and genuinely fun time. Reservations suggested. No credit cards.

Water's Edge, 44th Drive at the East River. Tel: 718-482 0033. With a sweeping view of the Manhattan skyline, this Long Island City (Queens) restaurant is another spot for splurging. The cuisine includes plenty of ocean catches like salmon and sole, all handled with flair. Free water-taxi service provided from East 34th St. Diners Club and American Express only. Reservations required. Lunch, dinner and Sunday brunch.

Reasonable/Inexpensive $$–$

Aesop's Tables, 1233 Bay St, in Rosebank. Tel: 718-720 2005. A small Staten Island restaurant where the menu tends towards seafood, with a Mediterranean touch. Book before you take a trip on the ferry. All major credit cards accepted. Closed Sunday.

Dominick's, 2335 Arthur Ave. Tel: 718-733 2807. Take a hike to the Bronx for this old-fashioned Italian eatery, where you share tables with other diners. No menu, no credit cards. A true New York experience.

Elias Corner, 24-02 31st St, at Astoria Blvd. Tel: 718-932 1510. A Greek taverna in Queens, with fish the main specialty. Expect to wait for a table. No menus, no credit cards here either, but great food.

Culture

Dance

Numerous renowned dance troupes are based in the city, including the Martha Graham Dance Company, Paul Taylor Dance Company, Alvin Ailey American Dance Theater and the Dance Theater of Harlem.

Performance venues include:

Aaron Davis Hall, City College, 138 Convent Ave. Tel: 650 7148.

Brooklyn Academy of Music, 30 Lafayette Ave, Brooklyn, tel: 718-636 4100.

City Center, 131 West 55th St. Tel: 581 1212.

Cunningham Studio, 55 Bethune St. Tel: 691 9751.

Danspace Project, St Mark's Church, Second Ave at East 10th St. Tel: 674 8194.

Dance Theater Workshop, 219 West 19th St. Tel: 924 0077.

The Joyce Theater, 175 Eighth Ave. Tel: 242 0800.

The Joyce Soho, 155 Mercer St. Tel: 431 9233.

Wave Hill, 249th St and Independence Ave, Riverdale, the Bronx. Tel: 718-549 3200. Beautiful spot with outdoor, site-specific performances (summer only).

Art Galleries

There are well over 400 art galleries in the Naked City, in various neighborhoods – in **Midtown** along 57th St between Sixth Ave and Park Ave, on the **Upper East Side** along upper Madison Ave, in **Chelsea** (particularly around West 22nd and West 24th streets near Tenth Ave), in the **Meatpacking District** around 13th and 14th streets between Tenth Avenue and the West Side

Highway and, of course, in **Soho**.

Some of Soho's best-known galleries have closed or moved to Chelsea (**Paula Cooper, Sonnabend, Gagosian, Sean Kelly, Center for Book Arts**) while others have fled to the more traditional environs of 57th St or Fifth Ave (**Mary Boone, Pace Wildenstein**). Many emerging artists have already fled to Brooklyn or Queens.

But despite its transformation into a shopping and dining mecca for the rich, the beautiful and the cheekboned, Soho is still home to close to 200 galleries, with a few of the major ones still on West Broadway (**O.K. Harris, Vorpal**, the **Dia Center for the Arts**) and others on adjoining streets such as Greene (**Phyllis Kind, Sperone Westwater**); Prince (**Louis K. Meisel**); Wooster (**Brooke Alexander, Tony Shafrazi**); Broome (**P.P.O.W.**); and along lower Broadway (**Thread Waxing Space, Exit Art**).

As with restaurants and clubs, galleries spring up overnight and disappear just as quickly. True art fans should consult the listings in weekly magazines like *New York* or *Time Out*, as well as the art section of *The New York Times* on Friday and Sunday. Or head down to Soho, where most galleries have free guides listing shows around town.

It's also worth checking out the following places, most of which have some sort of artist participation:

AIR, 40 Wooster St. A women's art collective.

Artists Space, 38 Greene St. New trends, new artists, also visual screenings and performance art.

New Museum of Contemporary Art, 583 Broadway. Video installations, sculpture and other works.

Printed Matter, 77 Wooster St. Books on, by and for artists.

P.S. 1 Contemporary Art Center, 22–25 Jackson Ave, at 46th Ave, Long Island City, Queens. Tel: 718-784 2084. Up-and-coming artists, multi-media installations, and much more.

White Columns, 320 West 13th St (entrance on Horatio St), in the West Village.

Photography

A score of galleries around Manhattan are devoted to photography, including:
Camera Club of New York, 853 Broadway. Tel: 260 7077.
Greenberg Gallery, 120 Wooster St. Tel: 334 0010.
PaceWildensteinMacGill, 32 East 57th St. Tel: 759 7999.
Witkin, 415 West Broadway. Tel: 925 5510.
The International Center of Photography, 1133 Sixth Ave, tel: 768 4682.

Multi-Media

Performance art, multi-media presentations and various uncategorizable events are held at spots around the city, including:
Dia Center for the Arts, 548 West 22nd St. Tel: 989 5566.
The Kitchen, 512 West 19th St. Tel: 255 5793.
La Mama, 74A East 4th St. Tel: 475 7710.
P.S. 122, 150 First Ave. Tel: 477 5288.
Symphony Space, 2537 Broadway (at 95th St). Tel: 864 5400.

Museums

There are over 150 museums in New York City, from world-renowned palaces of art to small, local establishments with quirky subject matter and appeal. Opening hours change depending on season; check out local publications or the Friday and Sunday arts sections of *The New York Times* before visiting. Or pick up a copy of the *Museums New York* guide, sold in bookstores and at some newsstands, which includes free tickets and discount coupons and also lists current shows as well as times. Major museums usually charge an admission fee; some of the smaller ones do not.

The largest group of important museums are located within easy walking distance of each other along upper **Fifth Avenue's "Museum Mile"** and on adjacent **Madison Avenue**. Some of them offer free admission on Tuesday or other evenings and most offer a discount to students and senior citizens.

Concert Halls

Lincoln Center for the Performing Arts, on Broadway, between 62nd and 66th St, is the city's pre-eminent cultural center. It's home to America's oldest orchestra, the New York Philharmonic, which gives 200 concerts annually in **Avery Fisher Hall**, while nearby **Alice Tully Hall** houses the Center's Chamber Music Society. The New York City Opera and New York City Ballet perform at different times in the **New York State Theater**. Also in this complex are the **Metropolitan Opera House**, home of the Metropolitan Opera Company and, in spring, the American Ballet Theater; the excellent **Vivian Beaumont Theater**, the **Mitzi E. Newhouse Theater**, and the **Walter Reade Theater** (where the New York Film Festival is held); the **Julliard School of Music**, and an excellent **reference library** of music and the arts. Tours of Lincoln Center are offered daily between 10am and 5pm; for details, call 875 5350. For information about current performances, call 546 2656.

New York's oldest joke concerns the tourist who asks how to get to **Carnegie Hall** and is told "Practice, practice." It's far quicker to take the N or R subway to 57th St and walk to Seventh Ave or catch a crosstown 57th St bus to this century-old hall, where the world's greatest performers have appeared. For information, call 247 7800.

Venues for classical (and other) music also include **Town Hall**, 123 West 43rd St, tel: 840 2824; **Merkin Concert Hall**, 129 West 67th St, tel: 362 8719; the **Kaye Playhouse**, 695 Park Ave at 68th St, tel: 772 4448; **Brooklyn Center for the Performing Arts**, Brooklyn College, tel: 718-951 4500; and the **Brooklyn Academy of Music (BAM)**, 30 Lafayette Ave, Brooklyn, tel: 718-636 4100.

Poetry Readings

Numerous readings take place, typically in bookstores, cafés and churches. Here are some leads, but always check first.
● **Housing Works Used Books Café**, 126 Crosby St. Tel: 334 3324.
● **92nd Street YM-YWHA**, 1395 Lexington Ave. Tel: 415 5500.
● **New York Public Library**, Fifth Ave and 42nd St. Tel: 930 0855.
● **Nuyorican Poets Café**, 236 East 3rd St. Tel: 505 8183.
● **Poetry Society of America**, 15 Gramercy Park. Tel: 254-9628.
● **St Mark's Church Poetry Project**, Second Ave and East 10th St. Tel: 674 0910.

Soho's Party Past

Once upon a time, in the mid-1970s, it was possible to wander down to Soho on your first Saturday in New York, get into conversation with one of the habitués at any gallery opening and find yourself in the evening at the best party of your life.

When the area first saw a major influx of artists decades ago, they came because the decline in the area's light manufacturing meant that large spaces were virtually going begging – perfect for conversion into artists' lofts and studios, and cheap too. Weekend partying became endemic; and the unspoken rule was that if you heard about a party you were invited. Back then, it was commonplace to climb three flights of stairs on Greene Street and find yourself among three or four hundred revelers. The dedicated "party circuit" pioneers used to meet in Fanelli's or the Broome Street Bar early on Saturday evening to swap addresses.

Opera

In addition to the grand-scale performances of the New York City Opera and the Metropolitan Opera at Lincoln Center, opera can be enjoyed at cozier venues, including: **Amato Opera Company Theatre**, 319 Bowery. Tel: 228 8200. **DiCapo Opera Theater**, 184 East 76th St. Tel: 288 9438.

Contemporary Music

Apollo Theater, 253 West 125th St. Tel: 749 5838.
Beacon Theater, Broadway at 74th St. Tel: 496 7070.
Madison Square Garden, Seventh Ave, between 31st and 33rd Streets. Tel: 465 6000 or 465 6741.
Radio City Music Hall, Sixth Ave and 50th St. Tel: 247 4777.
Symphony Space, 2537 Broadway. Tel: 864 5400.
Town Hall, 123 West 43rd St. Tel: 840 2824.
And just out of town at:
Continental Airlines Arena, The Meadowlands, East Rutherford, New Jersey. Tel: 201-935 3900.
Nassau Coliseum, Uniondale, Long Island. Tel: 516-794 9300.

Movies

Movie theaters are dotted all over town, with first-run films often shown at cinemas in Midtown, in the East 50s and 60s, on East 34th St near Third Ave, and in Greenwich Village. The city's daily newspapers, weekly papers and color magazines carry complete listings, as well as, usually, the performance times.

There are at least a score of venues that are devoted to showing revival, cult, experimental and genre films, including the **French Institute**, 55 East 59th St, tel: 343 2675, and the **Japan Society**, 333 East 47th St, tel: 832 1155, which specialize in foreign-language showings. Places such as **Anthology Film Archives**, 32 Second Ave, tel: 505 5181; **Cinema Village**, 22 East 12th St, tel: 924 3363; and the **Film Forum**, 209 West Houston St, tel: 727 8110, all show films of a special nature.

Independent and foreign films are a specialty at the BAM **Rose Cinemas** at the Brooklyn Academy of Music, 30 Lafayette Ave, Brooklyn, tel: 718-623 2770, and at the **Walter Reade Theater** at Lincoln Center, tel: 875 5600, where the annual New York Film Festival takes place every fall.

Rarely seen movies or obscure directors are featured at the **American Museum of the Moving Image** in Queens, tel: 718-784 0077,and the **Museum of Modern Art**, tel: 708 9400.

Dinner (or brunch) and a movie are offered in one setting at the **Screening Room**, 54 Varick St, tel: 334 2100. During the summer **Bryant Park**, behind the Public Library at 42nd St, shows free outdoor movies; call 512 5700 for a current schedule.

Theater

Very few Broadway theaters are actually on Broadway. The alternative to Broadway is off-Broadway, where performances scarcely differ in quality from the former category, although they are performed in smaller theaters. The vast majority of off-Broadway theaters, and indeed, the more experimental off-off-Broadway theaters, are Downtown – particularly in the East Village area. Here you'll find the influential **Joseph Papp Public Theater**, a complex of several theaters in one building at 425 Lafayette St. Tel: 260 2400. The **Theater for the New City** at 155 First Ave, tel: 254 1109 and **LaMama E.T.C.**, 74A East 4th St, tel: 475 7710, are both nearby and show new work by experimental theater artists.

Interesting off-Broadway productions can also be found around Union Square; in Soho; and in the West Village, including the **Lucille Lortel Theater**, 121 Christopher St, tel: 239 6200, and the **Cherry Lane Theater**, 38 Commerce St, tel: 727 3673. Near Times Square, the group of off Broadway theaters on West 42nd St between Ninth and Tenth avenues are known as **Theater Row**, of which the best-known is probably **Playwrights Horizons**, tel: 279 4200. On the Upper West Side the **Promenade Theater**, 2162 Broadway at 76th St, tel: 580 1313 is a fine venue.

The New York Times offers good listings (as do *The New Yorker* and *New York* magazines; these are worth checking regularly. A useful telephone number for ticket prices, availability and/or information about current shows are NYC/On Stage, tel: 768 1818, www.TDS.org.

Buying Broadway Tickets

The TKTS **booth**, at Broadway and 47th St, just north of Times Square, has discounted seats (25-50 percent off) for that night's performances. It is open Monday through Saturday 3pm to 8pm for evening performances; Saturday and Wednesday 10am to 2pm for matinees, and Sunday 11am to 7pm for matinees and evening shows. There is another booth at 186 Front Street near the South Street Seaport in Lower Manhattan. Lines form early and are long, so take a book to read. Tip: there tend to be fewer people waiting at the booth in Lower Manhattan. TKTS booths do not accept credit cards, so be sure to take traveler's checks or cash.

● Unsold tickets can often be purchased at theater box offices an hour or so before show time.
● There are also numerous (expensive) ticket brokers, many of whom can be contacted via hotel concierges.
● A useful website to visit for the latest theater information is www.theatredirect.com

Events

It's just possible that there may be somebody somewhere who comes to New York for a rest. But it's certainly the least likely place to choose because in The Big Apple there's something happening 24 hours, every day of the year.

A calendar of events is included in the *Official NYC Guide* published by the NYC & Company & Visitors Information Center, 810 Seventh Ave, New York, NY, 10019, tel: 397 8222; 809-NYCVISIT. Information is also available online at www.nycvisit.com, or call 484 1222 when you arrive.

JANUARY

National Boat Show, Javits Convention Center.
Outsider Art Fair, Puck Building, Lafayette St.
Winter Antiques Show, 7th Regiment Armory, Park Avenue.

FEBRUARY

Black History Month.
Chinese New Year Celebration in Chinatown (sometimes Jan).
Westminster Kennel Club Dog Show, Madison Square Garden.
The Art Show, 7th Regiment Armory, Park Avenue.
Empire State Building Run-Up race.

MARCH

New York City Opera (through April), Lincoln Center.
Artexpo New York, Javits Convention Center

International Cat Show, Madison Square Garden (sometimes Feb).
St Patrick's Day Parade Fifth Avenue.
Greek Independence Day Parade.
Greater New York Orchid Show, World Financial Center.
Circus Animal Walk, Ringling Brothers, Barnum & Bailey Circus, Queens Midtown Tunnel.
New Directors Film Festival. Museum of Modern Art.
Whitney Biennial exhibition, Whitney Museum.

APRIL

New York Yankees baseball season begins.
American Ballet Theater (to June) at Lincoln Center.
Easter Parade on Fifth Avenue.
Cherry Blossom Festival at Brooklyn Botanic Garden (sometimes May).
Macy's Spring Flower Show.
Greater New York International Auto Show, Javits Convention Center.

MAY

New York beaches open.
Belmont Racetrack opens.
New York City Ballet (to June) at Lincoln Center.
Great Five Borough Bike Tour Race & Festival, Staten Island.
Ninth Avenue International Food Festival.
Martin Luther King Jr Day Parade, Fifth Avenue.
Salute to Israel Parade, Fifth Ave.
Ukrainian Festival, 7th St and Second Avenue.
Fleet Week, Intrepid Sea-Air-Space Museum.
Washington Square Art Show.
Memorial Day Parade, Fifth Avenue.

JUNE

Free Metropolitan Opera performances in parks of all five boroughs (through August).
Central Park Summer Stage shows (through Aug), Rumsey Playfield, Central Park.

Midsummer Night Swing dancing at Lincoln Center (through July).
JVC Jazz Festival throughout the city.
Feast of St Anthony, Little Italy.
Puerto Rican Day Parade, Fifth Avenue.
Buskers Fare Festival, Lower Manhattan.
Mermaid Parade, Coney Island, Brooklyn.
Gay and Lesbian Pride Day Parade, Fifth Avenue.

JULY

Free New York Philharmonic concerts in major parks. Free concerts at South Street Seaport.
Museum of Modern Art Summergarden concerts.
Mostly Mozart Festival (to Aug) at Lincoln Center.
Macy's Fourth of July Fireworks, East River.
Washington Square Music Festival.
Thunderbird American Indian Midsummer Pow Wow, Queens County Farm Museum.
Dancing of the Giglio, Williamsburg, Brooklyn.

AUGUST

Harlem Week celebrations, including the Harlem Jazz and Music Festival.
Greenwich Village Jazz Festival.
US Open Tennis Championships, USTA National Tennis Center, Queens (through mid-Sept).
New York Giants football season begins.

SEPTEMBER

Metropolitan Opera (to April), Lincoln Center.
New York Philharmonic (to March), Lincoln Center.
West Indian American Day Carnival (Labor Day), Eastern Parkway, Brooklyn.
Richmond County Fair (Labor Day weekend), Staten Island.
Feast of San Gennaro Festival, Little Italy.

Washington Square Art Show.
"New York is Book Country" Fair,
Fifth Avenue.
UN General Assembly opens.
Mayor's Cup Race, South Street
Seaport.

OCTOBER

American Ballet Theater (to
mid-Nov), City Center.
Big Apple Circus (to Jan), Lincoln
Center.
Medieval Festival, Fort Tryon Park,
Manhattan
New York Rangers hockey and New
York Knicks basketball starts,
Madison Square Garden.
Aqueduct Race Track opens,
Queens.
Next Wave Festival (through Dec),
Brooklyn Academy of Music (BAM).
New York Film Festival (to Nov),
Lincoln Center
Pulaski Day Parade, Fifth Avenue.
Hispanic Day Parade, Fifth Avenue.
Columbus Day Parade, Fifth Avenue.
Halloween Parade, Greenwich Village.

NOVEMBER

New York City Ballet (through Feb),
Lincoln Center.
New York City Marathon, Staten
Island to Central Park.
Macy's Thanksgiving Day Parade.
Christmas Holiday Spectacular
(to Jan), Radio City Music Hall.
The Nutcracker (to Jan), New York
City Ballet at Lincoln Center.
Veterans' Day Parade, Fifth Avenue.
National Horse Show, Madison
Square Garden.
Singing Christmas Tree (through
Dec), South Street Seaport.

DECEMBER

Lighting of Christmas Tree,
Rockefeller Center.
**Lighting of Giant Chanukah
Menorah,** Fifth Avenue.
New Year's Eve Celebration in
Times Square.
New Year's Eve Midnight Run,
Central Park.

Nightlife

Clubs appear and disappear in New
York even more abruptly than do
restaurants. While flagships like the
Village Vanguard and Café Carlyle
seem eternal, others, especially the
ultra-chic dance clubs, are more
ephemeral, seeming to rise and fall
literally overnight. With clubs, it's
even more important to consult up-
to-date listings in the *New Yorker*,
New York magazine, *Time Out New
York* and the *Village Voice*.

The following represent a range
of clubs offering various types of
live and recorded music, as well as
comedy, cabaret acts and even
poetry readings. Because cover
charges, reservation policies and
show times vary from club to club
and act to act, you must call and
ask for details.

Jazz

DOWNTOWN

Blue Note, 131 West 3rd St. Tel:
475 8592. The West Village is
home to the most famous jazz clubs
in the world, and first and foremost
there's the Blue Note; it's been
packed virtually every night for
years. The reason is simple: the
club presents the very best of
mainstream jazz and blues, from
time-honored greats to more
contemporary acts. The line-up here
has featured such luminaries as the
Modern Jazz Quartet, Etta James,
Joe Williams, Betty Carter, the
Count Basie Orchestra... the list
goes on and on. For die-hard fans,
there's a late-night session that
jams until 4am, after the last set.
Cajun, 129 Eighth Ave at 16th St.
Tel: 691-6174. Jazz and blues
bands predominate here, although
the occasional 1930s Bix

Biederbecke-style bands slip in, as
do authentic Cajun bands,
washboards and all.
Small's, 183 West 10th St. Tel:
929 7565. As the name suggests,
this is a cramped and relatively
recent addition to the city's jazz
club roster, where things don't get
started until the early hours of the
morning and last until 8am. For
serious aficionados and those who'd
like to be. First set starts at 10pm.
Village Vanguard, 178 Seventh Ave
South. Tel: 255 4037. Born over
half a century ago in a Greenwich
Village basement, this flagship club
cut its teeth helping to launch
fabulous talents like Miles Davis
and John Coltrane. In its adulthood,
it hardly keeps up with the
"vanguard" anymore, but rather
presents the greats and near-greats
of what is now the mainstream. It's
a chance to catch acts that rarely
tour. A terrific evening out but an
extremely popular one – call the club
well in advance for reservations to
avoid disappointment.

Club Culture

● **What you pay:** Expect to spend
roughly $15 to $25 or more per
person for featured "name acts,"
and $4 or more for a drink,
although it varies (e.g. hotel bars
charge $10 and up per cocktail).
Jazz clubs often have a two-drink
minimum and a cover charge.
● **When you go:** Featured live
acts won't start before 9 or
10pm, although a few of the jazz
clubs also offer midday brunch
music on weekends. Dance clubs
don't wake up before midnight.
● **What you wear:** Dress codes
are casual to punk chic in most
music and comedy clubs, and
more dinner-jacket at nightclubs.
Dress is most crucial in dance
clubs, where being able to flash
the latest fashion can be the
difference between getting in or
being snubbed by the doorman.

MIDTOWN

Birdland, 315 West 44th St. Tel: 581 3080. Elegant jazz club and restaurant, formerly located on the Upper West Side. Big-name big bands are the norm, along with smaller well-known or up-and-coming groups holding sway from around 9pm, with a second set at 11pm.

The Jazz Standard, 116 East 27th St. Tel: 576 2232. Everything from duos to nine-piece bands and beyond in this basement club. There's a restaurant upstairs, but they serve food downstairs, too. Closed Monday.

Red Blazer, 32 West 37th St. Tel: 947 6428. A hefty dose of New Orleans-style jazz in comfortable, relaxed surroundings, plus dining and dancing.

UPTOWN

Iridium, 44 West 63rd St. Tel: 582 2121. Some people find this venue strangely disorienting – the decor being Gaudí-esque in the extreme. But since it opened in early 1994, this club and restaurant has also presented some of the jazz world's most gifted denizens. Definitely worth checking out, especially Monday night when guitar legend Les Paul is often holding court to dazzled admirers.

Showman's Cafe, 375 East 125th St. Tel: 864 8491. A landmark Harlem nightspot, reopened in a new location with seriously cool music played by top musicians on a nightly basis.

Rock, Dance, Blues

DOWNTOWN

Arlene Grocery, 95 Stanton St, between Ludlow and Orchard. Tel: 358 1633. A low-key, dress-down Lower East Side venue for rock, folk, funk and everything in between. No admission fee.

The Bitter End, 147 Bleecker St. Tel: 673 7030. A Greenwich Village landmark, the Bitter End books an

Avant-Garde

The Knitting Factory, 74 Leonard St, between Broadway and Church St. Tel: 219 3055. Deep in the heart of Tribeca, this eclectic music mecca is a good spot for catching the next wave in experimental jazz, rock, poetry, and every combination of the same. Leading lights of New

eclectic mishmash of folk, folk rock, soft rock, blues, some comedy and cabaret... whatever. A classic example of eternal bohemianism, it's very popular with young adult tourists and can be mobbed on weekend nights.

The Bottom Line, 15 West 4th St. Tel: 228 7880. A venerable, mostly folk and blues venue in the heart of Greenwich Village. Very popular with the college crowd, who will line up outside a week in advance to purchase tickets. And once inside, it's a mad scramble for the best seats. Still, the intimacy of the space and the top-quality bookings make the struggle well worthwhile.

Brownies, 169 Ave A at 11th St. Tel: 420 8392. Like Arlene Grocery, Brownies mostly showcases unknown local bands and attracts a young, beer-drinking crowd.

CBGB & OMFUG, 315 Bowery at Bleecker St. Tel: 982 4052. The club where punk started in America, still the quintessential grubby rock venue; in effect, a museum to the spirit of '77. In the midst of the Bowery, CBGB has a beaten-down anti-glamour that's quite charming if you can appreciate it. You may not have heard of any of the young bands, because CBGB continues to encourage up-and-coming groups with bad haircuts, although occasional name bands do show up. The newer, cleaner, all-acoustic **CB's 313 Gallery** next door might be more soothing to older ears.

Irving Plaza, 17 Irving Pl. Tel: 777 6800. A ramshackle hall near Union Square that's gone through more than one incarnation, currently featuring everything from top rock

York's "Downtown" music, like John Zorn, Elliot Sharp and the Lounge Lizards, are regulars, but the seven-nights-a-week bookings are far too wide-ranging to sum up in any single category. Amazingly casual for such a cool club and well worth the trip Downtown to spend an evening.

bands to Sunday swing dancing.

Mercury Lounge, 217 East Houston St. Tel: 260 4700. Intimate Lower East Side club with excellent acoustics, catering to a more sophisticated alternative music crowd than usual. A good line-up of rock and country bands about to make it big (and some that already have) can be heard here.

The Village Underground, 130 West 3rd St. Tel: 777 7745. For those who miss the eclectic mix that was Tramps in Chelsea, its former booker picks the groups that appear here.

Webster Hall, 125 East 11th St. Tel: 353 1600; www.websterhall.com. Discount passes available online for this large, crowded East Village club that attracts a young crowd to its theme rooms, theme nights, trapeze acts and other assorted craziness. Open Wednesdays to Saturdays from 10pm, it offers all-night dancing to everything from rock, reggae and R&B to house, techno and who knows; theme nights range from "runway parties" to psychedelia.

MIDTOWN

B.B. King's Blues Club & Grill 243 West 42nd St. Tel: 997 4144. In the heart of Times Square, the legendary bluesman's New York venture (there are others around the country, including Memphis) packs them in for the best of the biggest names in R & B. This often includes the King himself, stroking the only woman who's never let him down – his trusty guitar, Lucille.

Rodeo Bar, 375 Third Ave at East 27th St. Tel: 683 6500. Like the name says, this borderline-Murray Hill neighborhood music bar/ restaurant has a kitschy Wild West theme, a correspondingly loose and lanky atmosphere, and (sometimes) live performances by "cowboy rock" bands like Asleep At The Wheel.

Roseland, 239 West 52nd St. Tel: 247 0200. Historically, a venue for traditional ballroom dancing; lately, also for performances by alternative rock bands or DJ-driven dancing to classic R&B.

Swing 46, 349 West 46th St. Tel: 262 9554. An all-swing jazz and supper club that's an epicenter of the ongoing swing revival, with dance lessons every night and live bands like the Flipped Fedoras. George Gee and his 15-piece Make Believe Ballroom Orchestra get the joint jumping whenever they appear. Cover charge.

The Supper Club, 240 West 47th St. Tel: 921 1940. A romantic, violet-toned throwback to New York's heyday of the 1940s, with weekend dining and dancing to live big bands, and occasional onstage appearances by the likes of ex-Talking Head David Byrne or Bob Dylan during the week.

World Beat

S.O.B.'s, 204 Varick St at Houston St. Tel: 243 4940. The name of this Soho restaurant and music club stands for "Sounds of Brazil," but it has expanded its repertoire to become the premiere club in the city for internationalist dance music. A typical month's billings offers an exhaustive world music tour, from salsa to reggae to jazz; performers have included the West African funk band Les Amazones de Guinea; Brazilian singer Margareth Menezes; Jamaican reggae singer Alton Ellis; and Samoan rappers Boo-Yaa Tribe. Book for dinner, then dance the calories away.

OUT OF TOWN

Maxwell's, 1039 Washington St, Hoboken, New Jersey. Tel: 201-653 1703. Another rock club that dates to the glory days of punk, Maxwell's draws fans from "the City" as well as from "Joisey" by regularly booking the best of the independent label rock bands. The music here tends to be more adventurous and rambunctious than in other clubs. (Transportation options there and back include PATH trains and, more expensive, taxis.)

Comedy and Cabaret

DOWNTOWN

The Comedy Cellar, 117 MacDougal St, tel: 254 3480. A cramped basement room where the tables are packed so close together that, even if you don't get the jokes, you may make some new friends. Show starts at 9pm.

The Duplex, 61 Christopher St. Tel: 255 5438. A landmark of the gay West Village, attracting a friendly and mixed audience.

Boston Comedy Club, 82 West 3rd St. Tel: 477 1000. Remember the film *Animal House*? That's basically the atmosphere at this Downtown joint.

MIDTOWN

Caroline's Comedy Club, 1626 Broadway. Tel: 757 4100. A plush restaurant and club with a continuous roster of young comic hopefuls along with some of the biggest names in the "biz." An evening here can also be your chance to laugh your way onto American television; some of the shows are videotaped for national cable TV consumption.

The Campbell Apartments, 89 E 42nd St at Park Ave. Tel: 953 0409. This is a reclaimed elegant space in the recent restoration of Grand Central Terminal. A place to dress up and act sophisticated.

Danny's Skylight Room at the Grand Sea Palace, 346 West 46th St. Tel: 265 8130. A lively Theater District piano bar and cabaret room, in a Thai restaurant. Shows starts around 9pm during the week and earlier on weekends.

Don't Tell Mama, 343 West 46th St. Tel: 757 0788. Very jolly spot, long favored by a theatrical crowd. In the front there's often a sing-along at the piano bar. The back room is a non-stop cabaret featuring comedians and torch singers. Leave inhibitions behind, and bring cash (no credit cards accepted).

The Oak Room, Algonquin Hotel, 59 West 44th St. Tel: 840 6800. A dark, intimate piano bar with great singers (Harry Connick Jr played here before he made it big).

Michael's Pub at The Park Restaurant, 109 East 56th St. Tel: 758 2272. This Midtown restaurant and cabaret features a variety of top acts, ranging from Broadway stars to Big Band swing to jazz singers. The New Orleans Funeral and Ragtime Orchestra plays here every Monday night.

UPTOWN

Café Carlyle, 35 East 76th St. Tel: 570 7184. In the elegant Carlyle Hotel, an upper-crusty institution of sorts for the social set. Depending on who's singing, playing or both, there's a hefty cover charge and always a two-drink minimum. On Monday, Woody Allen sits in with the New Orleans Jazz Band headed by Eddy Davis.

Comic Strip, 1568 Second Ave at 82nd St. Tel: 861 9386. A casual, popular proving ground for young stand-up kamikazes, both known and unknown. Open seven days a week, with three shows on Friday and Saturday night.

Feinstein's at the Regency, 540 Park Avenue at 61st St. Tel: 307 4100. Singer Michael Feinstein is so devoted to cabaret that he opened his own high-end club in the luxurious Regency Hotel.

Shopping

Shopping Areas

Shopping is a major pastime in New York: there isn't much to be found anywhere that can't be found here, and usually more of it. **Art**, of course, is a good bet; apart from the major auctioneers, **Sotheby's** and **Christies**, where record prices are set for world-famous works, there are hundreds of art galleries in which to browse (if not to buy).

Antiques can be found in Greenwich Village along Bleecker St and on side streets off University Place; along upper Madison Ave, on 60th St near Third Ave; and on Lafayette St below Houston St, as well as at a few indoor "malls" around the city, including the **Manhattan Art & Antiques Center**, 1050 Second Ave, tel: 355 4400; **Metropolitan Art & Antiques Pavilion**, 110 West 19th St, tel: 463 0200; and the **Chelsea Antiques Building**, 110 West 25th St, tel: 929 0909.

The city's famous **department stores** offer something for almost everyone but differ somewhat in their clientele: the most famous are the bustling **Bloomingdale's** (1000 Third Ave at 59th St) and **Macy's** (151 West 34th St), which sell everything from housewares to furniture and clothing. **Lord & Taylor** (424 Fifth Ave at 39th St); and **Saks Fifth Avenue** (611 Fifth Ave) concentrate on clothes, with the latter offering the most upscale fashions. Soho and the Upper East Side are generally where the highest proportion of classy clothing boutiques can be found, with Madison Avenue Uptown thick with expensive possibilities. There's another stretch of elegance along

Fifth Avenue from Rockefeller Center to the Plaza Hotel, with **Takashimaya** (693 Fifth Ave), **Henri Bendel** (712 Fifth Ave), **Prada** (724 Fifth Ave) and **Bergdorf Goodman** (754 Fifth Ave). The Swedish import **H & M** has been a huge success at 640 Fifth Avenue just across from St Patrick's Cathedral.

Electronic and photographic suppliers can be found almost everywhere, including Times Square and on Lexington Avenue near Grand Central Terminal. A few outlets are less than scrupulous, so it's best to do some comparison shopping before actually buying. A better bet might be in the downtown City Hall district or on Fifth Avenue between 37th and 40th streets.

The real bargains are often Downtown: along Orchard St on the Lower East Side; in Chinatown; on Canal St between Sixth and Third avenues, and in the East Village, particularly the cross streets between First and Second avenues. Savvy New York shoppers also flock to Manhattan's **flea markets**, including the eclectic weekend **Chelsea antiques market** on Sixth Ave between 25th and 27th streets and the **Sunday flea market** at Columbus Ave and 77th St on the Upper West Side.

There are some excellent antiquarian and second-hand bookstores around town, especially the **Strand Book Store**, 828 Broadway at 12th St, tel: 473 1452, which claims to have two million volumes in stock and is a wonderful place to browse (There's also a Strand in the South Street Seaport, at 95 Fulton St, tel: 732 6070.)

The transformation of Soho from a pioneering art colony to a major shopping mecca has injected new life into lower Broadway, where good chains like **Pottery Barn** and **Eddie Bauer** draw hordes of shoppers, especially on weekends. East of Soho, a handful of interesting small boutiques can be found on Elizabeth and Mott streets, in Nolita ("North of Little Italy").

In Chelsea, meanwhile, **Old Navy**, **Filene's Basement** and other suburban franchises are doing a

booming business in the old "Ladies Mile" emporiums lining Sixth Avenue between 18th and 23rd streets.

The Upper West Side is home to the stylish shops of Columbus Avenue as well as to Manhattan's best-known gourmet delicatessen, **Zabar's**, at 2245 Broadway, tel: 787 2000.

Other food meccas around town include **Citarella**, at 2135 Broadway; **Dean & DeLuca**, at 560 Broadway in Soho; **Balducci's**, at 424 Sixth Ave in Greenwich Village; **Eli's Vinegar Factory** at 431 E. 91st St, and **Grace's Marketplace**, at 1237 Third Ave on the Upper East Side.

Major crosstown arteries (8th, 14th, 23rd, 34th, 42nd, 57th, 86th, 125th) are usually good for shopping. But in the final analysis, that special something you didn't even know you were looking for may turn up just where you least expect it, in some out-of-the-way shop discovered quite serendipitously.

One-stop Shopping

Don't overlook one-stop centers like the **Manhattan Mall** at Sixth Avenue and 33rd Street and the **South Street Seaport** at Fulton and Water streets.

Books

Barnes & Noble, 105 Fifth Ave. Tel: 807 0099.
Biography Bookshop, 400 Bleecker St. Tel: 807 8655.
Books of Wonder, 16 West 18th St. Tel: 989 3270. Children's books.
Borders Books & Music, 465 Park Ave. Tel: 980 6785.
Civilized Traveller, 864 Lexington Ave. Tel: 288 9190. Another branch of the store is at 2003 Broadway. Tel: 875 0306.
Complete Traveller, 199 Madison Ave. Tel: 685 9007.
Crawford Doyle Booksellers, 1082 Madison Ave. Tel: 288 6300.
Drama Bookshop, 723 Seventh Ave. Tel: 944 0595.

Gotham Book Mart, 41 West 47th St. Tel: 719 4448.

Murder Ink, 2486 Broadway. Tel: 362 8905.

Rizzoli, 31 West 57th St. Tel: 759 2424.

St Mark's Bookshop, 31 Third Ave. Tel: 260 7853.

Shakespeare & Co, 939 Lexington Ave. Tel: 570 0201.

Three Lives & Co, 154 West 10th St. Tel: 741 2069.

Clothing Stores

WOMEN'S CLOTHES

Agnès b, 1063 Madison Ave, tel: 570 9333; 116 Prince St, tel: 925 4649.

Betsey Johnson, 138 Wooster St. Tel: 995 5048.

D&G, 434 West Broadway. Tel: 965 8000.

Eileen Fisher, 1039 Madison Ave, tel: 879 7799; 341 Columbus Ave, tel: 362 3000; 103 Fifth Ave, tel: 924 4777.

OMO-Norma Kamali, 11 West 56th St. Tel: 957 9797.

Harriet Love, 126 Prince St. Tel: 966 2280.

April Cornell, 487 Columbus Ave. Tel: 799 4342.

MEN'S CLOTHES

Alfred Dunhill, 450 Park Ave. Tel: 753 9292.

Brooks Brothers, 346 Madison Ave. Tel: 682 8800.

J. Press, 16 East 44th St. Tel: 687 7642.

Paul Stuart, Madison Ave at 45th St. Tel: 682 0320.

Sean, 224 Columbus Ave, tel: 769 1489; 132 Thompson St, tel: 598 5980.

MEN'S AND WOMEN'S CLOTHES

A/X Armani Exchange, 568 Broadway. Tel: 431 6000.

Barneys New York, 660 Madison Ave. Tel: 826 8900.

Brooks Brothers, 346 Madison Ave.

Burberry's, 9 East 57th St. Tel: 371 5010.

Calvin Klein, 654 Madison Ave. Tel: 292 9000.

Comme des Garçons, 520 West 22nd St. Tel: 604 9200.

Emporio Armani, 110 Fifth Ave. Tel: 727 3240.

J. Crew, 91 Fifth Ave. Tel: 255 4848.

Polo-Ralph Lauren, 867 Madison Ave. Tel: 606 2100.

Urban Outfitters, 628 Broadway. Tel: 475 0009.

DESIGNER DISCOUNTS

Century 21, 122 Cortlandt St, tel: 227-9092 (located Downtown but loved by uptown ladies).

Daffy's, 111 Fifth Ave, tel: 529 4477 and branches.

Filene's Basement, 620 Avenue of the Americas, tel: 620 3100 (Chelsea) and at 2222 Broadway (79th St), tel: 873 8000.

Loehmann's, 101 Seventh Ave (Chelsea), tel: 352 0856.

Cameras, Computers and Electronics

B & H Photo-Video, 420 Ninth Ave. Tel: 444 600.

Circuit City, 52-64 East 14th St. Tel: 387 0730 (and other locations).

Fone Booth, 330 Seventh Ave. Tel: 564 0900. Anything about phones.

Harvey Electronics, 2 West 45th St. Tel: 575 5000.

J&R Computer World, 15 Park Row. Tel: 732 8600.

Sony Style, 550 Madison Ave. Tel: 833 8800.

Willoughby's, 136 West 32nd St. Tel: 564 1600.

Music Stores

West 48th Street is particularly good for music stores. You may want to check out more than one along here, but be sure to go to **Manny's Music** at 156 West 48th Street, tel: 819 0576.

Other music stops include:
Bleeker Bob's, 118 West 3rd St. Tel: 475 9677. Good for rare

Clothes Chart

The chart listed below gives a comparison of United States, European and United Kingdom clothing sizes. It is always a good idea, however, to try on any article before buying it, as sizes between manufacturers can vary enormously.

● **Women's Dresses/Suits**

US	Continental	UK
6	38/34N	8/30
8	40/36N	10/32
10	42/38N	12/34
12	44/40N	14/36
14	46/42N	16/38
16	48/44N	18/40

● **Women's Shoes**

US	Continental	UK
4½	36	3
5½	37	4
6½	38	5
7½	39	6
8½	40	7
9½	41	8
10½	42	9

● **Men's Suits**

US	Continental	UK
34	44	34
—	46	36
38	48	38
—	50	40
42	52	42
—	54	44
46	56	46

● **Men's Shirts**

US	Continental	UK
14	36	14
14½	37	14½
15	38	15
15½	39	15½
16	40	16
16½	41	16½
17	42	17

● **Men's Shoes**

US	Continental	UK
6½	—	6
7½	40	7
8½	41	8
9½	42	9
10½	43	10
11½	44	11

recordings and hard-to-find classics. **Colony Records**, 1619 Broadway. Tel: 265 2050. In business for almost 60 years and going strong. **HMV Record Store**, 42nd St and Seventh Ave (and branches). Tel: 348 0800.
House of Oldies, 35 Carmine St. Tel: 243 0500.Vintage vinyl in Greenwich Village.
J&R Music World, 23 Park Row. Tel: 732 8600. Downtown near City Hall; great jazz and classical recordings.
Jazz Record Center, 236 West 26th St. Tel: 675 4480. Chelsea's best place for jazz.
Sam Ash, 160 West 48th St. Tel: 719 2299. Good for seeking out musical instruments.
Tower Records, 692 Broadway (and branches). Tel: 505 1500.
Virgin Megastore, Times Square (and branches). Tel: 921 1020.

Sports Equipment & Clothing

Niketown, 6 East 57th St. Tel: 891 6453.
Paragon Sporting Goods, 867 Broadway. Tel: 255 8036.
Patagonia, 101 Wooster St. Tel: 343 1776.
Scandinavian Ski & Sports, 40 West 57th St. Tel: 757 8524.

Toys

Children's General Store, 2473 Broadway near 92nd St, tel: 580 2723; Grand Central Terminal, tel: 284 0004.
The Enchanted Forest, 85 Mercer St. Tel: 925 6677.
FAO Schwarz, Fifth Ave and 58th St. Tel: 644 9400.
Penny Whistle, 448 Columbus Ave, tel: 873 9090; 1283 Madison Ave, tel: 369 3868.
Toys R Us, Broadway at 44th St. Times Square megastore complete with working indoor Ferris wheel.

Sport

Participant Sports

New York offers a wide array of recreational facilities. Many are found in the city's **parks** – including Central Park, where roads are closed to traffic on summer weekends for the benefit of bicyclists and in-line skaters. For general information call the Department of Parks and Recreations at 1-800 201 PARK.

Tennis can be played in Central Park and various other parks; it's also available at private facilities such as the Midtown Tennis Club, 341 Eighth Ave, tel: 989 8572; the Manhattan Plaza Racquet Club, 450 West 43rd St, tel: 594 0554; and the HRC Tennis Club, Piers 13 and 14 near Wall St, tel: 422 9300.

Horses can be hired at the Claremont Riding Academy, 175 West 89th St, tel: 724 5100, for riding along Central Park's miles of bridle trails; at Kensington Stables in Brooklyn, tel: 718-972 4588, for riding in Prospect Park, and other places around the city.

Ice skating is available at both Wollman and Lasker Rinks in Central Park between October and April; also at Rockefeller Center, tel: 332 7654; and year-round at Sky Rink, Pier 61 at the Hudson River, tel: 336 6100, which is part of the Chelsea Piers complex (below).

Baseball and **softball** diamonds are located in city parks, as are miles of **jogging** tracks and trails. (The New York Road Runners Club maintains a running center at 9 East 89th St, tel: 860 4455.) And **rowboats** can be hired at the Central Park Lake boathouse (and at Prospect Park in Brooklyn, Kissena Park in Queens and Van Cortlandt Park in the Bronx), as can **bicycles**.

You'll find public **golf courses** at Pelham Bay Park, Van Cortlandt Park (both in the Bronx) and at Latourette Park in Staten Island, among other outer borough parks.

There are also several public indoor and outdoor **swimming pools** around the city including 348 East 54th St, and the Asser Levy Pool at 23rd St and the FDR Drive. Call 718-699 4219 for information. In addition, day rates are available at the YMCAs at 224 East 47th St. Tel: 756 9600 and 5 West 63rd St. Tel: 787 4400, both of which have swimming pools and exercise facilities. Manhattan hotels with pools include the Parker Meridien, Regal UN Plaza,and the Sheraton Manhattan.

For numerous sports in one place, try the **Chelsea Piers Sports and Entertainment Complex** (tel: 336 6666; www.chelseapiers.com), which stretches along the Hudson River between 17th and 23rd streets. Facilities include a multi-tiered **golf driving range**, **boating**, **bowling**, **horseback riding** and **in-line skating**; day passes are available at the sports/fitness center, which has an Olympic-size swimming pool, a sundeck, running track and **rock climbing** wall.

Spectator Sports

New York is understandably proud of its top-rated teams, the Mets and Yankees, who play **baseball** from April to October at Shea Stadium in Flushing, tel: 718-507 8499 and Yankee Stadium in the Bronx, tel: 718-293 6000. The New York Knicks (tel: 465 6741) play **basketball** between October and May at Madison Square Garden, where the New York Liberty (tel: 564-WNBA) professional women's team can be seen in summer. College team schedules are listed in the sports sections of daily papers.

Ice hockey season runs from October to April, with the the New York Rangers at Madison Square Garden (tel: 465 7561) and the Islanders playing at Nassau Coliseum on Long Island (tel: 516-

794 4100). Madison Square Garden is also the main site for important events in **boxing** and **tennis**, although the US Open is at the **National Tennis Center** in Flushing Meadows-Corona Park, Queens (tel: 718-760 6200) from late August to September.

The **football** season starts in late August and lasts through December or January, with both the New York Giants (201-935 8222) and New York Jets (tel: 516-560 8100) playing at Giants Stadium in the Meadowlands, East Rutherford, NJ.

Soccer, increasingly popular since the 1994 World Cup was hosted by the United States, takes place between March and September, when the MetroStars play matches at the Meadowlands (tel: 201-583 7000). **Cricket** matches are held on summer Sundays in Van Cortlandt Park in the Bronx, as well as on Randall's Island in the East River and various parks in Brooklyn and Staten Island.

The closest thoroughbred **horse-racing** is at Aqueduct Racetrack in Queens (subway from Eighth Ave and 42nd St) and Belmont Park in Elmont, Long Island (Long Island Railroad from Pennsylvania Station). Tel: 718-641 4700 for both.

Further Reading

General

AIA Guide to New York City by Elliot Willinsky and Norval White. Harcourt Brace Jovanovich, 1988.

A Natural History of New York City by John Kiernan. Fordham University Press, 1982.

The Beautiful Bronx: 1920–1950 by Lloyd Ultan. Crown, 1982.

At The Theatre: An Informal History of New York's Legitimate Theatres. Dodd Mead & Company, 1984.

The Encyclopedia of New York City, edited by Kenneth T. Jackson. Yale University Press, 1995.

George Balanchine, Ballet Master by Richard Buckle. In collaboration with John Taras. New York: Random House, 1988.

Here is New York by E.B. White. Warner Books, 1988.

History Preserved: A Guide to New York City Landmarks and Historic Districts by Harmon H. Goldstone and Martha Dalrymple. Schocken Books, 1976.

The Lincoln Center Story by Alan Rich. New York: American Heritage, 1984.

Literary Neighborhoods of New York by Marcia Leisner. Starhill Press, 1989.

Manhattan '45 by Jan Morris. Oxford University Press, 1987.

The Movie Lover's Guide to New York by Richard Alleman. Perennial Library/Harper & Row, 1988.

The New Chinatown by Peter Kwong. Hill & Wang, 1987.

New York by Djuna Barnes. Sun and Moon Press, 1989.

New York Art Guide by Deborah Jane Gardner. Robert Silver Associates, 1987.

New York: Heart of the City by J.P. MacBean. Mallard Press, 1990.

New York: An Illustrated History by Ric Burns, Knopf, 1999.

New York's Nooks and Crannies: Unusual Walking Tours in all Five Boroughs, written by David Yeadon.

New York: Charles Scribner and Sons, 1986.

New York Times Guide to Restaurants in New York City by Bryan Miller. Times Books, 1990.

New York Times World of New York by A.M. Rosenthal and Arthur Gelb. Times Books, 1985.

On Broadway: A Journey Uptown Over Time by David W. Dunlop. Rizzoli International Publications, 1990.

Poet in New York by Federico Garcia Lorca. Farrar, Straus, Giroux, 1988.

Slaves of New York by Tama Janowitz. Pocket Books, 1988.

Time and Again by Jack Finney. Simon & Schuster, 1970.

Up in the Old Hotel by Joseph Mitchell, Pantheon, 1997.

Uptown & Downtown: A Trip Through Time on New York Subways by Stan Fischler. E.P. Dutton, 1976.

You Must Remember This. An Oral History of Manhattan from the 1890s to World War II by Jeff Kisseloff. Harcourt Brace Jovanovich, 1988.

When Brooklyn Was the World: 1920–1957 by Elliot Willensky. Crown, 1986.

When Harlem Was in Vogue by David Levering Lewis. Oxford University Press, 1983.

Winter's Tale by Mark Helprin. Harcourt Brace Jovanovich, 1983.

The WPA Guide to New York City, Federal Writers Project Guide to 1930s New York. Pantheon, 1982.

New York Classics

If you read nothing else when you visit New York, take your pick from these five classics:

The Age of Innocence by Edith Wharton. Penguin, 1996.

Another Country by James Baldwin. Vintage, 1993.

A Tree Grows in Brooklyn by Betty Smith. Harperperennial Library 1998.

Bonfire of the Vanities by Tom Wolfe. Bantam Books 1988.

Washington Square by Henry James, Penguin, 1984.

Other Insight Guides

The *Insight Guides* series of over 200 books covers every continent and includes 40 titles devoted to the United States, from Alaska to Florida, from Seattle to Miami. Destinations include:

Insight Guide: Boston. An excellent team of writers and photographers celebrates Boston, one of America's most intriguing cities.

Insight Guide: San Francisco is essential reading to one of the most fascinating of American cities.

Insight Guide: New Orleans. The cream of the city's writers and photographers document the Big Easy in comprehensive, elegant detail.

Insight Pocket Guides act as a "substitute host" to a destination and present a selection of well-researched itineraries. They also include a large, fold-out map. *Insight Compact Guides* are miniature travel encyclopedias, carry-along guidebooks for on-the-spot reference. *Insight FlexiMaps* include attractions, color photos and a laminated finish.

Insight Pocket Guide: New York City. In the town of a thousand choices, personal recommendations and sightseeing routes take the big angst out of the Big Apple.

Recommended Books on New York City

Fifth Avenue: The Best Address by Jerry E. Patterson. Rizzoli International Publications, 1998. Describes the gradual development of the city's most famous boulevard, from rocky dirt path, to shanty row to elegant thoroughfare.
Flatbush Odyssey: A Journey Through the Heart of Brooklyn by Alan Abel. McClelland & Stewart, 1997. A fond reminiscence by an expat writer (now a Canadian) who grew up in one of Brooklyn's most picturesque neighborhoods.
Gotham: A History of New York to 1898 by Mike Wallace and Edwin G. Burrows. Oxford University Press, 1998. Pulitzer prize-winning narrative about the city's early years; in-depth, with an emphasis on some of its characters.
The Heart of the World by Nik Cohn. Alfred A. Knopf, 1992. A

British journalist's slightly cynical adventures in Manhattan, from subways to brief encounters.
Low Life by Luc Sante. Vintage Books, 1992. Everything you always wanted to know about the gangs, gangsters and riff-raff who thrived at the edge of New York's society in the 19th century.
Still Life in Harlem by Eddy L. Harris. Henry Holt and Company, Inc., 1996. A well-written autobiographical take on this famed Uptown neighborhood, with poignant details.
Writing New York: A Literary Anthology edited by Philip Lopate. The Library of America, 1998. Observations about life in New York by such literary folk as Henry David Thoreau, Walt Whitman, Maxim Gorky and F. Scott Fitzgerald. A must for city-philes.

Insight Compact Guide: New York. This slim, handy volume tells you all the facts, figures and low-down on New York City.

ART & PHOTO CREDITS

INSIGHT GUIDE
NEW YORK CITY
Cartographic Editor Zoë Goodwin
Production Linton Donaldson
Design Consultants
Carlotta Junger, Graham Mitchener
Picture Research Hilary Genin

Index

Numbers in italics refer to photographs

INSIGHT GUIDES

The classic series that puts you in the picture

Alaska	Dominican Rep. & Haiti	London	Rio de Janeiro
Amazon Wildlife	Dublin	Los Angeles	Rome
American Southwest	**E**ast African Wildlife	**M**adeira	Russia
Amsterdam	Eastern Europe	Madrid	**S**t Petersburg
Argentina	Ecuador	Malaysia	San Francisco
Arizona & Grand Canyon	Edinburgh	Mallorca & Ibiza	Sardinia
Asia, East	Egypt	Malta	Scandinavia
Asia, Southeast	England	Mauritius Réunion	Scotland
Australia	**F**inland	& Seychelles	Seattle
Austria	Florence	Melbourne	Sicily
Bahamas	Florida	Mexico	Singapore
Bali	France	Miami	South Africa
Baltic States	France, Southwest	Montreal	South America
Bangkok	French Riviera	Morocco	Spain
Barbados	**G**ambia & Senegal	Moscow	Spain, Northern
Barcelona	Germany	**N**amibia	Spain, Southern
Beijing	Glasgow	Nepal	Sri Lanka
Belgium	Gran Canaria	Netherlands	Sweden
Belize	Great Britain	New England	Switzerland
Berlin	Great Railway Journeys	New Orleans	Sydney
Bermuda	of Europe	New York City	Syria & Lebanon
Boston	Greece	New York State	**T**aiwan
Brazil	Greek Islands	New Zealand	Tenerife
Brittany	Guatemala, Belize	Nile	Texas
Brussels	& Yucatán	Normandy	Thailand
Buenos Aires	**H**awaii	Norway	Tokyo
Burgundy	Hong Kong	**O**man & The UAE	Trinidad & Tobago
Burma (Myanmar)	Hungary	Oxford	Tunisia
Cairo	**I**celand	**P**acific Northwest	Turkey
California	India	Pakistan	Tuscany
California, Southern	India, South	Paris	**U**mbria
Canada	Indonesia	Peru	USA: On The Road
Caribbean	Ireland	Philadelphia	USA: Western States
Caribbean Cruises	Israel	Philippines	US National Parks: West
Channel Islands	Istanbul	Poland	**V**enezuela
Chicago	Italy	Portugal	Venice
Chile	Italy, Northern	Prague	Vienna
China	Italy, Southern	Provence	Vietnam
Continental Europe	**J**amaica	Puerto Rico	**W**ales
Corsica	Japan	**R**ajasthan	Walt Disney World/Orlando
Costa Rica	Jerusalem		
Crete	Jordan		
Cuba	**K**enya		
Cyprus	Korea		
Czech & Slovak Republic	**L**aos & Cambodia		
Delhi, Jaipur & Agra	Las Vegas		
Denmark	Lisbon		

☂ INSIGHT GUIDES

The world's largest collection of visual travel guides & maps